# THE BEST OF
# HOCKEY

*Hockey's Greatest Players, Teams, Games, and More*

Morgan Hughes

Consultants:
Joseph Romain and James Duplacey

Publications International, Ltd.

Louis Weber, C.E.O.
Publications International, Ltd.
7373 North Cicero Avenue
Lincolnwood, Illinois 60646

Permission is never granted for commercial purposes.

Manufactured in U.S.A.

8 7 6 5 4 3 2 1

ISBN: 0-7853-1911-5

Library of Congress Catalog Card Number: 97-67076

Morgan Hughes is the former editor of *Hockey Stars* and *Hockey Heroes* and has written about hockey for such national publications as *Goal, Hockey Scene,* and *Inside Sports.* He authored *Hockey Legends of All Time,* co-authored *Hockey Almanac* and *20th Century Hockey Chronicle,* and served as consultant for *Great Book of Hockey.* A freelance writer, he has also contributed to *The Sporting News, Village Voice,* and *Sport.*

Joseph Romain was a librarian and curator with the Hockey Hall of Fame and Museum. He has published more than a dozen books about the history of hockey, including *Pictorial History of Hockey* and *Hockey Hall of Fame.* His current projects include *Ladies Day: The Women's Guide to Pro Baseball* and the fiction works *The Wagner Whacker* and *The West Windsor Nine.*

James Duplacey is the former curator of the Hockey Hall of Fame and Museum. He is the author of numerous books and articles on the history of hockey, including *Hockey Superstars: 1000 Point Players, Maple Leaf Magic,* and *Toronto Maple Leafs: Images of Glory.* He has served as managing editor of the *Official NHL Guide and Record Book.*

**Photo credits:**

Front cover: **Bruce Bennett Studios.**

Back cover: **Bruce Bennett Studios:** (bottom); **Graphic Artists/Hockey Hall of Fame and Museum:** (center); **Nevin Reid/Allsport USA:** (top).

**AP/Wide World Photos:** 15, 22, 35, 49, 69, 78, 83, 106, 115 (top), 171 (right), 176 (right), 180 (left), 183, 201 (right); **Allsport USA:** 56, 165, 172 (center), 201 (left); Glenn Cratty: 27, 53, 87, 92, 170 (right), 182 (right), 199 (center); Tim DeFrisco: 33; Tony Duffy: 162; Mike Powell: 129 (bottom), 148, 149; Steve Powell: 8 (left), 153; Harry Scull: 12; Jamie Squire: 68, 72; **Bruce Bennett Studios:** 5 (top), 7 (top), 8 (right), 9 (bottom), 17, 19, 21, 28, 36, 40, 41, 61, 65, 75, 77, 85, 94, 97, 99, 101, 105, 124 (left), 125, 126, 127, 128, 129 (top), 131, 141, 144, 146 (top), 147 (right), 163, 166, 167, 170 (left), 171 (left), 172 (right), 173 (right), 174 (right), 175 (left), 176 (left), 177 (right), 178 (left), 184 (top), 185 (left & right), 186 (left), 187 (top), 189 (right), 192 (left & center), 193, 194 (right), 196 (right), 197 (top), 198 (center), 202 (right), 206, 208 (left), 209, 211 (bottom); C. Andersen: 47; C. Berg: 196 (left); M. Campanelli: 192 (right), 197 (bottom); Melchior DiGiacomo: 7, 44, 64, 73, 80, 90, 122, 147 (left), 152, 160, 175 (right), 185 (center); J. Giamundo: 26, 172 (left), 177 (left), 198 (right), 203 (left); J. Leary: 207 (bottom); Scott A. Levy: 180 (center), 198 (left); Jim McIsaac: 182 (left); B. Miller: 50; S. Wachter: 96; Brian Winkler:

150, 151 (left), 170 (center), 180 (right); **Boston Globe Photo:** 200 (left); **Canapress Photo Service:** 199 (right), 205 (bottom), 208 (center); **Corbis/Bettmann:** 16, 43, 104, 114, 115 (bottom), 117, 121 (top), 123, 130, 134, 137 (right), 138, 139, 140, 145, 151 (right), 156, 159, 161, 164, 186 (right), 188, 189 (left), 190, 191 (left), 202 (left), 203 (right), 204, 205 (top), 211 (top); **Ralph Dinger/LaPresse:** 158; **Ernie Fitzsimmons Collection:** 18, 24, 51, 58, 71, 74, 84, 191 (right); William Gallaway Collection: 66; Turofsky Collection: 63, 70; **Hockey Hall of Fame and Museum:** 4 (center & bottom), 5 (bottom), 9 (top), 10, 11, 13, 14, 20, 23, 30, 34, 39, 45, 46, 48, 57, 59, 60, 62, 67, 76, 79, 81, 91, 93, 95, 98, 100, 102, 108, 109, 110, 111, 112, 118, 119, 120, 124 (right), 133, 135, 142, 146 (bottom), 154, 155, 168 (right) 169, 173 (left), 174 (left), 178 (right), 184 (bottom), 194 (left & center), 208 (right); William Gallaway Collection: 25, 55; Graphic Artists: 82, 89, 103, 107, 168 (left), 181; Imperial Oil Turofsky Collection: 31, 42, 54, 86, 88, 113, 132, 136, 137 (left), 143, 157, 179, 187 (bottom), 195, 199 (left), 207 (top); Doug MacLellan: 37; Frank Prazak: 32, 38, 52, 200 (right); James Rice: 29; **Michael Leonetti Collection:** 6, 116, 121 (bottom); **Additional Photography: Sam Griffith Photography; White Eagle Studio.**

# CONTENTS

# SELECTING THE BEST

Someone once said, "Maurice Richard may not have been the greatest hockey player ever, but he was the greatest goal-scorer." Sounds great, but it's pure opinion. The same honor could easily be attached to Gordie Howe or Wayne Gretzky or, in his own time, Phil Esposito. It's all an endless debate.

Who were the best goalies ever to stop an NHL puck? Certainly Jacques Plante rates. What about Patrick Roy and Terry Sawchuk? How about Gump Worsley and Tony Esposito? The answers are yes and no.

For the last century, these questions have been shot back and forth among hockey aficionados like so many pucks on frozen ponds across North America. The questions have raged since Richard became the first man to score 50 goals in 50 games, since Howe eclipsed the 800-goal plateau shortly before his retirement at the astonishing age of 51, and since Gretzky eclipsed everyone in every scoring category.

The opening section of *The Best of Hockey* focuses on the top 80 players of all time, including 25 centers, 25 wingers (left and right), 15 defensemen, and 15 goaltenders. Included among the choices in these categories are the "no-brainers," such as Bobby Hull, Bobby Orr, Plante, Sawchuk, and others, players whose sheer dominance and statistical accomplishments made them obvious picks. However, while the players included won't spark much argument, the omissions in these four categories are bound to ignite heated debates.

Terry Sawchuk, with his NHL-record 447 victories and league-best 103 shutouts, was atop everyone's list of best goalies.

Why wasn't Hall of Fame winger Dickie Moore of the Montreal Canadiens included? He won two Art Ross Trophies as the NHL's scoring champion and set a league record with 96 points in 1958–59. However, if Moore had been included among the 25 Best Wingers, what might have become of, say, Mike Gartner, the only player in NHL history to score a minimum of 30 goals in 14 consecutive seasons? That's a feat never matched by any of the greats—not Gretzky, not Hull, not Guy Lafleur.

How did defensemen Brian Leetch and Chris Chelios fail to make the cut despite their perennial placement at the top of the Norris Trophy voting? Leetch, a Norris Trophy winner in 1992, led the New York Rangers to the 1994 Stanley Cup title and was the playoff MVP. Chelios, who has three Norris Trophies to his name, is the heart and soul of the Blackhawks. And where is Al MacInnis, who remained the all-time scoring leader in Calgary years after he left the Flames for St. Louis? He, too, was a playoff MVP when he took Calgary to the Stanley Cup in 1989. When you look over the list of players who did make the final cut, and consider their accomplishments both individually (trophies, scoring records, etc.) and in terms of their respective teams (i.e., Stanley Cup titles), you may understand the dilemma facing the author, consultants, and editors of *The Best of Hockey* and appreciate the choices we made.

It took more than a single great performance to earn a place in the front section of this compendium. There was no room for any "flash in the pan" aspirants among the greatest 50 front-line skaters of all time. You won't find Chicago winger Troy Murray, who blasted 45 goals in 1985–86 in his one and only sen-

*The determined Bobby Clarke, winner of two Hart Trophies, is among the 25 best centers in hockey history.*

sational season. Nor will you read about Boston's Cam Neely, a regular 50-goal threat. Done in by injuries, his career was cut short at age 31. Flyers goalie Pelle Lindbergh was widely viewed as a potential Vezina Trophy dominator, winning the award in 1985, but he was killed in a car accident at age 26.

Quite a few Hall of Famers didn't get into *The Best of Hockey*, either. Detroit Red Wings great Sid Abel, who centered the Production Line with Gordie Howe and Ted Lindsay in the late 1940s and early 1950s, was the league's MVP in 1948–49 and won three Stanley Cups, yet his own statistical profile wasn't enough to put him ahead of such fellow star pivots as Syl Apps and Ted Kennedy.

Two of the most difficult omissions occurred among the legion of wonderful masked (and unmasked) men who've courageously tended goal in the NHL over the last century. New York Rangers puck-stopper "Fast Eddie" Giacomin, who won the Vezina Trophy in 1970–71, didn't make it into the 15 Best Goalies because he never carried his team beyond the final barrier, to a Stanley Cup. Meanwhile, Andy Moog, a 300-game winner and three-time Stanley Cup champion with the Edmonton Oilers, failed to find a place in this collection because those Oilers teams so clearly dominated with offense rather than with outstanding goaltending.

The 50 centers and wingers included in *The Best of Hockey* combined for 67 scoring championships and 49 Hart Trophies as league MVP. No fewer than 21 of them are 500-goal scorers, the most

*Wayne Gretzky displays the puck he used to break Gordie Howe's goal-scoring record on March 23, 1994.*

recent being Mario Lemieux, Mark Messier, Steve Yzerman, and Dale Hawerchuk, each of whom reached the mark during the 1995–96 season. In fact, the only retired player with 500 NHL goals who failed to make the lists of 25 Best Centers and 25 Best Wingers was Boston legend Johnny Bucyk, and he was perhaps the hardest cut of all.

The 15 defensemen who earned spots on these pages combined for 32 Norris Trophies. Boston Bruins legend Bobby Orr alone captured eight straight Norris Trophies from 1967–75 (during which time he also won two scoring championships and three MVP awards).

*Though huge underdogs, the U.S. hockey team defeated the Soviet Union 4–3 in the medal round of the 1980 Olympics—one of the most exciting games ever played.*

New York Islanders who won four straight from 1979–83? The Oilers who took four Stanley Cups in a five-year span from 1983–88? What about the Toronto Maple Leafs who, from 1946–49, became the first team ever to win three Stanley Cups in a row?

Which were the greatest games ever? How did the drama on the ice translate to the emotions of the fans in their seats and in front of the TVs and radios? How many watched and listened the night Toronto's Bill Barilko won the 1951 Stanley Cup with an overtime goal, his

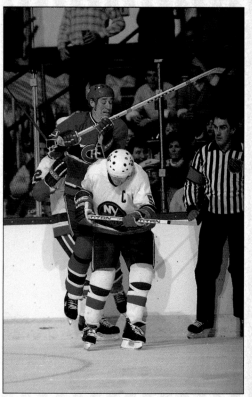

*In the early 1980s, Denis Potvin's Islanders succeeded Bob Gainey's Canadiens as hockey's newest dynasty.*

Canadiens Hall of Famer Doug Harvey finished his brilliant career with seven Norris Trophies in an eight-year span from 1955–62. Bruins star Ray Bourque earned his fifth Norris Trophy in 1994, outdoing Chris Chelios, Paul Coffey, Denis Potvin, and Pierre Pilote, each of whom earned three.

The list of 15 goalies judged to be the best ever actually excludes five of the winningest netminders in NHL history, including Tony Esposito (423 career wins), Rogie Vachon (355), Gump Worsley (335), Harry Lumley (333), and Moog. However, when these admittedly superb puck-stoppers were compared against those who did make the cut, such as Chicago's Charlie Gardiner and Philadelphia's Bernie Parent—who carried their respective teams to Stanley Cup titles with singularly heroic play—it proved that quality still wins out over sheer quantity. For instance, Esposito, who spent 15 years in Chicago and is third all-time in victories, never won the Stanley Cup.

And what about those Montreal clubs that have amassed more championships than any other team in the history of major professional sports? Which editions were the best? The team that won five straight Stanley Cups from 1955–60, or the one that took four in a row from 1975–79? Who rates with them? The

*Beefy Maple Leafs goalie Walter "Turk" Broda was certainly one of the game's 10 best personalities.*

last ever before an off-season plane crash claimed his life? How were the emotions of hockey-crazed Canadiens fans stirred the night, in 1952, when Rocket Richard, dizzy from a head injury, scored a series-winning goal against Boston's Sugar Jim Henry in what has been called the most courageous feat in hockey history?

What series best captured the spirit of Stanley Cup play? Certainly, the 1942 Finals, during which Toronto came back from a three-games-to-none deficit to beat Detroit in seven, is among the greatest series ever.

In the post–Boom Boom Geoffrion era, who had the biggest slap shots?

History has paid homage to the wreckage Andy Bathgate's huge shot visited on Jacques Plante in 1959, sending the goalie scurrying, bloody and stunned, for his revolutionary facemask in a moment that changed hockey forever. Hull authored more than 600 NHL goals and twice that number of nightmares for goalies, who had to face his 100-mph blasts.

In the book's Best of the Rest section, you'll find a comprehensive list of categories, from the fastest skaters to the worst goons, from *Slap Shot* (listed in 5 Best Films) to *Requiem for Reggie* (5 Best Books). A look at the 10 Best Personalities will shed light on some of the great humor that has always been part of the NHL.

Finally, if you're looking for the likes of Jaromir Jagr, Chelios, Leetch, and others, you may find them under 10 Best Europeans or 10 Best Americans. However, if you're looking for center Eric Lindros, goalie Mike Richter, or winger Paul Kariya—all of whom are certainly among the game's current trendsetters— you'll just have to wait for another edition of *The Best of Hockey*. For the time being, consider the choices made here and remember that they were made by folks, like you, who love the game and love to argue about its greatest players and greatest performances.

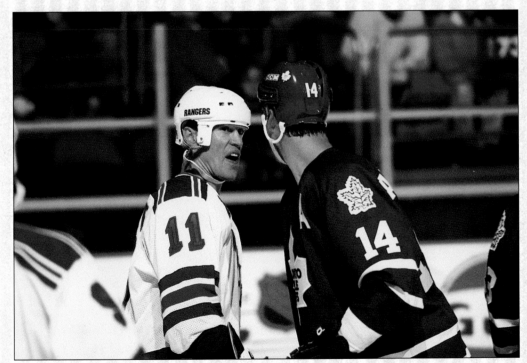

*Feared for his fists as well as his scoring punch and indomitable leadership, Rangers captain Mark Messier is one of hockey's 10 grittiest players.*

# Chapter 1

# 80 Best Players

Their styles ran the gamut, from conservative (Larry Robinson) to outlandish (Jacques Plante). What they all had in common, though, was supreme talent and relentless determination. Featured here are the best centers, wingers, defensemen, and goalies in hockey history.

Above: *Red Wing greats Alex Delvecchio (center) and Gordie Howe (left) played a combined 50 years in the NHL. Opposite page: Frank Mahovlich bear hugs fellow Leaf Red Kelly.*

## 25 BEST CENTERS

SYL APPS
JEAN BELIVEAU
MAX BENTLEY
FRANK BOUCHER
BOBBY CLARKE
ALEX DELVECCHIO
MARCEL DIONNE
PHIL ESPOSITO
WAYNE GRETZKY
DALE HAWERCHUK
TED KENNEDY
ELMER LACH
NEWSY LALONDE
MARIO LEMIEUX
MARK MESSIER
STAN MIKITA
HOWIE MORENZ
GILBERT PERREAULT
JOE PRIMEAU
HENRI RICHARD
DENIS SAVARD
MILT SCHMIDT
NELS STEWART
BRYAN TROTTIER
STEVE YZERMAN

Hockey's center position requires the greatest variety of skills. As the leader of the offensive attack, the centerman must possess speed afoot, nimble stick-handling, and deft passing skills. Those centers who rise above the crowd also possess an accurate shot and championship-style leadership. Of the 25 best centers in history, 13 led the NHL in scoring and 18 wore the captain's "C."

*After captaining the Edmonton Oilers to four Stanley Cups, Wayne Gretzky eyed a fifth Cup with the Los Angeles Kings, falling just short in 1993.*

# SYL APPS

**A** true gentleman of sport, Syl Apps was defined by his skill and sportsmanship. When he broke into the NHL in 1936–37, fresh from the 1936 Olympics where he competed in track events, he quickly established his credentials. With a league-best 29 assists to go with 45 points in 48 games, he beat out linemate Gordie Drillon to win the Calder Trophy as the NHL's top freshman.

Apps was rugged but clean, combining great athletic skill and intelligence in equal measures. His career at McMaster University in Hamilton, Ontario, included track and field, hockey, and football. When he signed with Toronto in 1936, he was as close to a "sure thing" as anything the Leafs had ever known.

As an NHL sophomore in 1937–38, Apps again teamed with Drillon and former Kid Line hero Busher Jackson, and again he won the league assist title (29), finishing second to Drillon in the overall points race with 50. Eventually an aging Jackson was replaced by Bob Davidson, and in 1941–42 the Drillon-Apps-Davidson trio led Toronto to its first Stanley Cup in a decade, ending a period of frustration during which the Maple Leafs took six trips to the Finals without winning a single title.

However, with captain Apps in command, a new era began with the most dramatic comeback in the history of playoffs. Down three games to none to the powerful Detroit Red Wings, Toronto incredibly won the next four games to grab its most unlikely playoff championship and set a new high-water mark for perseverance.

The Maple Leafs' championship reign was interrupted by World War II. A consummate team player and patriot, Apps put his skyrocketing career on hold to enter the military and serve his country in Europe. As a result, he missed the 1943–44 and 1944–45 seasons. He made a triumphant return to the NHL in 1945–46 and took up where he left off, now grouped with new linemates Wild Bill Ezinicki and Nick Metz. Apps led a successful charge to the Stanley Cup Finals in 1946–47 and scored five playoff goals—including the OT winner in Game 4—to help Toronto beat Montreal in six games and take the Stanley Cup.

In 1947–48, his swan song, Apps once more regained his status as the Maple Leafs' top center, flanked by Ezinicki and Harry Watson. Together this trio notched 58 goals and 125 points. Apps led the team in goals (26) and points (53) while goalie Turk Broda led the NHL in wins (32) and goals-against average (2.38). This powerful combination gave Toronto a first-place finish in the regular season, which the Leafs parlayed into yet another trip to the Stanley Cup Finals. Apps had four points in the Finals as Toronto swept Detroit to retain the championship. At the age of 33, Apps retired in 1948 with three Stanley Cup rings, a Calder Trophy, and the 1942 Lady Byng Trophy as the game's most gentlemanly player.

*Apps competed for Canada as a pole-vaulter in the 1936 Olympics, finishing in sixth place.*

### NHL STATISTICS

| GP | G | A | PTS | PIM |
|-----|-----|-----|-----|-----|
| 423 | 201 | 231 | 432 | 56 |

# JEAN BELIVEAU

In the aftermath of Maurice "Rocket" Richard's dominance of hockey in Montreal, it would take a man of herculean strength and talent to carry the Canadiens to their next plateau. Just such a man was Jean Beliveau, *Le Gros Bill,* a tall, elegant center whose career in Montreal included 10 Stanley Cup titles. Much-decorated during his two decades of service, Beliveau won every major NHL award and was one of the most respected skaters of his or any era.

Born in Trois Rivieres, Quebec, Beliveau was a much sought-after youngster coming out of Quebec juniors, where he was a scoring hero. Eventually secured by the Canadiens, he made his NHL debut in 1950–51, but he didn't really emerge until the 1954–55 season, when he scored 37 goals and 73 points in 70 games. The next year, he won the Art Ross Trophy as NHL scoring champ with 47 goals and 88 points. In the spring of 1956, he led all playoff scorers (19 points) as the Habs won the first of five straight Cups from 1956–60.

Injuries cost him 15 games in 1957–58, but the following year Beliveau was back on top of his game, leading the NHL in goals (45) and tallying a career-high 91 points. A terrific playmaker and passer, Beliveau led the NHL in assists on two occasions (1961 and 1966). In 1965, after notching 16 points in 13 playoff games and helping the Habs win another Stanley Cup, Beliveau earned the first-ever Conn Smythe Trophy as playoff MVP.

On November 5, 1955, Beliveau enjoyed one of the most amazing nights in an amazing career. Against the lowly Boston Bruins, Beliveau ripped a three-goal hat trick against Terry Sawchuk, the winningest goalie in NHL history. However, this was no ordinary hat trick. Beliveau beat Sawchuk three times in just 44 seconds during the second period of play. What is even more shocking is that this feat was not an NHL record. In fact, it took twice as long as the mark set by Chicago's Bill Mosienko, who had scored three goals in 21 seconds during the 1951–52 season.

For his consistent excellence, Beliveau won the regular-season MVP award—the Hart Trophy—twice, first in 1955–56 and again in 1963–64. He finished second in the voting four times.

On February 11, 1971, during his 20th and final season in the NHL, Beliveau became only the fourth man in NHL history to reach the 500-goal plateau when he beat Minnesota North Stars goalie Gilles Gilbert. He joined Rocket Richard, Gordie Howe, and Bobby Hull on this prestigious list. Later that spring, the magnificent center notched 22 points in 20 playoff games and helped the Canadiens win their 16th Stanley Cup—the 10th of his career.

Beliveau ended his career with 507 goals and 1,219 points in 1,125 games, an average of 1.08 points per game. Just as dangerous during the high-pressure playoffs, he notched 79 goals and 176 points in 162 Stanley Cup games. Only a man of such grace and skill could have stepped so effectively into the void created by Rocket Richard's retirement.

*The quintessential Canadien, Beliveau was viewed as hockey's greatest ambassador in the post–Rocket era.*

## NHL STATISTICS

| GP | G | A | PTS | PIM |
|-------|-----|-----|-------|-------|
| 1,125 | 507 | 712 | 1,219 | 1,029 |

# MAX BENTLEY

**K**nown for his fast skating and nifty puck-handling, Max Bentley earned the amusing nickname "Dipsy Doodle Dandy of Delisle" for his skill and pleasing style on the ice. In a career that stretched over a dozen seasons and was interrupted for two years while he served in the Canadian Army during World War II, Bentley enjoyed the highest level of personal achievement during his tenure in Chicago, although he chalked up his greatest overall accomplishments—including three Stanley Cups—while skating for the Toronto Maple Leafs.

One of three brothers to play in the NHL, Max was sandwiched between older sibling Doug and right winger Bill Mosienko on Chicago's fabled Pony Line in the 1940s. (Reg Bentley, the eldest of the three, also skated briefly but without distinction for the Black Hawks.)

During the 1942–43 season, Max put his name in the record books when he scored four goals in a single period against the New York Rangers during a 10–1 victory—matching the feat of Toronto's Busher Jackson in the 1930s. Though Doug Bentley finished that 1942–43 season with the NHL scoring title (73 points), Max later one-upped his big brother by winning a pair of scoring titles. He won his first scoring championship when he led the NHL with 61 points

in 1945–46—also winning the Hart Trophy as MVP. He took his second scoring title the very next year with a career-high 72 points.

But despite his thrilling style, Max was unable to carry the Hawks to a Stanley Cup title. Thus, in a blockbuster deal in 1947–48, following his return from military service, Bentley was traded to Toronto for Gus Bodnar, Ernie Dickens, Bob Goldham, Bud Poile, and Gaye Stewart. Though disappointed to leave his brother, Bentley dutifully

reported to the Leafs and paid immediate dividends, scoring 11 points in nine playoff games, leading the Leafs in assists (seven) and helping them win their second consecutive Stanley Cup.

But Bentley wasn't done yet. Playing behind Charlie Conacher and Teeder Kennedy at center, Bentley chipped in 19 goals in 1948–49 and scored the insurance goal in Game 4 of the Finals to complete the Leafs' sweep of Detroit. Toronto was ousted by the Red Wings in the 1950 semifinals, but the Leafs were right back in the hunt in 1951. Bentley, who enjoyed his second-best season ever, topping Toronto in scoring with 62 points (third best in the NHL), then led all playoff scorers with 11 assists and tied Rocket Richard for the overall points lead (13) while Toronto systematically erased Montreal in the Stanley Cup Finals.

Bentley retired following the 1953–54 season after reuniting briefly with his brother Doug on the New York Rangers. He finished his career with two scoring titles, a Lady Byng Trophy, a Hart Trophy, and three Stanley Cup titles among his most outstanding accomplishments.

*Before he joined the NHL in 1940, Bentley was told by doctors to quit hockey due to a heart ailment.*

## NHL STATISTICS

| GP | G | A | PTS | PIM |
|-----|-----|-----|-----|-----|
| 646 | 245 | 299 | 544 | 179 |

# FRANK BOUCHER

Over the years, the NHL has featured countless men of gentility and manners, but few have rivaled the class demonstrated by New York Rangers legend Frank Boucher. From 1928–35, the Ottawa native won the Lady Byng Trophy—emblematic of gentlemanly play and excellence—seven times. A marvelous playmaker who led the NHL in assists three times, Boucher was so widely revered that following the 1934–35 season he was given the Lady Byng Trophy—to keep! A second trophy was cast for annual winners.

Boucher stood barely 5'9", but he was strong and sleek on his skates. He debuted in the NHL in 1921–22 with the Ottawa Senators, scoring nine goals while being overshadowed by Cy Denneny, Frank Nighbor, and Punch Broadbent. Boucher went west and spent the next four years with the Vancouver Maroons of the Pacific Coast Hockey Association. When the New York Rangers arrived on the NHL scene in 1926–27, Boucher was acquired and paired with Bill and Bun Cook. This Bread Line would become one of the most potent in all of hockey.

In 1927–28, the Bread Line combined for 55 goals—Boucher potted 23—and the Rangers finished second in their division. After advancing past Pittsburgh and Boston in the playoffs, the Rangers faced the powerful Montreal Maroons, led by Nels Stewart. Boucher became a one-man wrecking crew. His sudden-death overtime goal in Game 2 tied the series 1–1; his goal in Game 4—the game's only goal—saved the Rangers

from elimination; and, finally, he scored both goals in a 2–1 squeaker over the Maroons in Game 5 to earn New York its first-ever Stanley Cup title.

Boucher's star continued to rise. In 1929–30, he notched 26 goals, had a career-high 62 points, and was runner-up for the NHL scoring title. In 1930–31, he helped his right winger, Bill Cook, score 30 goals. The next year, Cook and Conacher topped the charts with 34 goals apiece. In 1932–33, Boucher led the NHL in assists (28) while Cook led in scoring with 50 points.

Despite a third-place division finish, the Rangers skated past Montreal and Detroit to gain a berth in the 1933 Stanley Cup Finals against Toronto. Boucher's trio shared the spotlight with the team's second line of Butch Keeling-Murray Murdoch-Cecil Dillon, but it

*Boucher's Rangers won the Cup in 1940 (his first year as coach) and finished in first place in 1941–42.*

was Boucher's starboard sniper who gunned home the decisive goal in Game 5, at 7:34 of sudden-death, to give the Rangers their second Cup.

Boucher retired in 1938. At the age of 42, he made a brief 15-game comeback in 1943–44, notching four goals and 14 points. By then he had already won his third Stanley Cup—as a rookie coach for the 1939–40 Rangers. Boucher coached New York until the 1948–49 season.

## NHL STATISTICS

| GP | G | A | PTS | PIM |
| --- | --- | --- | --- | --- |
| 557 | 161 | 262 | 423 | 119 |

# BOBBY CLARKE

With the game face of a junkyard dog and the courage of a battalion of soldiers, Bobby Clarke overcame formidable health obstacles as a young man and carved out a Hall of Fame NHL career by playing with grit in both ends of the rink. During Clarke's tenure as captain of the Philadelphia Flyers, the organization evolved from expansion pushovers to two-time Stanley Cup champions.

A native of Manitoba, Clarke starred in junior hockey and was picked in the second round of the 1969 entry draft. A diabetic condition requiring daily insulin injections raised some doubts about his fitness for the rugged world of the NHL, but Clarke wasted no time silencing critics and winning support. As a rookie in 1969–70, he scored 15 goals and was the team's third-leading scorer (46 points). As a sophomore, he led the team with 63 points. Steadily improving, he topped the Philly charts again the next year, with 81 points, and was awarded the Bill Masterton Trophy for perseverance. In 1972–73, he topped the 100-point mark with 37 goals and 67 assists. For his efforts, he earned the Hart Trophy as league MVP.

It was clear that Clarke won the Hart with heart. Besides his diabetic condition, he was modestly built at 5'10", 185 pounds. He didn't have the fastest feet or the hardest shot. But he was a sensational passer, a great defensive center, and, said Punch Imlach, "He gives more of himself than anybody I've ever seen."

By 1973, Clarke was ringleader of a team known as the Broad Street Bullies,

*Clarke is one of four Flyers to have his number (16) retired, along with Barry Ashbee, Bill Barber, and Bernie Parent.*

thanks to their use of intimidation to win. Though Clarke rarely fought, he earned a reputation as a gritty battler who didn't mind spilling blood to get the job done. In 1973–74, Philly became the first of the 1967–68 expansion teams to win a Stanley Cup when it beat Boston in six games in the Finals.

In 1974–75, the Flyers faced their biggest challenge—to defend their Stanley Cup. In his finest season yet, Clarke led the NHL in assists (89) and won his second Hart Trophy with a 116-point year. The Flyers bulled through the playoffs, culminating with a six-game triumph over Buffalo in the Finals. Clarke counted a dozen playoff assists and scored the winning goal in Game 2. Though Flyers goalie Bernie Parent won his second straight playoff MVP award, Clarke was viewed as the heart and soul of the team. And his best effort was yet to come.

In 1975–76, with everyone gunning for them, the Flyers won 51 of 80 games and finished second overall. They led the league in goals (348), thanks to another stellar effort from their captain. Clarke once more led the NHL with 89 assists and skated off with his third Hart Trophy, chalking up a career-high 119 points. With Clarke dishing off brilliant passes, his linemates, Bill Barber and Reg Leach, scored 50 and 61 goals, respectively (with Leach leading the league).

Clarke later added a Selke Trophy as the NHL's best defensive forward to his list of awards, then retired after the 1983–84 season. He added 119 points in 136 playoff contests and won a pair of Stanley Cup titles. Clarke served as general manager for the Flyers, Minnesota North Stars, and Florida Panthers before returning to Philadelphia in the role of president and GM in 1994.

| NHL STATISTICS | | | | |
|---|---|---|---|---|
| GP | G | A | PTS | PIM |
| 1,144 | 358 | 852 | 1,210 | 1,453 |

# ALEX DELVECCHIO

Like Sid Abel before him, Alex Delvecchio faced the daunting task of complementing one of the most talented and dominant right wingers in NHL history, Gordie Howe. A gifted playmaker and passer, Delvecchio became the perfect foil for Howe, helping Mr. Hockey achieve some of his greatest scoring feats. In 1952–53, then just a sophomore, Delvecchio took Abel's place on the Production Line and notched 43 assists. That year, Howe won the NHL triple crown, leading the NHL in goals (49), assists (46), and points (95).

Delvecchio's rookie year (1951–52) featured just 15 goals in 65 games, but it concluded with a Stanley Cup title when Detroit rode Terry Sawchuk's brilliant goaltending to sweep Toronto and Montreal, an eight-game run that gave birth to the now-famous octopus ritual in the Motor City.

Delvecchio was moved off the Production Line in 1953–54, when coach Tommy Ivan installed Earl Reibel between Howe and Ted Lindsay. Ironically, the Red Wings became a juggernaut, winning the 1954 and 1955 Stanley Cup titles. But during the 1955 playoffs, it was Howe, Lindsay, and Delvecchio who topped the scoring charts with a combined 54 points.

In 1957–58, with Lindsay in Chicago and Abel in retirement, Delvecchio was again paired with Howe, though he would once more be replaced temporarily at center by Norm Ullman (with Alex moving to the left wing). In 1962–63, Delvecchio helped Howe win another scoring title, and the two remained line-

mates for the next eight years, until Howe retired in 1971. During that span, Howe and Delvecchio played with an assortment of highly respected left wingers, including Vic Stasiuk, Parker MacDonald, Paul Henderson, Dean Prentice, and Frank Mahovlich.

Though Delvecchio never won a major scoring trophy, he was rewarded for his great sportsmanship, winning three Lady Byng Trophies (1959, 1966, and 1969). A consistent player who rarely missed any action, Delvecchio scored at least 20 goals in 13 of 17 seasons from 1955–72. He enjoyed his finest goal-scoring production with a career-high 31 goals in 1965–66 and had his best overall campaign in 1968–69, when he notched 83 points.

Delvecchio's 24 NHL seasons rank second all-time. Named captain of the Red Wings in 1962–63, he remained a team leader until his retirement in 1973. He finished up at the age of 42 with 1,549 regular-season games to his credit (and 121 more in playoff action). Only his longtime linemate Gordie Howe played more NHL games. However, no Red Wing has ever matched Delvecchio's durability. From 1956–64, the man affectionately known as "Fats" set a franchise record by playing 548 straight games. In his career, he won three Stanley Cup rings to match his three Lady Byng Trophies.

*Named team captain in 1962, Delvecchio wore the "C" for 11 years, longer than any Red Wing until Steve Yzerman.*

### NHL STATISTICS

| GP | G | A | PTS | PIM |
| --- | --- | --- | --- | --- |
| 1,549 | 456 | 825 | 1,281 | 383 |

# MARCEL DIONNE

If there was ever a doubt that good things can come in small packages, Marcel Dionne dispelled all uncertainty. Just 5'9", the fleet-footed center played 18 years in the NHL and amassed the third-highest number of points in the history of the game—most of it on woefully weak teams.

A native of Quebec and a scoring champ in junior hockey, Dionne arrived in the NHL in 1971–72 as the second pick overall in the 1971 entry draft. Only Guy Lafleur was more coveted by NHL teams. In Detroit, a fifth-place finish was all Dionne and the team could muster. But Dionne led the Red Wings in assists (49) and points (77).

To put an exclamation point on his first season of excellence, Dionne shrugged off any sophomore jinx mythology by ripping 40 goals and again leading Detroit in scoring with 90 points in 1972–73. He could do nothing to avoid another fifth-place Detroit finish. After a dismal third year (24 goals, 78 points), the speedy pivot broke through in 1974–75. While the team continued to lose far more games than it won, Dionne exploded for 121 points, third best in the NHL, and 47 goals. For his sportsmanship and excellence, Dionne earned his first Lady Byng Trophy.

Ironically, Dionne's build may have been an asset. He was nimble and swift on his feet as well as a marvelous stickhandler. Around the goal, he relied on an assortment of tricky moves to put the puck in the net. Moreover, at 190 pounds, he was solid enough to withstand daily punishment.

After playing out his contract in Detroit, Dionne signed a controversial free-agent deal with the Kings in 1975. Six times in the next eight years he scored at least 50 goals and 100 points. In 1979–80, he notched a career-high 137 points, tying NHL rookie Wayne Gretzky for first overall. Dionne beat Gretzky in the goal-scoring column (53 to 51) and won his only Art Ross Trophy as scoring champ. That year, he enjoyed his greatest success when he teamed with Charlie Simmer and Dave Taylor. The so-called Triple Crown Line scored 146 goals and 328 points, out-producing Montreal's top line of Steve Shutt, Pierre Larouche, and Guy Lafleur (305 points).

Though he won just one Art Ross Trophy, Dionne was a runner-up three times. But his most prestigious honors came with a pair of Lester B. Pearson Awards, the MVP trophy voted by his fellow NHLers, which he took home in 1979 and 1980.

Ultimately, Dionne's consistency as a goal-scorer enabled him to become just the third man in NHL history to reach the 700-goal mark, joining Gordie Howe (801) and Phil Esposito (717). Dionne eventually surpassed Esposito and finished with 731 career goals before Gretzky totally reconfigured the record books once and for all.

After nearly a dozen years in Los Angeles, Dionne was traded to the New York Rangers, where he enjoyed a 31-goal swan song in 1987–88. He finally hung up his skates in 1989. At the time, he was the third-most prolific scorer in NHL history with 1,771 points. The only thing Dionne never achieved in his brilliant career was a Stanley Cup; in fact, he never even reached the Cup semifinals. In view of his surroundings, however, his accomplishments were huge.

*Dionne became the first man in NHL history to reach the 500-goal mark while playing for a non–Original Six team.*

| NHL STATISTICS | | | | |
|---|---|---|---|---|
| GP | G | A | PTS | PIM |
| 1,348 | 731 | 1,040 | 1,771 | 600 |

# PHIL ESPOSITO

Only three men in NHL history—Wayne Gretzky, Gordie Howe, and Marcel Dionne—scored more goals than Phil Esposito. The leader of the Big, Bad Bruins of the 1970s, Esposito had a simple plan: Fire the puck quickly and make sure it's on net, and the rest will take care of itself.

Esposito ruled the NHL before Gretzky's arrival, and though his game was neither complex nor a thing of beauty, he was arguably the most dangerous weapon of his day. In 1970–71, he shattered the single-season goal mark when he scored 76 times in 78 games. Camping in front of the enemy net, he used his long reach and powerful wrists to whip home centering passes from his two board-crashing worker bees, Wayne Cashman and Ken Hodge. And God save the goalie who left a loose puck in the slot. Espo's specialty was shoveling in rebounds, regardless of the abuse heaped on him by defensemen.

Born in Ontario, Phil apprenticed with Chicago's junior team at St. Catherines, Ontario, before turning pro. In 1964–65, his first full season in the NHL, he centered a line with Bobby Hull and counted 32 assists. After four modest seasons, he was traded to Boston with Ken Hodge.

In Beantown, Espo immediately exploded, recording career highs in goals (35) and points (84) while leading the NHL in assists (49). In 1968–69, he won his first scoring title (126 points) and the first of two Hart Trophies as MVP. Never had a change of scenery netted better results.

With Bobby Orr on defense, Gerry Cheevers in goal, and Espo on the front line, the Big, Bad Bruins dominated. In 1969–70, Esposito's production fell to 99 points, but he established himself as the NHL's top goal-scorer (43). In the 1970 playoffs, he ripped 13 goals and 27 points in 14 games to lead in all categories. Riding Espo's broad shoulders, Boston skated past the Rangers, Chicago, and St. Louis in the playoffs (made memorable by Orr's flying OT goal in the final game against the Blues) and won their first Stanley Cup in 29 years.

Over the next four years, Esposito won four Art Ross Trophies as the NHL's top point-getter. In 1970–71, he scored 76 goals and 152 points, levels once thought unreachable. Amazingly, Espo fired 550 shots on goal (more than seven shots per game), obliterating Hull's record of 414. In 1971–72, he scored 66 goals and led the NHL with 133 points—and put the Bruins back in the playoff hunt. With series wins over Toronto, St. Louis, and the Rangers in the Finals, the Bruins

*Espo did the majority of his scoring damage—and he did a lot of it—from within 15–20 feet of the enemy cage.*

raised their second Cup in three years. Esposito tied Orr atop the leader board with 24 playoff points.

Esposito won two more scoring titles, tallying 55 goals and 130 points in 1972–73 and 68 goals and 145 points in 1973–74, when he won his second Hart Trophy. Esposito enjoyed one more extraordinary season, scoring 61 goals and 127 points in 1974–75. On November 7, 1975, in one of the biggest trades in hockey history, Esposito was traded to the rival Rangers for Brad Park and Jean Ratelle.

While he never found the 100-point range again, he enjoyed one last 40-goal season (42 tallies in 1978–79). He took the Rangers to the Finals in 1979, but the team lost to Montreal. Espo retired during the 1980–81 season with five scoring titles, two Hart Trophies, and a pair of Stanley Cups among his accomplishments.

## NHL STATISTICS

| GP | G | A | PTS | PIM |
|---|---|---|---|---|
| 1,282 | 717 | 873 | 1,590 | 910 |

# WAYNE GRETZKY

The most accomplished player in NHL history, Wayne Gretzky arrived in the NHL as a fuzzy-cheeked teenager in 1979 and soon began rewriting the record books, winning every conceivable award, capturing championships, and reviving hockey in a part of the country (namely California) where shinny was all but dead.

Born in Ontario, Gretzky spent his childhood and teenage years competing against older, stronger competition. Yet he was always the best. Using unparalleled instincts and graceful skating, he was a superstar despite his sparse build.

While skating for a local team as an 11-year-old, Gretzky scored 378 goals and 517 points in 85 games, winning the goal-scoring race by 238. He wore No. 9, in a chilling homage to his idol, Gordie Howe.

In 1978, after two years of junior hockey, Gretzky signed a million-dollar contract with the WHA's Indianapolis Racers. Sold to the Edmonton Oilers, he entered the NHL in 1979–80. As a rookie, he tied Kings veteran Marcel Dionne for the scoring lead (137 points) but lost the Art Ross Trophy when Dionne edged him in goals (53 to 51). No matter, Gretzky simply went out and won the next seven scoring titles. In 1981–82, his third NHL season, he went into a new orbit, scoring his 50th goal in December and finishing with 92 goals and 212 points. To date, he is the only player ever to reach the 200-point level.

In 1983–84, Gretzky took the Oilers to the promised land, leading them to their first Stanley Cup while pacing all playoff scorers (35 points in 19 games). In the next four years, the Oilers won three more Cups, with a brief interruption of their "dynasty" in 1985–86 when Montreal took the title.

In nine brilliant seasons in Edmonton, Gretzky tallied 583 goals, 1,086 assists, and 1,669 points in 696 games, notched 43 hat tricks, and amassed 55 short-handed goals (all of which remain as franchise records). He won a truckload of awards, including seven Art Ross Trophies, eight Hart Trophies (MVP), five Lester B. Pearson Awards (players' choice as MVP), a pair of Conn Smythe Trophies (playoff MVP), and the first of four Lady Byng Trophies.

In 1988, Gretzky orchestrated his trade to Los Angeles, where he put hockey back on the map as entertainment. Moreover, he converted the Kings from doormats to playoff contenders. In 1993, he carried them all the way to the Stanley Cup Finals against Montreal. However, a series of heartbreaking sudden-death overtime goals spelled the Kings' doom. In the meantime, however, Gretzky proved he was "The Great One," winning three more scoring titles (1990, '91, and '94) and three more Lady Byng Trophies (1991, '92, and '94).

On October 15, 1989, Gretzky notched his 1,851st point, passing his hero Howe to become the NHL's all-time leading scorer. Five years later, on March 23, 1994, he tallied the 802nd goal of his career to become the all-time leader in that department as well.

Traded to St. Louis late in 1995–96, Gretzky failed to "click" with right winger Brett Hull. As a free agent in the summer of 1996, he signed with the Rangers, where he reunited with ex-Oiler teammates Mark Messier and Jari Kurri. Though 36 years old, Gretzky was still among the league leaders in scoring.

*Gretzky has more assists than any man in NHL history has total points, passing Gordie Howe in 1997.*

| NHL STATISTICS | | | | |
|---|---|---|---|---|
| GP | G | A | PTS | PIM |
| 1,335 | 862 | 1,843 | 2,705 | 535 |

# DALE HAWERCHUK

For some youngsters, no curse is more fatal than being chosen first overall in the entry draft. But for Dale Hawerchuk, this prestigious honor served as a launching pad to a career that has included a record-setting rookie season, an extended run as a bona fide franchise player, and, ultimately, a place among the game's most prolific all-time goal-scorers.

A native of Toronto, "Ducky" was named Major Junior Canadian Player of the Year in 1980–81 after he scored 81 goals and 183 points in 72 games for Cornwall. That summer, he became the first player selected in the 1981 draft, by the Winnipeg Jets. Though pressure on Hawerchuk was tremendous, he delivered, setting a team record for rookie goals (45) and points (103). His Jets were mediocre, but he stood out and won the Calder Trophy as the game's most outstanding rookie.

Following a minor blip in his scoring (his sophomore jinx season featured 40 goals and 91 points), Hawerchuk put together five straight seasons with at least 100 points. His finest season came in 1984–85 when he scored 53 goals and 130 points, third overall in the league.

Despite Hawerchuk's excellence, the Jets played inconsistently from year to year. After nine years with the Jets, during which he scored 379 goals and 929 points, Hawerchuk asked for a trade in 1990. Ultimately, the Jets sent their all-time leading scorer to Buffalo for Phil Housley. The Jets also got a draft pick who would become their next franchise player, Keith Tkachuk.

In 1984–85, Hawerchuk was runner-up to Wayne Gretzky in voting for the Hart Trophy.

In 1992–93, though he notched only 16 goals, Hawerchuk recorded a career-high 80 assists and came within four clicks of his seventh 100-point season. In 1993–94, he resurrected his scoring touch and fired home 35 goals, his highest total in five years.

A durable player who missed only 16 games in his first 13 seasons, Hawerchuk was suddenly stymied by various aches and pains in 1994–95, the lockout season, playing only 23 of 48 games. With an eye toward the future, the Sabres let the 32-year-old's contract expire, and Dale signed with St. Louis for the 1995–96 campaign. On January 31, 1996, in Toronto, playing before a crowd of hometown friends and family, Dale scored his 500th career goal, making him the 23rd player in NHL history to reach that mark.

Unfortunately, Hawerchuk's stint in St. Louis failed to last an entire season. One of several high-buck veterans on the team, he found himself traded to Philadelphia late in the year. Many observers felt that, in moving away from St. Louis, Hawerchuk had been given a chance to redeem an otherwise disappointing season. And indeed, he finished the regular season with a flourish and was often the Flyers' best player in the playoffs.

## NHL STATISTICS

| GP | G | A | PTS | PIM |
| --- | --- | --- | --- | --- |
| 1,188 | 518 | 891 | 1,409 | 742 |

# TED KENNEDY

It would take a man of great skill and grace to follow successfully in the footsteps of such a hero as Syl Apps, who captained the Toronto Maple Leafs to two straight Stanley Cups. Such a man was Ted "Teeder" Kennedy, who took the "C" when Apps retired in 1948 and provided plenty of heroics of his own.

An Ontario native, Kennedy was playing junior hockey in his home province when former NHL great Nels Stewart discovered him. At the age of 17, Kennedy turned pro with Toronto and made his mark in 1943–44, when he scored 26 rookie goals, second to team veteran Lorne Carr (36).

In 1944–45, he led the Leafs in scoring (29–25–54) as Toronto finished third behind Detroit and Montreal. In the playoffs, Kennedy was instrumental in helping the Leafs knock off the Canadiens in the first round and survive a seven-game thriller against Detroit to win the Stanley Cup, eight months before his 20th birthday. He scored a hat trick in Game 4 and finished second only to Detroit's Joe Corvath for the most playoff points (nine).

When Kennedy missed all but 21 games of the 1945–46 season with injuries, the Leafs stumbled out of playoff contention. His return to form in 1946–47 sparked Toronto's return to success. Centering the team's top line with Vic Lynn and Howie Meeker, Kennedy led the way in goals (28), assists (32), and points (60) and was fifth best in the league in all categories. More important, by finishing second overall, the Leafs were back in the Stanley Cup hunt. Again, Kennedy was the hero. In the Finals against Montreal, he scored the winning goal in Game 2, added an insurance marker in Game 3, then scored the Stanley Cup-clinching goal 14:39 into the third period of Game 6 to give Toronto the title.

With the Maple Leafs now dominating the NHL, Kennedy's greatest moments lay ahead. In the 1948 playoffs, after relinquishing his team scoring leadership to Apps one last time, he helped the Leafs charge through a five-game opening-round series win over Boston before training his sights on Detroit in the Finals. After Toronto outscored Detroit 11–5 in three straight wins, Game 4 was barely three minutes old when Kennedy first struck. Later, in the second period, his eighth playoff goal provided the insurance as Toronto cruised to a 7–2 win and a sweep of its arch-rival. Kennedy's 14 playoff points topped the charts.

Despite his reputation for clean play, Kennedy's career was not without controversy. In the 1950 playoffs, Kennedy nearly killed Gordie Howe without ever touching him. After ducking a locomotive check from Howe, Kennedy watched as Howe catapulted headfirst into the boards, fracturing his skull and requiring lifesaving surgery. Kennedy was later exonerated, but his popularity in Detroit was never great.

Kennedy took Toronto to one last Stanley Cup (in 1951) and won a Hart Trophy (in 1955) before quitting in 1957. Following his retirement, his No. 9 jersey was taken out of circulation.

*Though he wasn't the smoothest skater, Kennedy was known for putting out a bigger effort than anyone else on the ice.*

| NHL STATISTICS | | | | |
|---|---|---|---|---|
| GP | G | A | PTS | PIM |
| 696 | 231 | 329 | 560 | 432 |

# ELMER LACH

The key man behind one of the greatest feats in NHL history—Rocket Richard's 50 goals in 50 games in 1944–45—Elmer Lach played much of his career in the shadow of legendary NHLers. But his own achievements (a Hart Trophy and two scoring championships) were more than enough to get him into the Hall of Fame. Lach's gifts in the pivot were his hands and his eyes. He not only could find the open winger in the heat of action, but he had the skills to get the puck to his linemates, who, for many years, were Rocket Richard and Toe Blake on the famed Punch Line.

A Saskatchewan product, Lach made his NHL debut in 1940–41, then broke his arm in the 1941–42 season opener and didn't play again that year. Back in the saddle in 1942–43, he scored 18 goals and 58 points while tying for fifth overall in assists (40). Around the NHL, folks quickly recognized a terrific playmaker in Lach. In 1943–44, united with Blake and Richard, Lach reached a career-high 72 points. After dominating the regular season with a 38–5–7 record, the Habs roared into the 1944 playoffs, ousting Toronto in five games before sweeping Chicago in the Finals. The lethal Blake-Lach-Richard line led all scorers with 18, 13, and 17 points, respectively.

In 1944–45, Lach led the NHL in assists (54) and points (80), establishing new personal highs. He won the scoring title and took the Hart Trophy as well. Still, much of his thunder was muffled by the explosive Rocket Richard, whose 50 goals in 50 games set an almost unthinkable new standard. The campaign ended in frustration as Montreal was a first-round playoff loser to the eventual Stanley Cup champion Maple Leafs.

Powered by the Punch Line, the Canadiens finished the 1945–46 season first overall. While Lach led the NHL in assists (34), his production fell to 47 points.

In the playoffs, however, he turned up the heat and carried Montreal to a first-round sweep of Chicago and a five-game victory over Boston. In nine games, Lach set up a dozen goals and led all scorers with 17 points.

Injuries carved a huge notch out of Lach's career. In 1946–47, he played just 31 games. And though he rebounded in 1947–48, winning a second scoring title (61 points), he then sat out much of the 1948–49 season. With Lach ailing, his Habs were hard-pressed to make much hay in the playoffs. They made the Finals three times between their 1946 Cup win and their next in 1953, but Lach managed just 10 points in 28 playoff games in that span.

In 1952–53, Lach played 53 games and tallied 41 points, showing some of his trademark intensity in the playoffs. After a spirited seven-game tussle with Chicago, the Habs outscored the Bruins 15–9 in the first four games of the Finals. Game 5 was 0–0 after regulation. At 1:22 of sudden-death, Lach scored the final playoff goal of his career, beating Sugar Jim Henry to give Montreal the Stanley Cup. Lach hung up his skates for good in 1954.

*Lach won three Stanley Cups, assisting the Cup-winning tally in 1946 and scoring the clincher himself in 1953.*

### NHL STATISTICS

| GP | G | A | PTS | PIM |
|-----|-----|-----|-----|-----|
| 664 | 215 | 408 | 623 | 478 |

# NEWSY LALONDE

**L**ong before Gordie Howe, Bobby Hull, Wayne Gretzky, and Mario Lemieux graced the NHL, the first superstar of pro hockey was already a legend. Newsy Lalonde—who played in the National Hockey Association, the Pacific Coast Hockey Association, and ultimately the National Hockey League —combined speed, great puck-handling ability, and a ferocious temper for an all-around game that was as effective on the scoreboard as it was in the trenches.

Born in Ontario, Edouard Lalonde (nicknamed "Newsy" following a short apprenticeship on a newspaper) turned pro in Sault Ste. Marie at the age of 18. In 1910–11, at just 23, he won his first NHA scoring title as a member of the Canadiens, banging home 38 goals in just 11 contests. In 1911, the truculent forward walked away from the Canadiens and traveled west to play in the rival PCHA, taking advantage of more lucrative salary opportunities. With Vancouver in 1911–12, he scored 27 goals and won that league's scoring title.

However, the lure of money wasn't enough to hold Lalonde in the West, and he returned to eastern Canada permanently in 1912–13, where he continued to create havoc.

Lalonde was a skater whose inventiveness and resourcefulness created scoring chances other players couldn't imagine. However, he was also known as a hatchetman, a player who would use his stick to do more than shoot the puck. A nastyboy of the first order, he staged some epic and bloody battles with "Bad Joe"

Hall and the Cleghorn brothers, Odie and Sprague. During one such episode, in 1912, Newsy hammered Odie Cleghorn with a check that not only reduced Odie to rubble but launched Odie's brother Sprague into a rage. The elder Cleghorn avenged his brother by attacking Lalonde with his stick, opening a 12-stitch gash across Newsy's forehead.

In 1917–18, when the NHL formed its present structure, Lalonde continued his scoring exploits, though he faced stiff competition from Joe Malone in Ottawa. The following year, Lalonde won his first of two scoring titles, leading the NHL with 32 points (including 23 goals) in 17 games. Two years later, he won his second scoring title with 33 goals and 41 points in 24 games.

In 1921–22, Lalonde's production dwindled to just nine goals, and he was swapped to Saskatoon of the Western league for Aurel Joliat, the next superstar of the Canadiens. In 1926–27, Lalonde made his way back to the NHL as a coach, spending a year with the New York Americans and actually playing one game. He moved on to Ottawa for two

seasons, then, after a one-year hiatus, was hired by the Canadiens, where he spent two and a half years. Despite his intensity, Lalonde never coached a team past the first round of playoffs.

Though his NHL career spanned just 99 games, Lalonde was one of hockey's most audacious and prolific performers, a legend in his own time.

*The most colorful player of his era, Lalonde played for nine teams in his 21-year career.*

| NHL STATISTICS | | | | |
|---|---|---|---|---|
| GP | G | A | PTS | PIM |
| 99 | 124 | 27 | 151 | 122 |

# MARIO LEMIEUX

Since his NHL debut in 1984, when he scored against Boston on the first shift of his first game, Mario Lemieux has been forced to withstand the awesome burden of carrying a franchise on his shoulders. Like all great players, he has delivered.

A native of Quebec, Lemieux was a junior scoring ace and Canadian Junior Player of the Year prior to Pittsburgh making him the first overall pick in the 1984 entry draft. As a rookie, he stockpiled 100 points and was unchallenged for rookie-of-the-year honors. As a sophomore, he won the Lester B. Pearson Award as the players' choice for MVP. In 1986–87, Lemieux broke the 50-goal barrier for the first time (54). And though Wayne Gretzky continued to own the overall scoring race for the next two years, Lemieux finally crested in 1987–88, scoring a league-high 70 goals, 98 assists, and 168 points, ending Gretzky's seven-year Art Ross Trophy domination. Lemieux also won his first Hart Trophy as MVP as well as his second Lester B. Pearson Award.

Lemieux took his game to another level in 1988–89, coming within one point of the 200-point plateau, where only Gretzky had gone before. Despite missing four games, Mario totaled 85 goals and 199 points to win his second straight Art Ross Trophy.

As injuries began to plague him, Lemieux played just 59 games in 1989–90. Despite his 123 points, the Pens failed to make the playoffs, and there were rumblings that, unlike his rival

Gretzky, Mario couldn't take his team to a playoff title. Though diminished by a herniated disc that caused excruciating pain, Mario continued to battle. Limited

*In his final year of junior hockey at Laval (Quebec), Lemieux scored 133 goals and 282 points in just 70 games.*

to only 26 games in 1990–91, he returned in time for the 1991 playoffs and spearheaded Pittsburgh's first real assault on a championship. With 16 goals and 44 points in 23 playoffs games, Lemieux

carried the Pens to their first Stanley Cup, taking the Conn Smythe Trophy as playoff MVP.

If all his critics were not yet silenced (and there were still some who called him selfish), Lemieux penned another dramatic chapter in his story when he won the 1991–92 scoring title with 131 points, despite missing 20 games. As a coda to a brilliant year, he guided the Penguins to another Stanley Cup with 34 playoff points in 15 games and won his second Smythe Trophy.

For Super Mario, the best—and worst—was yet to come. In 1992–93, well on his way to another scoring title, Lemieux was diagnosed with Hodgkin's disease and had to sit out 24 games while undergoing radiation therapy. In a legendary comeback, Mario returned to action and won his fourth Art Ross Trophy (161 points), his third Lester B. Pearson Award, his second Hart Trophy, and the Bill Masterton Trophy for perseverance. He also won over the last of his doubters. After taking a year off to recuperate in 1994–95, Lemieux rejoined the Pens in 1995–96 and won his fifth scoring title (69 goals and 161 points in 70 games). He also won the Hart Trophy for the third time. Lemieux retired in 1997 after copping yet another scoring crown.

| NHL STATISTICS | | | | |
|---|---|---|---|---|
| GP | G | A | PTS | PIM |
| 745 | 613 | 891 | 1,494 | 737 |

# MARK MESSIER

Measured against the greatest centers in NHL history, Mark Messier will always face comparison with longtime friend and teammate Wayne Gretzky, with whom he shared four Stanley Cup titles in Edmonton. Unlike Gretzky, who tried and failed to bring Stanley Cups to both Los Angeles and St. Louis after leaving Edmonton, Messier not only captained the Oilers to a fifth playoff title after No. 99 departed in 1988, but he then guided the 1993–94 Rangers to their first Stanley Cup in 54 years. He became the first man ever to captain two franchises to championships.

An Edmonton native, Messier made his NHL debut with the Oilers in 1979–80 following an uneventful year in the WHA. He grew quickly into his role as second-line center behind Gretzky, and in his third season (1981–82) he finished with 50 goals and 119 points.

While Gretzky rewrote the record books, Messier evolved into the backbone of the Oilers, the spiritual guide and jungle-tempered squad sergeant. In 1983–84, the Oilers knocked off the four-time defending-champion New York Islanders to capture their first playoff title. Even in Gretzky's huge shadow, Messier's performance—26 points in 19 games—shone through, and he was voted the Conn Smythe Trophy as MVP of the 1984 playoffs.

Though the Oilers were a dominant team from 1984–88, it wasn't until Gretzky left for Los Angeles that Messier earned the recognition his achievements merited. The team went through a brief rebuilding period in the immediate wake of Gretzky's exit, and Messier struggled with knee injuries that many feared would shorten his career. But he showed his trademark intensity and courage and regained both his health and his All-Star form. In 1989–90, he scored 45 goals and a career-high 129 points and won both the Hart Trophy and Lester B. Pearson Award as players' choice for MVP. Moreover, he took the Oilers to their fifth Stanley Cup in seven years. In the playoffs, he led all players with 22 assists and won his second Conn Smythe Trophy.

In 1991–92, Messier went to Broadway and faced his biggest challenge: to end the longest Stanley Cup drought in NHL history. Messier was an instant smash. Not only did he lead the Rangers to a Presidents' Trophy as the top regular-season team, but he notched his sixth 100-point season (35 goals, 107 points) and was awarded a second Hart Trophy and a second Pearson Award. In 1993–94, despite many intense challenges, primarily from New Jersey in the Stanley Cup semifinals, Messier would not let the Rangers lose in the playoffs. His dramatic Game 6 hat trick against the Devils staved off elimination and allowed New York to play a seventh game, which the Rangers won in sudden-death overtime. With Messier at the front, New York went on to beat Vancouver in the 1994 Finals.

During the 1995–96 season, Messier scored his 500th career goal. Only a late-season rib injury stopped this future Hall of Fame inductee from recording his second 50-goal season. One more chapter in the Messier saga was written in 1996–97, when Gretzky signed with the Rangers. Despite the presence of the Great One, Messier continued to wear the captain's "C."

*In 1996–97, Messier did what no NHLer before him could—turn Rangers teammate Wayne Gretzky into a second-line center.*

| NHL STATISTICS | | | | |
|---|---|---|---|---|
| GP | G | A | PTS | PIM |
| 1,272 | 575 | 977 | 1,552 | 1,596 |

# STAN MIKITA

On February 22, 1977, three months shy of his 37th birthday, Chicago Black Hawk legend Stan Mikita beat Vancouver goalie Cesare Maniago for his 500th NHL goal, ensuring his place in the Hall of Fame. It was a crowning moment in the career of a man who had survived abject poverty in his native Czechoslovakia, who had endured difficult years as a child immigrant in Ontario, and who had lived through an early pro hockey tenure characterized more by brutality than by skill.

Sent as a child by his parents to live with more prosperous relatives in eastern Canada, Stan Mikita (born Stanilsav Gvoth) was a gifted athlete as a boy, though he was small and spoke with an accent that made him a target of bullies. He grew a tough hide and learned to stand up for himself. After an eye-catching junior hockey career at St. Catherines, Mikita turned pro in 1958.

In 1960–61, Mikita got his first and only taste of Stanley Cup success. After scoring 19 goals playing on the Hawks' second line with Kenny Wharram and Ab McDonald, he led all playoff scorers with six goals and set up McDonald's Cup-clinching goal in Game 6 of the Finals against Detroit. A pitiless soldier who could make a dandy pass or drop his gloves and fight if you looked at him sideways, Mikita would soon become known as one of the game's best, and nastiest, players.

In 1963–64, Mikita won his first scoring title with 89 points. But he was also the game's leading "bad boy" with 149 penalty minutes. He repeated his

*Inventor of the "banana blade," Mikita was deadly with his weapon—until the NHL imposed curve limitations.*

excellent playmaking in 1964–65, topping the charts in assists (59) and points (87), and rang up a career-high 154 PIM. In a five-year span from 1963–68, "Stash" won four scoring titles and finished second to teammate Bobby Hull the other time.

In 1965–66, a dramatic change altered the course of Mikita's career. Though he continued to play with brilliant creativity, the 25-year-old abandoned his hot-tempered style in favor of more genteel conduct. So extreme was his reversal that he went from 154 PIM to just 54 in one year. In 1966–67, when he won his third Art Ross Trophy with 97 points, he also won the Hart Trophy as MVP and the Lady Byng Trophy for sportsmanship, making him the game's first triple crown winner. No player had ever won three major awards in a single season.

In 1967–68, the clever pivot reached a career high in goals (40) and won his final scoring title (87 points) while taking a second Hart Trophy and Lady Byng Trophy in the process. Though he never got the Black Hawks to another Stanley Cup title, they made it to the Finals in 1965, 1971, and 1973, losing all three times to Montreal.

Mikita retired in 1979–80 as the team's all-time leading scorer (1,467 points), while leading in games played (1,394) and assists (926).

## NHL STATISTICS

| GP | G | A | PTS | PIM |
|---|---|---|---|---|
| 1,394 | 541 | 926 | 1,467 | 1,270 |

# HOWIE MORENZ

One of the largest crowds ever to fill the Montreal Forum didn't come to watch a hockey game, but to pay respects to perhaps the most thrilling player ever to grace their rink. In March 1937, thousands of fans passed the coffin of Howie Morenz as he lay in state at center ice. Morenz, who died suddenly at 35 while recovering in the hospital from hockey injuries, was arguably the greatest player ever to wear the *bleu, blanc, et rouge* of *Les Habs*.

A native of Ontario, Morenz came up through juniors in the early 1920s, when area NHL teams controlled players and teams. In a monumental gaffe, the Maple Leafs failed to recognize star power in the smallish Morenz, so he joined Montreal at 21 and made his NHL debut in 1923–24. With great skating and puck-handling ability, Morenz quickly won over Canadiens fans.

As a rookie, he got his name on Montreal's first NHL Stanley Cup when the Habs won a two-game set against Calgary of the Western Canada Hockey League. Morenz ripped a hat trick in Game 1 (a 6–1 rout), then scored the opening goal, the winner, in a 3–0 Cup-clinching victory in Game 2.

With explosive skating speed that earned him the nickname "Stratford Streak" (for the Ontario town of his origin), Morenz began to dominate in 1927–28, when he led the NHL in goals (33) and won his first scoring title with 51 points in 43 games. He also took home the Hart Trophy as MVP.

Playing on a front line with Aurel Joliat and Art Gagne (and later, Johnny "Black Cat" Gagnon), Morenz became one of the game's prominent snipers. In 1928–29, he was third overall in points (27), then scored a career-high 40 goals the following year, third behind Bruins Cooney Weiland (43) and Dit Clapper (41). However, it was Morenz who led the Canadiens over Boston in the two-game Stanley Cup Finals—and Morenz who scored the Cup-winning goal late in the second period of Game 2, a closely fought 4–3 conquest.

In 1930–31, the Habs ruled the NHL. Morenz led all scorers, taking his second scoring title (28 goals, 51 points) and second Hart Trophy. In the playoffs, Montreal dispatched Boston in the semifinals, then squeaked out a five-game series victory over Chicago. Morenz was quiet until the final game. With Montreal holding a 1–0 lead late in the game, Morenz beat Charlie Gardiner for his only goal of the Finals, ensuring Montreal's victory.

Morenz won his last Hart Trophy in 1931–32, after which his scoring began to fade. In 1934–35, he was traded to Chicago, where he stayed less than two years before moving briefly to the Rangers. He rejoined the Habs in 1936–37, a shadow of his former self, then suffered a badly broken leg during the campaign. While hospitalized, he suffered a fatal heart attack. All of Canada mourned the fallen hero.

*Only a series of nagging injuries kept Morenz from finishing his career with 300 goals and point-per-game status.*

## NHL STATISTICS

| GP | G | A | PTS | PIM |
|-----|-----|-----|-----|-----|
| 550 | 270 | 197 | 467 | 563 |

# GILBERT PERREAULT

In the spring of 1970, the expansion Buffalo Sabres were welcomed into the NHL. Not long after, the Sabres made the first overall pick in the annual entry draft and, to nobody's surprise, selected Montreal Jr. Canadiens scoring ace Gilbert Perreault, the MVP of the Ontario juniors. Perreault's assignment was clear: Carry the fledgling Sabres from obscurity to playoff contention.

A stocky center who had pistons for legs and a rocket-launcher for a shot, Perreault quietly accepted his commission and immediately set about bringing credibility to Buffalo. As a rookie in 1970–71, he scored 38 goals, led the team in points (72), and was voted rookie of the year.

In his second season, he reunited with Rick Martin, a former junior teammate, who took up his familiar post on Perreault's left side. Together, the fast-skating, hard-shooting pair notched 70 goals and 148 points. Unfortunately, they could not undo the team's woeful losing trend as the team finished 16–43–19. The final piece of the puzzle arrived the following year, 1972–73, when ex-Leafs prospect Rene Robert came from Pittsburgh in a deal for veteran Eddie Shack.

Robert was installed on Perreault's right side, and a deadly new trio, dubbed the French Connection Line, was born. The effects were immediate and dramatic. The line scored 105 goals and 244 points, and the team went 37–27–14 and made the playoffs for the first time, though it was quickly eliminated by the Canadiens. Perreault's 60 assists were fifth best in the league, and he won the Lady Byng Trophy for his combined sportsmanship (10 PIM) and excellence (88 points).

In 1973–74, a knee injury wrecked Perreault's year. He played only 55 games, and the team failed to get into the playoffs. But in 1974–75, in a newly aligned NHL, the Sabres cut a path to the top of the Adams Division with a 49–16–15 record. The French Connection Line combined for 131 goals and 291 points and carried the Sabres to the Stanley Cup playoffs.

The Sabres won their first-ever playoff series, against Chicago in the 1975 quarterfinals, then upset the Canadiens in the semis to earn a berth in the Stanley Cup Finals. Their opponents were the defending-champion Philadelphia Flyers. Though they were shut down by Philly in the first two games, the French Connection Line enjoyed a moment of high drama in Game 3, when Perreault and Martin assisted Robert's sudden-death OT winner to cap a comeback victory. The Sabres tied the series the following night, and Perreault scored his sixth goal of the playoffs. But the Flyers hammered Buffalo with two straight wins to win the Cup. Still, Perreault and his team had proven they were a force to be reckoned with. Sadly, the Sabres never got back to the Finals, losing in the first or second round each of the next 10 seasons.

Perreault, who made the Hall of Fame in 1990, played 17 seasons and had his No. 11 jersey retired following his retirement in 1987.

*With a huge skating stride, Perreault struck fear into the hearts of even the most confident and capable defenders.*

| NHL STATISTICS | | | | |
|---|---|---|---|---|
| GP | G | A | PTS | PIM |
| 1,191 | 512 | 814 | 1,326 | 500 |

# JOE PRIMEAU

One mark of a great player is his ability to evolve as the game around him changes. Few players in NHL history so dramatically exploited a rules change as did Joe Primeau, a tricky, little playmaker who took full advantage of the NHL's decision, in 1927, to allow forward passes in the offensive zone. In a relatively short career that spanned only seven full seasons, Primeau led the league in assists three times.

For much of his NHL tenure, he was teamed on Toronto's top line between Charlie Conacher and Busher Jackson, known as the Kid Line. In 1931–32, Primeau notched a league-high 37 assists, Conacher tied for the league lead in goals (34), and Jackson won the scoring championship (53 points)—the first time a line had dominated all scoring categories. For his part in the brilliant performance of the unit, Primeau won the Lady Byng Trophy, for his clean play and high degree of excellence.

Primeau made his NHL debut in 1927–28, but he played only two games for the Leafs that year and appeared in just six the next season. He was not very tall and was extremely lean—he tipped the scales at 153 pounds—and some doubted that a player of Primeau's nonabrasive style could survive in the rough-and-tumble world of the NHL. But he had some powerful allies, not the least of whom was Frank Selke Sr., who had found him playing junior hockey in Ontario and brought him to the attention of Leafs boss Conn Smythe in the first place.

It wasn't until the 1929–30 season that Primeau "arrived," still at the tender age of 23. In 1930–31, he led the NHL in assists (32) for the first time and quickly established himself as one of the craftiest playmakers of his era. It didn't hurt to know that if he dished the puck to Conacher, on the right side, he could rely on one of the strongest shots in the game, or that if he went the other way, to left winger Busher Jackson, he could expect his mate to conduct an artful and deadly attack on the enemy goal.

The following season (1931–32), Primeau's Kid Line began to display a frightening ability to dominate. They not only carried the Leafs all the way to the Stanley Cup Finals, where they faced New York, but were a critical force in the Leafs' charge to a Stanley Cup. Toronto scored 18 goals in their three-game sweep of the Rangers. The Kid Line—as a unit and individually—had a hand in 13 of those goals.

With Primeau's trio at the helm, the Maple Leafs returned to the Finals three times from 1933–36. Unfortunately, they were unable to win another Stanley Cup,

losing to the Rangers in 1933, the Montreal Maroons in 1935, and the Red Wings in 1936.

"Gentleman Joe" Primeau retired following the 1935–36 season, just 30 years old. Noticing his skills beginning to erode, he decided he wouldn't be a hanger-on. He left the NHL with 66 goals and 243 points, plus one Stanley Cup title.

*Primeau came closest to winning a scoring title in 1931–32, when he finished three points behind linemate Busher Jackson.*

### NHL STATISTICS

| GP | G | A | PTS | PIM |
|----|----|-----|-----|-----|
| 310 | 66 | 177 | 243 | 105 |

# HENRI RICHARD

Henri Richard originally came into his famous nickname, "Pocket Rocket," by virtue of being the younger (and physically smaller) brother of hockey's most intense superstar, Maurice "Rocket" Richard. In later years, however, Henri proved that although he was short (just 5'7"), he had all the explosiveness the family name had come to connote.

During a 20-year career with Montreal, Richard played in 180 playoff games, went to the Finals 12 times, and won 11 Cups, losing only in the 1967 Finals to Toronto. During this stretch of excellence, Richard also became one of only eight men in NHL history to score two Stanley Cup-clinching goals.

Richard came to the Canadiens in 1955–56, during the 14th year of Rocket Richard's reign. The brothers, separated by 15 years, occasionally teamed on a line. The younger sibling, who was at first given only a small chance of surviving in the NHL because of his stature, had to carve out every ounce of respect he could from the opposition. As a rookie, he scored 19 goals.

In his first five NHL seasons, Richard's playoff record was perfect. Five trips to the postseason; five Stanley Cups. He also developed into a more dangerous scorer during those years, raising his total to 30 goals by 1960.

In 1966, the Habs faced the Red Wings in the Finals. Richard already owned six Stanley Cup rings by then, and he had been very quiet in these playoffs, with no points against Toronto in the semifinals and just four assists in the first five games against Detroit. With Game 6 of the Finals tied 2–2 after 60 minutes, the teams headed to sudden-death OT. Richard, who had 24 goals in 80 previous playoff games, awoke and added his name to the history books when he scored on Roger Crozier just 2:30 into the extra session to give Montreal its 13th Stanley Cup championship.

A good but not great playmaker and goal-scorer, Richard never won a scoring title during his two decades of NHL service, although he was runner-up to Dickie Moore in 1957–58 when he notched 80 points. In 1959–60 and 1962–63, he finished fourth overall. Consistency was his greatest trait—particularly in high-pressure situations.

In Game 7 of the 1971 Finals against Chicago, Richard again displayed the backbone that had enabled him to thrive despite the enormous weight of his family name. With the decisive game knotted at 2–2, Richard beat Tony Esposito to give his Habs a lead. Montreal rookie goalie Ken Dryden held the Black Hawks at bay, and the Canadiens held on to win the Cup, Richard's 10th.

Scrappy and talented, the Pocket Rocket put his name on one last Cup (1973) and was rewarded for his perseverance with the 1974 Masterton Trophy before quitting in 1975.

*Richard (right) went to the playoffs 18 times and won a record 11 Stanley Cups.*

| NHL STATISTICS | | | | |
|---|---|---|---|---|
| GP | G | A | PTS | PIM |
| 1,256 | 358 | 688 | 1,046 | 928 |

# DENIS SAVARD

Growing up in Quebec, it was Denis Savard's childhood dream to win a Stanley Cup with the Montreal Canadiens. Although it took him until he was 32, Savvy finally made the grade in 1993. Before he ever donned a Montreal jersey, however, he spent 10 brilliant seasons in Chicago.

A scoring ace in the Quebec juniors, Savard scored 109 goals and 339 points in 142 games over his last two years and became the third player picked in the 1980 entry draft, after Montreal took Doug Wickenheiser and Winnipeg chose Dave Babych. Deeply disappointed to have been passed over by the Canadiens, Savard joined the Black Hawks in 1980–81 and scored 28 rookie goals. Over the next five years, he steadily increased his goal production, from 32 to a career-high 47 in 1985–86. Meanwhile, Wickenheiser proved to be one of the biggest busts in draft history.

A dynamic skater with explosive speed and catlike agility, Savard was responsible for creating the "Spin-o-rama," a move in which he executed a 360-degree turn in front of the defender, all the while maintaining control of the puck, then swooping in on the goalie. Other skaters have tried to copy the move, but precious few have enjoyed Savvy's success.

In 1987–88, Savard reached a career-high 131 points while centering a line with tough guy Al Secord and ironman Steve Larmer. Earlier, during the 1982–83 season, Savard had worked a special kind of magic, transforming Secord from a one-dimensional brawler into a bona fide goal-scoring threat.

*A brilliant playmaker, Savard (No. 18) is second all-time on the Chicago assists list, trailing only Stan Mikita.*

With Savard setting him up, Secord ripped 54 goals in 1982–83, then, after suffering through two terrible seasons of injuries, rebounded with 40 goals in 1985–86, again thanks largely to the playmaking ability of his centerman, Savard.

The beginning of the end for Savard in Chicago came in 1988–89, when the Black Hawks hired Mike Keenan to run the bench. Failing—or refusing—to recognize Savard's gifts, Keenan attempted to change Savard from a highly accomplished artiste into just another cog in the wheel. The chemistry between Keenan and Savard was slightly less volatile than gasoline and fire, but not much. In the summer of 1990, Keenan convinced the Hawks to ship Savard to Montreal for Chris Chelios, who happened to have been born and raised in Chicago.

After a pair of 28-goal seasons in Montreal, Savard's role began to dwindle. In 1992–93, he played only 63 games and was often scratched. However, he remained a valuable team player who would give a total effort every time he hit the ice, and in the spring of 1993 he was rewarded as the Habs eliminated Los Angeles in the Stanley Cup Finals.

Savard enjoyed a renaissance in 1993–94, scoring 18 goals for Tampa Bay. And when Jeremy Roenick was seriously injured late in the 1994–95 season, Savard was reacquired by the Hawks, where he was one of the team's most valuable veterans.

| NHL STATISTICS | | | | |
|---|---|---|---|---|
| GP | G | A | PTS | PIM |
| 1,196 | 473 | 865 | 1,338 | 1,336 |

# MILT SCHMIDT

From 1924–97, the Boston Bruins won the Stanley Cup five times. Hall of Fame center Milt Schmidt was largely responsible for two of those titles, emerging as a rising star in the 1939 playoffs and two years later setting up the Cup-winning goal in 1941. Some say Schmidt was the Phil Esposito of his era, a player known for his offensive skill and leadership. Others insist that Esposito, who came years later, was the Milt Schmidt of his era.

Schmidt was both consistent and capable of scorching hot streaks. In fact, as hot streaks go, the Ontario native enjoyed one of the greatest of all time during the 1941 Stanley Cup Finals. The driving force of Boston's fabled Kraut Line, Schmidt either scored or set up all four game-winning goals in the Bruins' masterful sweep of Detroit.

In Game 1, he assisted Pat McCreavy's goal to give the Bruins an insurmountable 3–0 lead as they won 3–2. Two nights later, he set up Roy Conacher's only goal of the playoffs, the winner in a 2–1 thriller that wasn't decided until just 2:15 remained to play in the game. In Game 3, won by Boston 4–2, Schmidt untied a 2–2 nail-biter 59 seconds into the middle frame. His goal stood up as the winner. Finally, in Game 4, he set up Boston's first two goals as the Bruins erased a 1–0 deficit, tied the game, and went ahead to stay midway through the second period. Schmidt's 11 playoff points that year topped all players. Had there been a Conn Smythe Trophy in those days, Schmidt would have been a unanimous choice.

The Kraut Line, consisting of Schmidt and his two childhood buddies, Woody Dumart and Bobby Bauer, was a mighty force in the NHL during the late 1930s and early 1940s. Schmidt made his NHL debut during the 1936–37 season, but he didn't begin to shine until 1938–39 when he notched a modest 32 points in 41 games before playing so well in the playoffs. In 1939–40, he led the NHL in assists (30) and won the scoring championship with 52 points. Bauer and Dumart tied for second with 43 points apiece. In the playoffs, the Bruins ran into a hot goalie in the semifinals (Davey Kerr of the New York Rangers) and saw their hopes of defending the Cup dashed.

In 1940–41, Boston played with a vengeance, leading the NHL in goals (168) and points (67). An assortment of Bruins had starring roles. Bill Cowley won the scoring title (62 points). Roy Conacher was second overall in goals (24). Schmidt was fourth in assists (25), but his greatest moments were yet to come in the Finals against Detroit.

Sadly, the history books reflect as much about potential as they do about achievement for Schmidt and his cohorts, for the Kraut Liners lost three crucial years (1942–45) when they left the NHL to fight in World War II. Schmidt returned to play another decade and won the Hart Trophy in 1950–51 with a career-high 61 points, but he never tasted Stanley Cup champagne again. He retired in 1955.

*Not only a great scoring threat, Schmidt was also the enforcer on Boston's Kraut Line, flexing his muscles as necessary.*

### NHL STATISTICS

| GP | G | A | PTS | PIM |
|-----|-----|-----|-----|-----|
| 778 | 229 | 346 | 575 | 466 |

# NELS STEWART

W hen the phrase "complete package" is attached to an athlete, it typically denotes a rare capacity in such a player to thrive in various aspects of his sport. One such complete package was Nels "Old Poison" Stewart, whose NHL career spanned 15 years from 1925–40. Big and strong, he was both graceful with the puck as well as fearsome with his fists; he was a goal-scoring champion and penalty-minute leader.

Stewart, who hailed from Montreal, made his NHL debut in 1925–26 with the Maroons. His first tour of duty in the NHL was a smashing success. He led all goal-scorers (34), won the scoring title (42 points), and bashed his way to 119 penalty minutes. Only Toronto's Bert Corbeau had more penalty time (121 minutes). Moreover, Stewart then spearheaded Montreal's four-game triumph over Victoria of the Western Hockey League in a best-of-five Stanley Cup title series. Taking the weight of the playoffs on his muscular shoulders, Stewart scored all three winning goals—in Games 1, 2, and 4—and counted six tallies in the series.

The sophomore jinx descended on Stewart in 1926–27, when his goal production was halved, from 34 to 17. But his truculence was even more pronounced, as he led the league with 133 penalty minutes. Stewart was back in form in 1927–28, scoring 27 goals (third in the league) and finishing fifth overall in points (34). By now Howie Morenz had emerged as the rival Canadiens' ace, and Stewart was hard-pressed to push his

Maroons ahead of the Habs in the standings. That year, Stewart's team did upset the Canadiens in the Stanley Cup semifinals but couldn't solve the New York Rangers in the Finals, losing in five dramatic games.

Old Poison was at his most potent in 1929–30, when he notched a career-high 39 goals, centering the awesome Big S Line with Babe Siebert and Hooley Smith. The trio combined for 74 goals and 118 points, and the Maroons finished first in the Canadian Division. For his part, Stewart was awarded his second Hart Trophy. But that was as far as he and his team got, as Boston knocked them off in the Cup semifinals, winning three of four games, with Games 1 and 3 going to triple and double overtime, respectively.

At the age of 30, Stewart was traded to the Bruins. He spent three years in Boston, though his skills were on the decline and his numbers were dropping. In 1935–36, he joined the New York Americans, then went back to Boston briefly in 1936–37 before finishing his career with the Amerks. That year, with 23 markers, Stewart tied Detroit's Larry Aurie for the league goal-scoring lead in what was his last moment of NHL glory.

Old Poison packed it in after the 1939–40 season, counting 324 goals and 515 points over his career in the NHL. He was hockey's most prolific goal-scorer until Maurice Richard passed him during the 1952–53 season. More than 50 years after his final game, Stewart remains one of the top 100 goal-scorers in NHL history.

*Though he wasn't the most nimble skater, Stewart had a way of getting into position to unleash his huge wrist shot.*

### NHL STATISTICS

| GP | G | A | PTS | PIM |
|-----|-----|-----|-----|-----|
| 650 | 324 | 191 | 515 | 953 |

# BRYAN TROTTIER

One reason Bill Torrey will be remembered as a great GM is that he had the wisdom to acquire vastly gifted players through the entry draft, chief among them Denis Potvin and Bryan Trottier. While Potvin was the nerve center of the Islanders' defense with his hard-nosed play, Trottier—a scrappy center with Hall of Fame talent—emerged as the team's heart and soul, a player who faced competition from such stars as Bobby Clarke, Gilbert Perreault, and Wayne Gretzky and yet was considered the best two-way pivot in the game during much of his 18-year career.

Tough as nails and blessed with the grace of a natural playmaker, Trottier, the 22nd player picked in the 1974 draft, led the Western juniors in assists (98) in 1974–75. He then debuted with the Isles in 1975–76 and was voted rookie of the year based on his 32 goals and 95 points. Two years later, in 1977–78, Trottier led the Isles in scoring with 123 points (including 46 goals) and made the NHL First All-Star Team.

Teamed with rugged Clark Gillies to the left and sniper Mike Bossy to the right, Trottier soared to new heights, winning the 1979 scoring title with 134 points, including a league-high 87 assists. That year, Bossy scored 69 goals and Gillies finished tied for ninth in points (91). Trottier also won the Hart Trophy as MVP. Favored to go all the way to the Stanley Cup Finals, Trottier and his team endured the last "growing pains" when they were upset by the Rangers in the 1979 semifinals.

In 1979–80, Trottier took the Isles to hallowed ground. After enjoying his third of six 100-point seasons, he led all playoff scorers with 12 goals and 29 points. The Isles won their first Stanley Cup on a Game 6 sudden-death overtime goal from Bobby Nystrom and began an era of eminence that would place them among the great dynasties of all time. Voted the Conn Smythe as the playoffs' MVP, Trottier entered his salad days as a team leader, a role in which he was unrivaled.

Over the next three years, the Islanders won three more Stanley Cups. While Trottier had given up hope of winning another scoring title (as Gretzky was entrenched as the game's top scorer), his effectiveness at the helm sustained. In 1981–82, he led all playoff scorers with 29 points, and the Isles hoisted their third straight Cup. The Islanders ultimately managed to defend their playoff title through the 1983 playoffs before injuries and age took the final toll.

After 15 years with the Isles, Trottier signed with Pittsburgh in 1990–91. In a supporting role, he played two years, taught the young Pens how to win, and added two more Stanley Cups to his impressive resume. After one year of retirement, Trots suited up for 41 games with Pittsburgh sin 1993–94 before finally calling it quits.

*While other centers had more finesse, bigger shots, and more speed, few could match Trottier's sheer determination.*

### NHL STATISTICS

| GP | G | A | PTS | PIM |
|---|---|---|---|---|
| 1,279 | 524 | 901 | 1,425 | 912 |

# STEVE YZERMAN

Hockey fans in Detroit are among the luckiest in the NHL, for they've been privileged to watch some of the greatest players ever— Gordie Howe, Terry Sawchuk, Ted Lindsay, to name just three—play their greatest hockey. And, of course, in more modern times they've had Steve Yzerman, Motown's other Stevie Wonder, to marvel at as well.

Yzerman came to the NHL in 1983–84 as the fourth overall pick in the 1983 entry draft. A good scorer in juniors, he missed lots of action due to injuries in his last two years, but he made an immediate impact when he ripped

*Yzerman was named Detroit's captain at age 21 and was the NHL's Comeback Player of the Year in 1986–87 at age 22.*

39 goals and 87 points as an NHL freshman. He was outvoted by Buffalo goalie Tom Barrasso for the Calder Trophy but did win a spot on the NHL All-Rookie Team. After a strong second season, he was injured badly in 1985–86 and played only 51 games.

To date, Yzerman had not yet lived up to the expectations of many who had seen superstar qualities in the young Ontario native. When Red Wings coach Jacques Demers pasted the captain's "C" on his jersey, Yzerman seemed to come alive. In 1987–88, fully recovered from his torn-up knee, he began an era of elite productivity that earned him a place in team history as one of the greatest centers to wear the flying wheel crest. Using his great speed, agility, and puck-handling skill, he put together four successive seasons with 50, 65, 62, and 51 goals, while notching 102, 155, 127, and 108 points. His performance in 1988–89, when he scored 65 goals and 155 points, earned him the Lester B. Pearson Award (the players' choice for MVP) and made him one of only four men in league history to notch as many as 150 points in a season.

From 1987–93, Yzerman put together six straight 100-point years. Another serious injury knocked

him out of 26 games in 1993–94, and the lockout-shortened schedule in 1994–95 cut into his scoring. In 1995–96, when the Red Wings were the pride of the NHL, Yzerman overcame public notions that he had been reduced to second-banana status behind Sergei Fedorov and finished with 95 points.

On January 17, 1996, with the flick of his wrists and a natural-born sniper's accuracy, Yzerman corralled a loose puck in the slot and quickly lifted it into the top corner of the Avalanche net over fallen goalie Patrick Roy. The goal, one of 36 on the season, enabled him to enter the record books as only the 22nd player in NHL history to score 500 career goals. The moment was one of many high points in a season that saw Detroit dominate the NHL and set a record with 62 wins. Yzerman also scored an overtime goal in Game 7 of the conference semifinals against St. Louis. However, the team failed yet again to win the Stanley Cup despite its status as overwhelming playoff favorite, thus extending the Detroit drought to 41 years.

The subject of trade rumors for more than a couple of years, Yzerman proved during the 1995–96 campaign that he was not only one of hockey's most gifted performers (with a points-per-game average in the 1.3 range), but also one of its classiest—never complaining, just doing his job with grace and skill.

| NHL STATISTICS | | | | |
|---|---|---|---|---|
| GP | G | A | PTS | PIM |
| 1,023 | 539 | 801 | 1,340 | 694 |

# 25 BEST WINGERS

Andy Bathgate
Toe Blake
Mike Bossy
Charlie Conacher
Bill Cook
Yvan Cournoyer
Cy Denneny
Babe Dye
Mike Gartner
Bernie Geoffrion
Rod Gilbert
Michel Goulet
Gordie Howe
Bobby Hull
Brett Hull
Busher Jackson
Aurel Joliat
Jari Kurri
Guy Lafleur
Ted Lindsay
Frank Mahovlich
Joe Malone
Lanny McDonald
Maurice Richard
Sweeney Schriner

When you're a winger on your team's top line, you have one major responsibility: Put the puck in the net. The right and left wingers listed here did so in a big way. Eleven lit the lamp at least 500 times in their NHL careers; 13 led the league in red lights at least once. Loved by their centermen, feared by opposing goalies, these are the 25 best wingers of all time.

*Few could keep pace with the "Golden Jet," Bobby Hull, who netted a mind-boggling 1,018 goals in the NHL and WHA (regular season and playoffs).*

# ANDY BATHGATE

**R**ugged and elegant, Hall of Fame right winger Andy Bathgate epitomized the best qualities of an athlete in a rough-and-tumble world where violence was likely to erupt at any moment. During his 18-year NHL career, he was a regular member of the NHL's elite playmaking corps, always near or at the top of the assists leader board while consistently maintaining his status among the game's most dangerous goal-scorers. On two occasions, he was runner-up for the Art Ross Trophy. He lost to Bobby Hull in 1961–62, though both players had 84 points; Hull had 50 goals to Bathgate's 28.

Born in Winnipeg, Bathgate made his NHL debut in 1952, at the age of 20, but didn't establish himself as a bona fide pro star until he cracked for 20 goals in 1954–55. Big and strong, Bathgate displayed his knack for playmaking when he teamed with Larry Popein and Dean Prentice in 1955–56 and finished the year with 47 assists, second only to Montreal's Bert Olmstead, who had Jean Beliveau and Rocket Richard to finish his plays.

For eight consecutive seasons, 1955–63, Bathgate was the Rangers' leading scorer, and he claimed a spot among the NHL's top five scorers in each of those campaigns. He led the league in assists twice, with 56 helpers in 1961–62 and 58 more playing for New York and Toronto in 1963–64. He also finished second no fewer than three times, and on four other occasions he was among the top four in the league in assists.

However, Bathgate wasn't just a crafty setup man. He was also an extremely proficient goal-scorer, a winger with a rifle shot and a keen sense for finding small openings. He was not above using his big slap shot to intimidate goalies. Often he would shoot high to get a goalie ducking, thus creating room in the top of the net. Once, in fact, he hammered Jacques Plante in the forehead with one of his patented slap shots and thus triggered the permanent use of masks by goalies in the NHL (many of whom were ready to make the switch but had done so only in practice, resisting in games due to peer pressure and the fear of making a career mistake).

Bathgate had his finest year in 1958–59, scoring 40 goals and 88 points and winning the Hart Trophy. The big knock on him was he couldn't take the Rangers to a Stanley Cup. In 1963–64, he was dealt to Toronto, where the defending Cup champs were struggling to keep pace with Montreal and Chicago. Bathgate finished the year with the Leafs, then scored five playoff goals—including the winner in Game 4 and the Cup-clincher in Game 7.

Bathgate played two mediocre seasons in Detroit (1965–67), then went to Pittsburgh in the 1967 expansion draft. After scoring 20 goals in 1967–68, he decided to call it quits. The classy winger made a brief return in 1970–71, then quit again until Vancouver of the WHA coaxed him out of retirement in 1974–75, but only for 11 games. He left with the reputation as one of the true gentlemen of the sport.

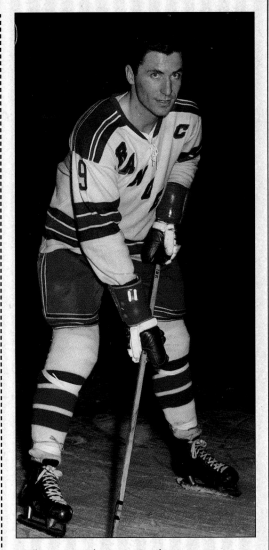

*The power-shooting Bathgate was a star on Broadway for over a decade, but he didn't become a champion until he went to Toronto.*

## NHL STATISTICS

| GP | G | A | PTS | PIM |
|------|-----|-----|------|------|
| 1,069 | 349 | 624 | 973 | 624 |

# TOE BLAKE

The product of a poor mining town in Ontario, Hector "Toe" Blake learned early in life the importance of hard work. Throughout his NHL career, spanning 15 years as a player and 13 more as a coach, he was rarely flashy. Instead, he was simply one of the most dedicated, consistent, and hard-working men ever to lace up skates.

Blake spent two unproductive years in the Montreal Maroons system before switching to the Canadiens in 1935–36. The following year, he played on Montreal's second unit behind the brilliant line of Aurel Joliat, Howie Morenz, and Johnny Gagnon. In 43 games he scored 10 goals, and the Habs eked out a narrow division title before losing to Detroit in the Stanley Cup semifinals. Blake increased his production to 17 goals in 1937–38, then copped the scoring chamionship in 1938–39 with 47 points while playing with Gagnon and Paul Haynes. He also won his only Hart Trophy as league MVP. But the Habs were not a power, finishing closer to the bottom of the league standings each season.

In 1942–43, Blake and Elmer Lach were teamed on a line with Joe Benoit. The following year, Benoit was replaced by Maurice Richard and history was about to be made. The Punch Line clicked almost instantly. In 1943–44, the trio counted 82 goals and 185 points and carried the Habs to a runaway regular-season title, finishing 25 points ahead of

Detroit. They then won the Stanley Cup (Montreal's first in 13 years) by knocking off the Maple Leafs in five semifinal games and sweeping Chicago in the Finals. The Punch Line finished 1–2–3 in playoff scoring.

*Though only 5'9", Blake was a huge talent, winning both the Hart and Art Ross Trophies.*

While the 1944–45 season was monopolized by Richard's 50 goals in 50 games, Blake also continued his consistent play,

scoring a career-high 29 goals and 67 points as the Habs roared to another regular-season title. The Punch Line finished atop the scoring list, as Lach won the scoring title with Richard and Blake, the NHL's top two goal-scorers, right behind. However, Toronto shocked Montreal in the semifinals, erasing its playoff hopes in six games.

The Canadiens played with a singular focus in 1945–46. Blake scored 29 goals and led the team in points (50), third overall, before leading Montreal to the Stanley Cup. He shared the goal-scoring lead with Richard (seven) and banged home the Cup-clinching goal in Game 5 as Montreal capped a five-game triumph over Boston. With just two penalty minutes all year, Blake won the Lady Byng Trophy as well.

Six years older than Lach and nine years Richard's senior, Blake quit in 1947–48 when, at 36, he suffered a badly broken ankle. A terrific Stanley Cup performer, he had a higher playoff points-per-game average (1.08) than he did in the regular season (0.91). Ironically, this Hall of Fame winger, who won only two Stanley Cups as a player, won eight more championships as coach of the Canadiens, earning a place as one of the great coaches of all time.

| NHL STATISTICS | | | | |
|---|---|---|---|---|
| GP | G | A | PTS | PIM |
| 578 | 235 | 292 | 527 | 272 |

# MIKE BOSSY

In a career marked by intense concentration, great willpower, and extraordinary grace, Hall of Fame right winger Mike Bossy established himself as one of the most dangerous snipers of his day—starting right from his debut season (1977–78) when he scored 53 goals, setting an NHL record for first-year players, and continuing until his untimely retirement in 1987.

A native of Quebec, Bossy played junior hockey at Laval (whence Mario Lemieux later emerged) and scored an astonishing 308 goals in just 260 games over four years before the New York Islanders picked him 15th overall in the 1977 amateur draft. A sleek skater with a rifle shot, Bossy made the rapid transition to the NHL at 20 and won the Calder Trophy, showing great offensive skills (53 goals, 91 points) and remarkable sportsmanship (just six penalty minutes). He was named to the NHL's Second All-Star Team—an extremely rare feat for a first-year player.

As a sophomore, he shed any worries about following up his terrific rookie year by leading the NHL in goals (69) and earning another Second All-Star Team nomination. The Isles, led by the offensive line of Bossy, Bryan Trottier, and Clark Gillies, became the powerhouse of the league, and in 1979–80 they ascended to the throne with their first of four straight Stanley Cup titles. Bossy not only led the offensive charge, but he was the class of the team, the model of sportsmanship.

In fact, this gifted winger, who had been a constant target of thugs throughout his junior and NHL tenures, often decried the unnecessary violence of the game and vowed never to stoop to retaliation. And despite constant attacks against him, he would not drop his gloves to fight back, getting his sweet revenge as a power-play weapon.

In 1980–81, Bossy again led the NHL in goals (68) and matched Rocket Richard's record of 50 goals in 50 games (scoring the final two goals with 4:10 and 1:29 remaining in the 50th game). He then set a record for points in a playoff year (35) and carried the Isles to their second straight Cup. A picture of consistency and excellence, Bossy ripped 64 goals in 1981–82 and enjoyed his second straight 17-goal playoff year. The Islanders raised the Stanley Cup for the third time, and Bossy was presented with the Conn Smythe Trophy as the postseason MVP.

A five-time First All-Star Team member, Bossy cranked 60 goals in 1982–83. In sitting out just 20 penalty minutes, he earned his first of three Lady Byng Trophies. He helped the Islanders extend their Stanley Cup dynasty to four when he scored 17 playoff goals—again—to top the charts.

A dark cloud hovered in Bossy's future, however. As a result of the physical abuse he'd absorbed over the years, Bossy developed a cranky back that was further aggravated by skating. In 1986–87, he was forced to sit out 17 games, and his string of 50-goal seasons ended at nine. He finished with 38 tallies, then spent the entire 1987–88 season on the sidelines before sadly announcing his retirement at just 30. Though he never won a scoring title, Bossy finished his career with 573 goals in 752 games, plus three Lady Byng Trophies (1983, 1984, 1986) and four Stanley Cups.

*Throughout his career, Bossy condemned hockey's tolerance of goon tactics and refused to be goaded into fighting.*

## NHL STATISTICS

| GP | G | A | PTS | PIM |
|-----|-----|-----|-------|-----|
| 752 | 573 | 553 | 1,126 | 210 |

# CHARLIE CONACHER

Some spectacular right wingers have blessed the NHL in the last 50 years—Howe, Richard, Lafleur, Bossy, Kurri. But long before these heroes carved their names into the record books there was Charlie Conacher of the Toronto Maple Leafs, a powerful shooter who led the NHL in goal-scoring no fewer than five times. Known as "Bomber" because of his big shot, Conacher patrolled the right side of Toronto's Kid Line, along with center Joe Primeau and left winger Busher Jackson.

A native of Toronto, Conacher came up through the famed Marlboros junior system and turned pro with the Leafs in 1929. In his first NHL game, against Chicago, he scored the first of his 225 career goals. He finished his rookie campaign with 20 tallies.

In 1930–31, as an NHL sophomore, Conacher led the league in goals (31) and was third overall in points (43), trailing only Howie Morenz (51) and Detroit's Ebbie Goodfellow (48). He helped the Leafs to a second-place finish in the Canadian Division. That year, the Leafs' top center, Primeau, led the league in assists (32). It wouldn't be long before the team united its best players.

In 1931–32, Conacher replaced Ace Bailey on Toronto's front unit with Primeau and Jackson, and the trio combined for 75 goals and 151 points. Conacher led the league in goals (34), Primeau was the top assist-maker (37), and Jackson won the overall scoring title (53 points). Despite their second-place finish behind Montreal in the Canadian Division, the Leafs were poised for greatness. In the 1932 playoffs, Toronto dispatched Chicago in the semifinals, then swept the Rangers in the Finals to win its first Cup

*Known as "The Bomber," Conacher had one of the hardest shots in the pre–slap shot era. He led the NHL in goals five times and in scoring twice.*

in 10 years. Conacher scored six goals, including the winning goal in the decisive third game to complete the sweep.

The following year, the Kid Line dropped to 52 goals and 109 points as a unit. Conacher missed eight games due to injuries, and his goal production fell to 14 goals, but the Leafs took the top spot in the division and got back to the Finals. However, the Rangers avenged the previous year's loss, eliminating Conacher and the Leafs three games to one in their best-of-five series.

Conacher won his first scoring title in 1933–34, when he led the NHL in goals (32) and points (52) and took the Leafs to another division title. But Toronto dropped a five-game semifinal series to Detroit and ended the year in disappointment. If he was dispirited, Conacher showed no signs of it in 1934–35. With the Kid Line still dominating but no longer kids, the Leafs topped the division, as Conacher won his second scoring title, leading the way in goals for the fourth time (36) and notching a career-high 57 points.

Conacher played only 34 games from 1936–38 as injuries waylaid his career. In 1938 he went to Detroit, where he played just one season before joining the New York Americans. There he finished his career in 1941. Conacher retired after a dozen NHL seasons and later coached his kid brother, Roy, in Chicago.

## NHL STATISTICS

| GP | G | A | PTS | PIM |
|----|----|----|-----|-----|
| 460 | 225 | 173 | 398 | 523 |

# BILL COOK

Oil and vinegar, salt and pepper, sweet and sour. Though the components are natural opposites, each combo is a proven success in its own right. Such was the magic between Frank Boucher, one of the most gentlemanly players ever to skate in the NHL, and Bill Cook, a hard-nosed, no-nonsense winger who cruised Boucher's right side in the 1920s and 1930s. With chiseled features and a hard glare, Cook was an intimidating force on the ice, a precursor to the multitalented firebrands who would follow, men like Gordie Howe, Mark Messier, and others.

Born in Brantford, Ontario (Wayne Gretzky's hometown), Cook and his kid brother, Fred (also known as "Bun"), joined the Rangers in 1926 and were paired with Boucher. Together the trio accounted for 60 goals. Bill Cook, who didn't begin his NHL career until he was already 30 after serving in World War I, immediately set about showing his prowess with the puck, scoring a league-high 33 goals and winning his first scoring title with 37 points.

In 1927–28, the Rangers finished the regular season behind Boston in the American Division, although the line of Boucher and the Cook brothers was back in top form. In the 1928 playoffs, Boucher and Cook spearheaded the Rangers' attack, together amassing 15 points in seven games. In the Finals, Cook assisted Boucher's two critical goals in Game 5 as the Rangers eked out a dramatic best-of-five series win over the Maroons, overcoming the loss of their goalie, Lorne Chabot, in Game 1. Coach Lester Patrick donned the big pads and went between the pipes to save the day.

*Long before Gordie Howe, Cook was the prototypical power forward, combining toughness, leadership, and scoring ability.*

Cook reached the 30-goal mark in 1930–31 (just one shy of league leader Charlie Conacher), then scored a career-high 34 goals in 1931–32 (tying his nemesis Conacher for the league lead). During those two seasons, Cook twice finished fourth overall in total points.

In 1932–33, at the age of 36, when many players his age were over the hill or beginning to plan for retirement, Cook demonstrated quite clearly that he still had a fire burning inside when he won his second scoring title. Along the way he again led the league in goals (28) as well as in total points (50). That year, the Rangers finished the regular season in third place behind Boston and Detroit. In the Stanley Cup playoffs, the Blueshirts won a two-game shootout with Montreal, eight goals to five, then upset Detroit in the semifinals, six goals to three. In the Finals against the Maple Leafs, Cook went head-to-head with Conacher and emerged as the hero. First, he scored the winning goal in Game 2, then he capped off his brilliant season by winning the Stanley Cup for New York with a sudden-death OT goal in Game 4, as the Rangers beat Toronto three games to one. His opposite number, Conacher, scored just one playoff goal and was held scoreless in the Finals.

Age and injuries ultimately took their toll on Cook. He played only 21 games in each of his last two seasons (1935–36 and 1936–37) and retired in 1937.

| NHL STATISTICS | | | | |
|---|---|---|---|---|
| GP | G | A | PTS | PIM |
| 452 | 229 | 138 | 367 | 386 |

# YVAN COURNOYER

To those who said he was too small to play in the NHL, Hall of Fame right winger Yvan Cournoyer offered a 428-goal rebuttal in his own defense, delivered at high speed and with great finesse over the course of 16 years, all with the Montreal Canadiens.

Standing just 5'7", Cournoyer compensated for his lack of physical size by skating like the wind, proving correct the age-old hockey adage "you can't hit what you can't catch." After a five-game cup of coffee with the Habs in 1963–64, Cournoyer, who earned the nickname "Roadrunner," arrived permanently in 1964–65, scoring modestly (seven goals, 17 points). While his regular season was less than phenomenal, Cournoyer received an accelerated indoctrination into the Stanley Cup playoffs. In the 1965 playoffs, he scored three goals, the last coming in Montreal's Game 7 win over Chicago that gave them the Cup.

Cournoyer scored 18 goals as a sophomore and won another Stanley Cup in 1965–66 before exploding with 25 goals in 1966–67, the final pre-expansion season. As his production steadily grew, the Roadrunner became a more integral part of the Habs' attack. In 1967–68, he scored 28 goals and put his name on a third Stanley Cup, assisting J. C. Tremblay's Cup-clinching goal in Game 4 against St. Louis. He was second in playoff assists (eight) and tied for second in points (14). In 1968–69, Cournoyer earned a spot on the Canadiens' top line and paid immediate

dividends with a career-high 87 points and 43 goals (best on the team in both categories). The Habs returned to the

*The Roadrunner won 10 Stanley Cups and was MVP of the 1973 playoffs.*

Stanley Cup Finals against St. Louis in 1969 and the Quebec native earned his championship ring.

After a minor glitch when the Canadiens went from league standouts to playoff spectators in 1969–70, Cournoyer scored 37 goals in 1970–71, then enjoyed three straight seasons in the 40-goal range. In 1971–72, he fired home 47 goals, then scored 40 more the next year. But his best was to come in the postseason. During the 1973 playoffs, the Habs fought off valiant challenges from Buffalo and Philadelphia to gain a berth in the Finals against Chicago. Along the way, the tiny winger banged home 15 goals—including the winner in Game 2 and the Cup-clinching goal in Game 6—and led in points (25) en route to winning the Conn Smythe Trophy as playoff MVP. It was also Cournoyer's sixth Stanley Cup in nine years.

After notching 40 goals in 1973–74, the Roadrunner finally began to slow. Over time, he was replaced by a young hotshot named Guy Lafleur. However, Cournoyer remained a consistent goal-scorer and team leader to the end. In 1977–78, his last full NHL season, he scored 24 goals (his lowest number since his sophomore season), then played 15 games in 1978–79 before hanging up his skates. By then, he had added two more Cups (in 1976 and 1978), bringing to 10 the number on which his name appears. Truly, his impact was as great as his physique was small.

### NHL STATISTICS

| GP | G | A | PTS | PIM |
|-----|-----|-----|-----|-----|
| 968 | 428 | 435 | 863 | 255 |

# CY DENNENY

**I**t's nearly impossible to compare great players from disparate eras, for how can the deeds of a skater like Cy Denneny, who starred in the fledgling NHL during the 1920s and who still holds the third-best goals-per-game average of all time, truly be analyzed against the exploits of, say, Wayne Gretzky, the greatest player of the modern era? The game has changed so much, the players have evolved so dramatically. Yet, even by current standards, Denneny's achievements are worthy of high praise and respectful observance.

Denneny was a hard-shooting left winger who teamed successfully with Frank Nighbor and Jack Darragh to spark the Ottawa Senators' attack. In 1920–21, he scored six goals against Hamilton goalie Howie Lockhart in a game won by the Sens 12–5. That year, Denneny, whose older brother Corbett patrolled the port side of Toronto's attack, finished with 34 goals in just 24 games, an average of 1.42 goals per game. By modern standards, such a GPG average would give a player more than 115 tallies over an 82-game season. Amazingly, Denneny finished only second in the goal-scoring race, as Toronto right winger Babe Dye notched 35 goals.

An Ontario product, Denneny broke into the NHL at 20 during the league's first season (1917–18) and blasted 36 goals in 22 rookie games for Ottawa (a 1.64 GPG average). Montreal's Joe Malone ripped 44 goals to win the scoring title, but Denneny's prowess was well established. Ironically, two years later the Senators won their first Stanley Cup under NHL sanction, beating Seattle three games to two. Denneny was held without a goal in those five games.

In 1920–21, the Senators eked out a hard-fought five-game series victory over Vancouver in the playoff Finals—successfully defending their championship—and this time Denneny contributed a handful of goals and set up Darragh's Cup-clinching goal midway through Game 5. He won another Cup in 1923, scoring the sudden-death winner in Game 1 of the Finals against Edmonton before Punch Broadbent's lone goal in Game 2 decided the series. In the 1926–27 Finals, Denneny scored the Cup-winning goal against Boston in Game 4 of their series, playing the hero and winning his third Stanley Cup.

A regular runner-up in the annual points race (1921, 1922, and 1923), Denneny finally won a scoring title with 22 goals and 23 points in 1923–24. With more stalwart goaltending in place around the NHL (including Georges Vezina in Montreal), goal-scorers no longer ruled. Still, Denneny's terrific campaign featured 22 goals in just 21 games, proof that he was still a fearsome lamplighter. In 1924–25, Denneny was back in his familiar place as the league's runner-up in scoring, finishing with 42 points to Babe Dye's 44. His last hurrah came in 1928–29, with the Bruins. After a dismal regular season, he put his name on one last Stanley Cup, then retired. His 246 career goals in 326 games cemented his status as a hero of his era and earned him a place among the great scoring threats of all time.

*Denneny notched 26 NHL hat tricks, including one six-goal effort, despite possessing substandard skating ability.*

## NHL STATISTICS

| GP | G | A | PTS | PIM |
|-----|-----|-----|-----|-----|
| 326 | 246 | 69 | 315 | 176 |

# BABE DYE

The Babe Ruth of the early NHL, Cecil "Babe" Dye was the ultimate big-goal scorer, the home run hitter who could win important games with dramatic style and authority. A powerfully built right winger, Dye played 11 seasons in the NHL (1919–31), three times led the league in goals, and twice was the league's top point-getter.

A native of Ontario, Dye made his NHL debut with the Toronto St. Pats (later renamed the Maple Leafs). He took no time establishing his skill as a goal-scorer. In 1920–21, he scored 35 goals in just 24 games, edging Ottawa's Cy Denneny for the league goal-scoring championship. It was the beginning of great things for Dye, who'd grown up in difficult circumstances as his father passed away when Babe was just a small child. An excellent all-around athlete who later received an offer to pursue a baseball career with the Philadelphia Athletics, Dye concentrated on his ice game and quickly became a dominant force.

In 1921–22, he banged home 30 goals while playing on a line with Corbett Denneny (Cy's big brother) and Reg Noble. Second in goals and third in points (37), he led Toronto to a second-place finish, then sparked a five-game win over Vancouver in the Stanley Cup Finals. He scored the winning goal in Game 2, set up the winner in Game 4, then scored four times (including the Cup-clincher) in Game 5 for nine playoff goals and 10 points, tops among all players. Had there been a playoff MVP award, Dye would have won hands down.

No flash in the pan, Dye built on his brilliant playoff performance and continued his onslaught against NHL goalies. In 1922–23, he led the league in goals yet again (26 tallies in 22 games) and won his first scoring title, with 37 points. However, Toronto finished only third in the league standings and didn't make the playoffs. The team failed to qualify again in 1923–24, as Dye played only 19 games due to nagging injuries. Nevertheless, his 17 goals were second best in the league.

Dye was back in top form in 1924–25, when he knocked home 38 goals and captured his second scoring title with a career-high 44 points. Toronto's defense surrendered a league-high 114 goals as the team fell all the way to sixth place in 1925–26, Dye's last with the St. Pats. In 1926–27, he went to Chicago and, teaming with Dick Irvin and Mickey MacKay, notched 25 goals and helped the Black Hawks lead the league in scoring (115 goals).

Dye suffered a broken leg at the start of the 1927–28 season and played only 11 games. Without their scoring star, the Hawks fell all the way to last place in the American Division. In 1928–29, Dye played 42 games for the New York Americans but shockingly failed to score even a single goal. After a one-year retirement, Dye attempted a comeback with Toronto in 1930–31, but he was without a single point in six games before hanging up the skates for good. He left the NHL with 202 goals in 270 games and a reputation as one of the most exciting game-breakers the game had ever known.

*Dye scored four goals in the finale of the 1922 Stanley Cup Finals.*

### NHL STATISTICS

| GP | G | A | PTS | PIM |
|-----|-----|-----|-----|-----|
| 269 | 202 | 41 | 243 | 205 |

# MIKE GARTNER

Tough as nails, clean as a whistle, fast as greased lightning... there are barely enough clichés to describe a player of Mike Gartner's sheer talent. No player in the history of the game has done what Gartner has done—specifically, put together 15 consecutive 30-goal seasons—or come close to playing with his combination of consistency and sportsmanship. He's a fleet-footed winger who can outskate 99 percent of the players in the NHL, but he's also tough enough, durable enough, and level-headed enough to put up with the physical abuse that comes with the job—and rarely commit the faux pas of retaliating.

Gartner was a high-scoring junior at Niagara Falls before turning pro with Cincinnati in the WHA at just 19. After a modest 27-goal season, he left the sinking ship of the WHA and reported to Washington, which had drafted his NHL rights (fourth overall in 1979) in time for the 1979–80 season. As a rookie, he ripped 36 goals, then added 48 more the following year, staking out his ground as a deadly sniper on the right wing.

Solidly built with pistons for legs, Gartner used speed and a tremendous slap shot to intimidate the enemy. During the next decade, he would become the league's most consistent winger. In 1984–85, he reached a personal high when he banged in 50 goals and finished with 102 points. During 10 years in Washington, the Caps rode Gartner's

back to six playoff berths. The only knock on Gartner, however, was that he was a subpar playoff performer, and his 16 goals in 47 postseason contests with the Caps provided credence to the claim. In 1989, he was traded to Minnesota for

*Gartner recorded his 500th goal, 500th assist, 1,000th point, and 1,000th game all in the same year (1991–92).*

a short stay, then moved on to the New York Rangers during the 1989–90 season.

On October 14, 1991, Garts ripped his 500th career goal. Ironically, the momentous goal came against the Capitals, for

whom he had done so much previous damage. Later that year, he notched the 1,000th point of his career. But he was far from done. On March 9, 1994, Gartner scored against the Canadiens in Montreal to become the sixth player in NHL history to record 600 goals. Soon he passed Bobby Hull to become hockey's fifth-most prolific scorer ever.

Gartner's most trying season came in 1994–95. An active member of the players' union, he was heavily involved in labor talks between the NHLPA and ownership. Because he insisted that the union stand strong, the season was a short one and he watched his record-setting string of 15 straight 30-goal seasons end when he managed only 12 goals in 38 games. Following the 1995–96 season, the Leafs, heavily burdened by high-dollar salaries, traded Gartner to Phoenix despite his team-leading 35 goals.

As the 1996–97 season ended, Gartner needed only four goals to reach 700, putting him in reach of Phil Esposito (717) and Marcel Dionne (731) for third all time. Though Gartner has never won a single major NHL award, he is surely headed for the Hall of Fame when he finally hangs up the skates.

| NHL STATISTICS | | | | |
|---|---|---|---|---|
| GP | G | A | PTS | PIM |
| 1,372 | 696 | 612 | 1,308 | 1,135 |

# BERNIE GEOFFRION

Hot-tempered and moody on some days, his face creased with a huge smile on others, right winger Bernie Geoffrion arrived in the NHL like a clap of thunder, changed the game in one of its most significant ways, and then faded into an inexplicable oblivion that in no way reflected the flashes of greatness in his 16-year NHL career.

It was both a curse and a blessing for Geoffrion to play in the shadow and aftermath of Maurice "Rocket" Richard. When he came out of Quebec junior hockey in 1950–51, Geoffrion showed boundless potential. In his first NHL game, he proved he wasn't afraid to get "involved." Checked into a goal post, he skated off the ice with a broken nose and a bloody mouth where 14 missing teeth once resided. And he was ready for more.

In 1951–52, his official rookie year, he scored 30 goals, tops on the Habs and third best in the league, and won the Calder Trophy as rookie of the year. The next year, he dropped to 22 goals but won his first Stanley Cup as Montreal took a seven-game series from Chicago before pounding Boston in the Finals. Geoffrion was second in playoff points with 10.

Geoffrion turned the game in a new direction and earned his famous nickname, "Boom Boom," when he took up and perfected the slap shot. His moniker came from the sound of his stick hitting the puck and the puck hitting boards (although it often went into the net). Geoffrion also turned a few heads in the spring of 1953, when he married Marlene Morenz, the daughter of former Canadiens star Howie Morenz.

In 1954–55, Boom Boom won his first Art Ross Trophy, although he failed to enjoy the rapture of the home crowd. In fact, he was vilified by Montreal fans who wanted the Rocket to win his one and only scoring title. When Richard was suspended for punching a referee, Geoffrion took the scoring championship with 75 points. Richard sat out three games and finished with 74.

During his 14-year tenure in Montreal, Geoffrion experienced terrific and horrific moments. He won five straight Stanley Cups from 1956–60. He counted assists on three Cup-clinching goals (Richard's in 1956, Dickie Moore's in '57, and Jean Beliveau's in '60). And he scored a Cup-winning goal of his own in 1958. On the other hand, in 1959 he suffered an intestinal rupture during a morning practice and nearly died.

In 1960–61, Geoffrion again visited the fourth dimension of abject frustration when he scored 50 goals (tying Richard's mark) but saw his achievement diminished in the public eye. At the same time, Canada heaped its praise on Toronto superstar Frank Mahovlich, whose pursuit of the same 50-goal plateau fell short at 48. Even a second Art Ross Trophy (with 95 points) and a Hart Trophy as MVP did little to assuage the sensitive Geoffrion.

A six-time Stanley Cup champ, Boom Boom retired in 1964, tried coaching (but was too tightly wrapped), then made a brief comeback with the Rangers in 1966–67.

*The confident Geoffrion once said, "If I saw a player score two goals in a game, I said, 'Uh-uh, I'm gonna get three.'"*

### NHL STATISTICS

| GP | G | A | PTS | PIM |
|-----|-----|-----|-----|-----|
| 883 | 393 | 429 | 822 | 689 |

# ROD GILBERT

Dashing and suave, as famous as a Manhattan bachelor as he was as an NHL scoring star, Rod Gilbert spent nearly two decades patrolling the right wing for the New York Rangers and was an integral member of the famed GAG (or goal-a-game) Line with Vic Hadfield and Jean Ratelle.

A native of Montreal, the sleek winger came perilously close to seeing his NHL career erased before it could begin. As a junior in the OHA, he suffered a broken back, and in subsequent years endured a series of surgical procedures, including a bone graft and a difficult spinal fusion. After wearing a brace for several seasons, Gilbert was finally able to play unencumbered.

In 1962–63, Gilbert finished his rookie NHL season with a modest 11 goals in 70 games, playing third banana to fellow right wingers Andy Bathgate and Andy Hebenton. The following year, he was moved to a line with Phil Goyette and Camille "The Eel" Henry. This slick trio led the Rangers with 77 goals.

With Bathgate's trade to Toronto in 1964, Gilbert became the team's ace right winger. In 1964–65, he led New York in goals (25) and points (61). Gilbert's 1965–66 season was wrecked by injuries, and he played just 34 games. That year, the team dropped to last place.

In 1967–68, Rangers GM-coach Emile Francis formed the Gilbert-Ratelle-Hadfield trio, then watched them grow into a dominant forward line. Paying immediate dividends, the GAG Line carried the Rangers to a second-place finish in the Eastern Division, although they would be upset in the playoffs by Chicago. Ratelle (78) and Gilbert (77) finished fourth and fifth overall in points, respectively.

As an antidote to Boston's powerful Wayne Cashman-Phil Esposito-Ken Hodge line, the GAG Line stayed together through the 1973–74 season, when Hadfield was dealt to Pittsburgh. Though they never overcame the playoff obstacles that extended the team's protracted Stanley Cup drought, the Rangers had some moments of high drama, thanks to Gilbert and company.

the Bruins in a mammoth trade for Phil Esposito. The league honored Gilbert with a Masterton Trophy for dedication and perseverance following the difficult 1975–76 campaign.

A player of great class and style, Gilbert watched helplessly when former Montreal nemesis John Ferguson was hired as coach and general manager in January 1976. Fergy exercised his full authority to "retire" No. 7 from duty. Gilbert, who to this day remains a crowd favorite in Manhattan, left the game during the 1977–78 season.

In 1971–72, Gilbert reached a career-high 43 goals and 97 points. In 1974–75, with youngster Greg Polls in Hadfield's spot, Gilbert led the team in points (97). In 1975–76, "Rocky" led the team with 86 points despite losing his lifelong friend and longtime linemate, Ratelle, to

*Gilbert notched 406 NHL goals (including his 300th against Detroit in 1974).*

## NHL STATISTICS

| GP | G | A | PTS | PIM |
|---|---|---|---|---|
| 1,065 | 406 | 615 | 1,021 | 508 |

# MICHEL GOULET

**B**ig and strong, tough yet graceful with the puck, Michel Goulet embodied elegance and grit during his 15-year NHL career. Sadly, a serious concussion suffered when he catapulted head-first into the boards at the Montreal Forum near the end of the 1993–94 season forced an early conclusion to his career.

Goulet played two years of junior hockey in his native Quebec before signing a pro contract with Birmingham of the WHA, where, as a member of the "Baby Bulls," he scored 28 goals skating alongside such underage future stars as Wayne Dillon, Rick Vaive, Craig Hartsburg, Rob Ramage, and goalie Pat Riggin. Drafted 20th overall by the Nordiques in the 1979 entry draft, the club's first-ever draft pick, Goulet scored his first NHL goal in November 1979 and finished the year with 22 goals.

Goulet scored 32 goals as a sophomore in 1980–81, then launched a campaign of terror against NHL goalies that included four straight 50-goal seasons. In 1982–83, he ripped 57 goals and 105 points, then followed up with 56 more goals the next year. His totals began to ebb slightly, to 55 goals in 1984–85 and 53 in 1985–86.

During the stretch from 1983–88, Goulet became the NHL's preeminent left winger, notching four 100-point seasons and earning two Second All-Star Team selections and three more as a First All-Star Team pick. Only an injury that knocked him out of 11 games in 1984–85 kept him from recording an almost-certain fifth 100-point season. He led the Nordiques in goals six years running (1982–88) and twice led the team in points (1983–84 and 1986–87).

Because of his exceptional physical strength, Goulet was able to compete in the slot for loose pucks and rebounds.

*Goulet's 548 career goals are third all-time among left wingers. In 1983–84, he tallied 56 goals and 121 points.*

His soft hands allowed him to score on a high percentage of ricochets.

Goulet played nearly 11 full seasons in his home province of Quebec before he was traded to the Chicago Blackhawks toward the end of the 1989–90 season. He had seen the best and worst of times with the Nordiques, including several last-place division finishes and a first-place finish as well. When the team began to fade again in the late 1980s, and Goulet's production slipped out of the 40- to 50-goal range into the more mortal 20- to 30-goal range, the Nords decided it was time to unload his expensive contract. In Chicago, Goulet demonstrated that he still possessed great leadership qualities, a strong work ethic, and some of the old scoring magic.

On February 16, 1992, Goulet scored against Calgary goalie Jeff Reese and entered the record books as the 17th player in league history to reach the 500-goal plateau. Goulet, who went from junior hockey to the WHA to the NHL without ever playing a single game in the minors, was 34 when he hung up his skates in 1994. He finished his NHL career with 548 career goals and 1,152 points in 1,089 games, an average of 1.058 points per game. At the time of his retirement, he ranked third all time among left wingers for goals and points, trailing only Bobby Hull (610 goals and 1,170 points) and Johnny Bucyk (556 goals and 1,369 points). As the NHL prepared to begin the 1996–97 season, Goulet remained in place as the 13th all-time leading goal-scorer.

### NHL STATISTICS

| GP | G | A | PTS | PIM |
|---|---|---|---|---|
| 1,089 | 548 | 604 | 1,152 | 825 |

# GORDIE HOWE

The long and storied career of right winger Gordie Howe was speckled with moments: significant historical dates, notable incidents, and spectacular achievements. Together, these moments contributed to creating the enduring legend of "Mr. Hockey." There was the night he crashed head-first into the boards and was nearly killed . . . the night he pummeled Lou Fontinato into a bloody pulp, all but ending Leapin' Louie's career as an enforcer . . . the night he surpassed Rocket Richard as the NHL's all-time leading goal-scorer . . . the night he debuted with his sons, Mark and Marty, on a line while playing for Houston in the WHA . . . the night he made his tri-umphant return to the NHL at the unheard-of age of 51.

A Saskatchewan native, Howe debuted in the NHL in 1946–47 with the Red Wings. In his first three NHL seasons, he scored seven, 16, and 12 goals and rarely looked like a world-beater. Ted Lindsay and Sid Abel, his Production Line mates, took turns leading the league in goals, but Howe's totals were modest at best. Then, in 1949–50, Howe ripped 35 goals and finished third overall in points (68) behind Lindsay (78) and Abel (69).

In 1949–50, the Red Wings finished atop the league standings and were favorites to win the Stanley Cup. But they'd have to do it without Howe. In Game 1 of the semifinals, he threw a check at Toronto's Teeder Kennedy, missed, and flew into the boards, fracturing his skull. Emergency surgery saved his life, but he missed Detroit's first Stanley Cup in seven years.

Over the next five years, Detroit won three more Stanley Cups (1952, '54, and '55) and Howe established his credentials as bona fide superstar. In 1950–51, fully recovered from his near-fatal head injury, he won his first of six Art Ross Trophies, leading the NHL in goals (43), assists (43), and points (86). The following season (1951–52), he won his second Ross Trophy (with 86 points) and took home his first of six Hart Trophies as league MVP.

On March 14, 1962, Howe rifled his trademark wrist shot past Rangers goalie Gump Worsley to become only the second NHLer ever to enter the 500-goal club. An intense competitor not known for resting on past achievements, Howe continued his onslaught, and on November 10, 1963, he scored the 545th goal of his career, passing Rocket Richard. A dominant force, Howe earned scoring titles in 1951, 1952, 1953, 1954, 1957, and 1958 and was named league MVP in 1952, 195, 1957, 1958, 1960, and 1963.

Howe retired in 1971 with 786 goals and 1,809 points. Three years later, he returned to play with his sons in the WHA. And after six years in Houston and New England, he reentered the NHL in 1979–80, at 51, and concluded his NHL career with 801 goals and 1,850 points and the title of hockey's greatest treasure, a claim he would hold until the arrival of Wayne Gretzky. There are many who still insist that Howe, who was tough and skilled and possessed amazing longevity, is the greatest player ever to skate in the NHL, bar none.

*Known as "Mr. Hockey" by fans and historians, Howe was referred to by some of his opponents as "Mr. Elbows."*

## NHL STATISTICS

| GP | G | A | PTS | PIM |
|---|---|---|---|---|
| 1,767 | 801 | 1,049 | 1,850 | 1,685 |

# BOBBY HULL

Rocket Richard and Boom Boom Geoffrion were the NHL's first two 50-goal scorers, reaching the magical mark in 1944–45 and 1960–61, respectively. But Bobby Hull, with 15 brilliant seasons in Chicago, was the first NHLer to do it more than once. Known for his speed and great physical strength, Hull scored 50 goals five times, relying on a devastating slap shot to overpower goalies.

An Ontario native, Hull broke into the NHL with the Black Hawks in 1957–58 and was placed on the front line. He scored 13 goals and showed great potential, but the Hawks were a weak club, finishing out of the playoffs. In 1958–59, the team improved to third place and the Golden Jet scored 18 goals, but the season ended after just six playoff games against Montreal.

Hull emerged as a full-bore superstar in 1959–60, when he scored a league-high 39 goals and won his first Art Ross Trophy with 81 points. The Hawks finished third once more, only to be swept by Montreal in the opening round of playoffs. Hull took a back seat to Geoffrion in 1960–61, as the Habs dominated the regular season and Boom Boom stole the show with his 50-goal season. But revenge was sweet for the Hawks, as Chicago eliminated Montreal in the first round of playoffs, then overcame a tough Red Wings squad to annex their first Stanley Cup in 23 years. Hull had 14 playoff points and assisted the Cup-clinching goal in Game 6.

The Hawks fell to third place once more in 1961–62. Hull won his second Art Ross Trophy and joined Richard and Geoffrion in the record books when he scored 50 goals and topped the scoring charts with 84 points. From 1963–69, Hull led the NHL in goals on five more occasions, with 54 goals in 1965–66, 52 in 1966–67, 44 in 1967–68, and a career-high 58 in 1968–69. He added a third Art Ross to his trophy case in 1965–66, with 97 points. Hull reached the 100-point mark just once in his NHL career, when he chalked up 107 points in 1968–69. A hard-nosed winger who fought some epic battles with Canadien John Ferguson, Hull also played with great sportsmanship, winning a Lady Byng Trophy and his first of two Hart Trophies in 1964–65 (39 goals in 61 games). He added a second Hart Trophy the following year.

The Golden Jet scored his 500th NHL goal at the tail end of the 1969–70 season, adding his name alongside those of Rocket Richard and Gordie Howe, then added 104 more before dramatically jumping to the World Hockey Association in 1972–73 as that fledgling league's top box-office draw. Hull spent seven years in Winnipeg, scoring 303 goals and 638 points in just 411 games. When the Jets entered the NHL in 1979–80, the 40-year-old Hull returned to his former league and notched six more goals.

Hull retired in 1980 with three scoring titles, two MVP trophies, and a Stanley Cup. In a 23-year pro career, Hull scored 913 goals in 1,504 total games. His closest rival, Howe, notched 975 goals in 2,186 combined games over 32 years.

*Hull scored 604 goals in Chicago before joining Winnipeg in the WHA in 1972 as that league's first million-dollar star.*

## NHL STATISTICS

| GP | G | A | PTS | PIM |
| --- | --- | --- | --- | --- |
| 1,063 | 610 | 560 | 1,170 | 640 |

# BRETT HULL

Despite his thoroughbred lineage, there were critics early on who felt Brett Hull, son of Hall of Fame left winger Bobby Hull, didn't have the right stuff to play in the NHL. Sent to play Junior B as a teen, Hull scored 104 goals in 56 games at Penticton. He earned a scholarship to play at the University of Minnesota-Duluth, but was picked 117th overall in the 1984 entry draft by the Calgary Flames.

In two years in the WCHA, Hull scored 84 goals for the UMD Bulldogs, then turned pro with the Flames at the end of the 1985–86 season. Hull spent most of the 1986–87 season in the AHL, scoring 50 goals. Brett made the Flames' roster in 1987–88 and scored 26 goals in 52 games, but Calgary, still doubtful, shipped him to St. Louis at the end of the 1987–88 season, little suspecting he would become the dominant goal-scorer of the 1990s.

In 1988–89, Hull rocketed 41 goals with his lightning wrist shot and quick-release slapper, then emerged as a legitimate superstar when he led the NHL in 1989–90 with a whopping 72 goals, breaking Jari Kurri's NHL record for goals by a right winger (71). That year, Hull recorded his first 100-point season (113) and won the Lady Byng Trophy with just 24 penalty minutes.

The best was yet to come, as Hull followed up in 1990–91 with 86 goals, setting a new standard for right wingers in the history books. He also notched a career-high 131 points, and though he finished second to Wayne Gretzky in the league scoring race, he was rewarded for his tremendous play with a Hart Trophy.

*Through 1996–97, Brett and his father had scored more than 1,600 goals in the NHL and WHA, including playoffs.*

In 1991–92, Hull "dropped" to 70 goals, giving him 228 in just three seasons of play, then added seasons of 54 and 57. From 1989–94 Hull bent the ropes 339 times (an average of 67.8), the most goals by any player in the NHL during the same span. For much of that period, he was teamed with center Adam Oates. Not so surprisingly, Hull's incred-

ible goal-scoring pace dropped to simply magnificent after Oates was traded to Boston for Craig Janney, a deal that backfired in a huge way so far as Brett Hull was concerned. In Oates's absence, the Blues have yet to find a playmaker who fits Hull the way Oates did. Even Gretzky, who played briefly for the Blues at the end of the 1995–96 season, couldn't find the rhythm with his longtime buddy, the Golden Brett.

In 1995–96, despite playing under tremendous pressure from a hard-driving coach in Mike Keenan, Hull overlooked heavy criticisms of his approach (which often appeared lazy even when Hull was giving 100 percent) and fired 43 goals, bringing him to within 15 markers of his 500th. In 1996–97, Brett notched his 500th goal in his 693rd career game. By comparison, it took Rocket Richard 863 games, Gordie Howe 1,045 games, and Brett's own father, Bobby Hull, 861 games to score No. 500. With several seasons still ahead of him, the Golden Brett has every chance of becoming the most prolific goal-scoring member of the Hull family.

## NHL STATISTICS

| GP | G | A | PTS | PIM |
|---|---|---|---|---|
| 735 | 527 | 388 | 915 | 339 |

# BUSHER JACKSON

In some ways, left winger Harvey "Busher" Jackson was the Rodney Dangerfield of the Toronto Maple Leafs' famed Kid Line. His center, Joe Primeau, was widely admired for his classy playmaking ability. Wingmate Charlie Conacher had a great shot and led the NHL in goals five times. Jackson, admittedly possessing the least dramatic flair of the three, failed to garner the individual respect afforded his linemates.

A Toronto native, Jackson turned pro with the Maple Leafs in 1929–30, at 18, and scored a dozen goals. The team's fourth-place finish eliminated it from playoff contention, but a new line had emerged, with obvious chemistry among Jackson, Primeau, and Conacher. In 1930–31, the Leafs took second in the Canadian Division. The Kid Line sent two members to the top of the NHL scoring list; Conacher led in goals (31) and Primeau in assists (32). Jackson had 18 goals.

Sparked by the Kid Line in 1931–32, the Leafs finished second again. Conacher took his second goal-scoring title (34) and Primeau once more topped the charts in assists (37). But now Jackson had joined his cohorts as a major scoring threat. With 28 goals and 25 assists, he won the league scoring title with 53 points.

In the 1932 Stanley Cup playoffs, the Leafs skated past Chicago in the first round and the Montreal Maroons in the semifinals to earn their first trip to the Finals in a decade. In three games against the Rangers, Toronto scored 18 goals. Jackson ripped a hat trick against Johnny Roach in Game 1, won by the Leafs 6–4. He chipped in another goal in Game 2, a 6–2 victory. In Game 3, the unsung hero potted his fifth playoff goal and helped Toronto complete the sweep.

In 1932–33, Jackson chalked up 44 points, second overall. The following year, Jackson accounted for just 20 goals. Though the Leafs won the Canadian Division title, they were ousted from the playoffs by Detroit.

In 1934–35, Jackson finished fifth in scoring (44 points) while Conacher won another scoring title with 57 points. The club was swept by the Maroons in the Stanley Cup Finals despite Jackson's team-leading five points.

Jackson was sent to the New York Americans for Sweeney Schriner in 1939, and his career began to dwindle. He moved on to Boston in 1941, then retired at the conclusion of the 1943–44 season. Unlike his Kid Line mates, Jackson's road to the Hall of Fame was fraught with naysayers and critics. But he made it in 1971, 27 years after his retirement.

*On the ice, Jackson was a polished winger who won a scoring title, but off the ice he was a rebel with a "party boy" reputation.*

## NHL STATISTICS

| GP | G | A | PTS | PIM |
|-----|-----|-----|-----|-----|
| 636 | 241 | 234 | 475 | 437 |

# AUREL JOLIAT

During the 1920s and 1930s, the NHL was a ruthless world of violent explosions. The game was played by big, strong men willing to spill blood, their own and that of their enemies, to win. Into this mix there came in 1922 a man so small in stature that his presence among the tough guys might have been laughable had he not been so talented, so competitive, so gifted. Hall of Fame left winger Aurel Joliat stood only 5'6" and tipped the scales at no more than 135 pounds, but his presence on the ice made him a giant. In fact, his playmaking was so spectacular that he was credited with transforming Howie Morenz into a superstar—credited by Morenz himself.

Born in Ontario, Joliat joined the Canadiens in 1922–23. Returning from western Canada, where he'd been playing hockey and football, Joliat teamed with Odie Cleghorn and Billy Boucher and scored 13 rookie goals. The following season (1923–24), Morenz replaced Cleghorn, and the Joliat-Morenz-Boucher line carried the Habs to a two-game sweep of PCHL champion Vancouver in the semifinals, as well as a two-game sweep of WCHL champion Calgary in the Stanley Cup Finals.

In 1924–25, Joliat finished second in the NHL in goals (29) behind Babe Dye (38) and was third in points (40). The Canadiens went to the Finals in 1925 but lost badly to Victoria of the WCHL, then dropped all the way to last place in 1925–26 after the death of goalie Georges Vezina. The Habs rebounded in 1926–27, and Boucher was replaced on Joliat's line by Art Gagne. In 1927–28, Montreal made it back to the Stanley Cup Finals as Morenz and Joliat led the NHL in goals, with 33 and 28 respectively, and were 1–2 in points, with 51 and 39. But the Rangers upset the Canadiens, holding Joliat and Morenz pointless.

In 1929–30, Nick Wasnie replaced Gagne on the Joliat-Morenz line, and the Habs finished second in the division. After dispatching Chicago in the quarterfinals and the Rangers in the semis, Montreal swept Boston in the Finals as Joliat raised his second Stanley Cup. The Habs were right back at the top of the division standings in 1930–31, and the Joliat-Morenz unit welcomed a new winger, Johnny "Black Cat" Gagnon. Joliat counted 22 assists, fifth best in the NHL, and helped Morenz win the scoring title with 51 points.

After squeaking past Boston in the 1931 Cup semifinals, the Habs played Chicago for the Stanley Cup. After a Game 1 victory, Montreal lost Game 2 in double overtime and Game 3 in triple OT. Facing elimination, Montreal turned to its leaders. In Game 4, which was tied 2–2 late in the third period, Joliat fed Pit Lepine, who beat Charlie Gardiner and tied the series. In the deciding fifth game, Joliat set up Gagnon for a goal midway through the game and Habs goalie George Hainsworth blanked the Hawks to win the Cup.

Joliat captured the Hart Trophy as league MVP in 1933–34, even as Toronto's Kid Line dominated the scoring charts, but he never got the Habs to another Stanley Cup. A three-time Stanley Cup winner, Joliat retired in 1938 with 270 goals in 654 games.

*One of the smallest NHLers ever at 5'6", 135 pounds, Joliat's skating and puck skill earned him a Hart Trophy in 1934.*

### NHL STATISTICS

| GP | G | A | PTS | PIM |
|-----|-----|-----|-----|-----|
| 654 | 270 | 190 | 460 | 757 |

# JARI KURRI

**I**n a debate rivaling the chicken-and-the-egg controversy, hockey experts will forever dissect and dispute the theory of whether Wayne Gretzky's incredible playmaking skill created the Jari Kurri scoring machine, or if it was Kurri's uncanny ability to find chinks in the armor of NHL goalies that resulted in extraordinary assist totals for No. 99. Either way, during the 1980s Kurri and Gretzky gave the Edmonton Oilers one of the deadliest scoring combinations in league history.

Born in Helsinki, Finland, Kurri joined the Oilers in 1980–81. He and Gretzky clicked immediately as Jari finished his rookie season with 32 goals, then repeated that total as a sophomore. In 1982–83, Kurri notched 45 goals and enjoyed his first of five straight 100-point seasons. A smart, very adept two-way player, Kurri proved he was as valuable in a checking role as he was in a scoring mode, finishing second in Selke Trophy voting (for the league's best defensive forward) to Philly's Bobby Clarke.

Kurri reached the 50-goal plateau for the first time in 1983–84 and scored five goals in one game. In the playoffs, he led all scorers in goals (14) as Edmonton won its first Stanley Cup title. As a follow-up to his brilliant 52-goal year, Kurri exploded for 71 goals in 1984–85, setting an NHL record for goals by a right wing (later eclipsed by Brett Hull, with 72) and

becoming only the third player in NHL history to score 70 goals in a season. He then set single-season playoff records for goals (19) and most goals in a series (12). He also captured his second Stanley Cup as the Oilers successfully defended their title. Kurri added a Lady Byng Trophy to cap a great year.

*Kurri, from Helsinki, Finland, is the NHL's second all-time leading scorer among Europeans, trailing Stan Mikita.*

In 1985–86, Kurri led the NHL in regular-season goals (68) and was fourth in points (131), but the season ended badly as Edmonton lost in the second round of playoffs and Kurri had but two goals in 10 postseason games. Kurri lost another scoring title to Gretzky in 1986–87, collecting 108 points, but for the third time in four years he led all playoff scorers in goals (15). He helped the Oilers to a third Cup with five game-winning goals,

including the Cup-clincher in the seventh game of the Finals against Philadelphia.

Kurri "slumped" to 96 points in 1987–88 but was his usual playoff self, winning a fourth Cup and leading in goals (14). In 1988–89, playing his first season without Gretzky, who had gone to the Kings, Kurri led the Oilers in points (102) but couldn't carry the team past the first round of playoffs. He scored just 33 goals in 1989–90, but he recorded the 1,000th point of his career and helped a surprisingly strong, rebuilding Oiler team win its fifth Stanley Cup.

Kurri left the NHL to play in Milan, Italy, in 1990, but he returned after one year and reunited with Gretzky in Los Angeles. On October 17, 1992, he scored his 500th career goal, and the following year he became the second-highest scoring European in league history when he passed Peter Stastny. After five years in L.A., he played briefly for the Rangers in 1995–96 before moving to Anaheim in 1996–97. He currently stands third all time among right wingers in goals, assists, and points, and is sure to gain entry into the Hall of Fame.

## NHL STATISTICS

| GP | G | A | PTS | PIM |
|------|-----|-----|-------|-----|
| 1,181 | 596 | 780 | 1,376 | 533 |

# GUY LAFLEUR

Two decades after Jean Beliveau graduated from junior hockey in Quebec and left raucous crowds at the Quebec Colisée screaming for more, Guy Damien Lafleur came along and did the very same. Like Beliveau before him, Lafleur dominated juniors in his home province and was eagerly sought by NHL teams. Montreal negotiated heatedly to obtain Lafleur as the No. 1 pick in the 1971 draft.

After scoring 233 goals and 379 points in 118 junior games, Lafleur made his NHL debut in 1971–72 and netted 29 goals in 73 games. The Habs were a strong team on the verge of domination as Lafleur found his stride. In 1972–73, he scored 28 goals, then rode the Habs' tidal wave to a Stanley Cup as Montreal beat Buffalo and Philadelphia to reach the Finals against Chicago, winning in six. Lafleur struggled in his third season, finishing 1973–74 with just 21 goals. The year ended badly when Montreal lost in the first round of the playoffs to the Rangers.

After three fitful seasons in which he showed flashes of greatness and suffered through stretches of uncertainty and inconsistency, Lafleur blossomed in 1974–75, scoring 53 goals for Montreal's league-leading offense. But the Habs were upset by Buffalo in the semifinals and Lafleur's triumphant season was tainted by team failure.

In 1975–76, the Canadiens put the NHL on notice. Not only were they going to dominate with big offense, they were going to crush all opposition in the postseason as well. Lafleur led the charge, netting 56 goals and winning his first of three straight Art Ross Trophies with 125 points. In the playoffs, Montreal lost only one game in three series en route to sweeping Philly in the Finals. Lafleur led the Habs with 17 playoff points and scored the Cup-clinching goal in Game 4.

Lafleur continued his personal domination of the NHL in 1976–77, winning his second Art Ross Trophy and leading the NHL in assists (80) and points (135). In the playoffs, Lafleur led all scorers with 26 points. In Game 4 of the Finals, he set up Jacques Lemaire's OT winner against Boston to win a second straight Stanley Cup. For his work, Lafleur earned the Conn Smythe Trophy as playoff MVP. He also took the Hart Trophy as regular-season MVP as well as the Lester B. Pearson Award as the players' choice for MVP.

In 1977–78, Lafleur scored a career-high 60 goals, tops in the NHL, and won his final Art Ross Trophy with 132 points. His 10 playoff goals led the Canadiens to a third straight Cup. Lafleur added 52 goals in 1978–79, tied for the playoff scoring lead with teammate Jacques Lemaire (23 points), and hoisted another Cup, the fifth of his career.

Lafleur enjoyed one more 50-goal season (1979–80) before his skills began to dwindle. He left the Habs in controversy in 1984 and sat out more than three years before making a dramatic comeback with the Rangers, after he'd been inducted into the Hall of Fame. He played one year in New York before finishing his career with Quebec, in the building where it all began. He retired in 1991.

*Lafleur was the fourth Canadien to net 500 goals, joining Rocket Richard, Jean Beliveau, and Frank Mahovlich.*

## NHL STATISTICS

| GP | G | A | PTS | PIM |
|-----|-----|-----|-------|-----|
| 1,126 | 560 | 793 | 1,353 | 399 |

# TED LINDSAY

Hall of Fame left winger Ted Lindsay had a name for his stick. Not a pet name, like "Woody" or "The Big Splinter." No, he called it "The Great Equalizer." A terrific goal-scorer who once led the NHL in goals and later won an Art Ross Trophy as the game's most prolific point-getter, Lindsay was also a mean cuss on the ice, the kind of rink rat who'd just as soon take a chunk out of his opposition with a slash as with a goal. At just 5'8" and 160 pounds, Lindsay wasn't big, but once the game started he had the temperament of an abused junkyard dog.

A native of Renfrew, Ontario, where professional hockey had its roots, Lindsay was the son of a pro hockey player (Bert Lindsay of the Renfrew Millionaires). He played junior hockey at St. Michael's College in Toronto and was a member of the 1944 Memorial Cup champion Oshawa Generals before signing with the Detroit Red Wings. Lindsay, who quickly earned the nickname "Terrible Ted" for his gritty tenacity on the ice, scored 17 rookie goals in 1944–45, although he fell victim to the sophomore jinx when he potted just seven goals the next season.

In 1947–48, the Red Wings assembled a line with Lindsay, Sid Abel, and Gordie Howe. Lindsay emerged as the line's finisher, taking advantage of Abel's playmaking and leading the NHL in goals (33). The unit was dubbed the Production Line. In 1948–49, Lindsay and Abel tied for third in the NHL in points (54) and progressed to the Stanley Cup Finals before being swept by Toronto.

In 1949–50, the Red Wings led the NHL in total goals (229), and the trio of Lindsay, Abel, and Howe finished 1–2–3 in scoring, with Lindsay taking the Art Ross Trophy on the strength of his league-best 55 assists and 78 points. Abel (69 points) and Howe (68) weren't far behind. Detroit appeared unstoppable as the playoffs approached. But in their first game against Toronto in the semifinals, the Red Wings were dealt a near-fatal blow as Howe fractured his skull crashing into the boards and was lost for the season. Without Howe, the Production Line wasn't the same. Lindsay notched just four goals in 13 games as Detroit barely got past Toronto in seven and then survived the Rangers in seven games to hoist a hard-won Cup.

The Red Wings captured the Stanley Cup again in 1952 and then put together back-to-back titles in 1954 and 1955. Lindsay's five playoff goals paced Detroit in 1952. And while he had a quiet series in 1954, his 12 assists were tops in 1955 as Detroit beat Montreal in seven games to win its fourth Stanley Cup in six years.

After 13 years in Detroit, Lindsay was traded to Chicago in 1957. He spent three years with the Black Hawks before retiring in 1960. He made a brief comeback in 1964–65 with Detroit but scored only 14 goals and, at nearly 40, packed it in with 379 goals and 851 points in 1,068 games. Lindsay also counted 1,808 penalty minutes over a 17-year career, which culminated with his 1966 induction into the Hall of Fame.

*Though well loved in Detroit, Lindsay was exiled to lowly Chicago in 1957 after he tried to organize a players' union.*

### NHL STATISTICS

| GP | G | A | PTS | PIM |
|---|---|---|---|---|
| 1,068 | 379 | 472 | 851 | 1,808 |

# FRANK MAHOVLICH

Hall of Fame left winger Frank Mahovlich was different things to different people. To some he was a brooding superstar whose introverted nature made him difficult to idolize; to others he was the missing link who could turn a team into a champion, something he did on several occasions during his 18-year NHL career.

Born in Ontario, Mahovlich debuted with the Maple Leafs in 1956–57 but played only three games. In 1957–58, he scored 20 goals and won the Calder Trophy as rookie of the year. It was the only major award the Big M would ever win, not counting a handful of Stanley Cups.

In 1960–61, his fourth year in Toronto, Mahovlich used his huge slap shot to rifle home 48 goals, coming that close to tying Rocket Richard's record 50-goal performance. While the Big M was chasing down a piece of history, Canadiens right winger Boom Boom Geoffrion did reach the hallowed milestone. Ironically, Mahovlich received a warmer hero's reception in his failed attempt than the Boomer did for his successful one.

Mahovlich took control of the Leafs in 1961–62, leading the team in points for the second straight season (71) and tying for second in the league in goals (33). After dispatching the Rangers in the semifinals, the Leafs overpowered Chicago in the Finals. Mahovlich scored the winning goal in Game 1 and added

another in Game 5 as the Leafs won their first Cup in 11 years.

Toronto ascended to the top of the NHL standings in 1962–63. Mahovlich was third in goals (36) and fourth in points (73). In the playoffs, the Leafs needed just 10 games to defend their Stanley Cup, ousting Montreal in five

*A quietly intense player, Mahovlich won four Cups in Toronto and two more in Montreal before finishing up in the WHA.*

and then rolling over Detroit in five in the Finals. Oddly, after his terrific regular season, Mahovlich went dry and was held without a goal in the playoffs.

The Big M finished the 1963–64 season with just 26 goals, and the Leafs

dropped to third behind Montreal and Chicago. In the playoffs, they survived a seven-game series against Montreal before taking on Detroit once more in the Finals. Mahovlich led the Leafs with 15 points and was the top assist-maker in the postseason as Toronto pulled off a seven-game thriller.

The Leafs won their last Cup in 1966–67, but Mahovlich and Leafs boss Punch Imlach were feuding. In 1967–68, the Big M was traded to Detroit. His stay in Motown lasted only until the 1970–71 season, when Montreal acquired him for the playoff drive. If anyone thought that Mahovlich was over the hill, he proved them wrong by leading all playoff scorers with 14 goals and 27 points. His outburst helped Montreal win another Stanley Cup, his fifth. During the 1972–73 season, he scored the 500th goal of his career and chipped in 23 points during the playoffs to add a sixth Stanley Cup to his impressive résumé.

In 1974–75, Mahovlich returned to Toronto to play in the WHA. He played four years (in Toronto and Birmingham) before retiring in 1978. His NHL career featured 533 goals, 1,103 points and six Stanley Cups for two different teams.

| NHL STATISTICS | | | | |
|---|---|---|---|---|
| GP | G | A | PTS | PIM |
| 1,181 | 533 | 570 | 1,103 | 1,056 |

# JOE MALONE

The first superstar of hockey, Malone scored goals in 14 straight games in 1917–18 on his way to 44 goals in 20 games.

**M**odern historians often overlook Joe Malone when cataloging the greatest players in NHL history, for he played in a bygone era when hockey was vastly different from today's lightning-quick and explosive game. But before the advent of slap shots, huge pads, and aluminum hockey sticks, Malone earned his colorful nickname, "Phantom," not only for his skating but for his astonishing ability to elude the goalie with the puck.

Malone was the NHL's first superstar goal-scorer. When the NHL was born in 1917–18, Malone, a 27-year-old veteran of many years in the National Hockey Association, formed a line with Newsy Lalonde and Didier Pitre and scored a whopping 44 goals in just 20 games for the Montreal Canadiens. Despite the huge output of today's stars, Malone's 2.2 goals-per-game average ranks as the most deadly of all time. Considering the fuss created by Rocket Richard's 50-goal performance in 1944–45, achieved in 50 games, Malone's explosion of 1917–18 is even more amazing.

Born in Quebec, Malone began his pro hockey career in the NHA, joining the Quebec Bulldogs as a 19-year-old in 1909. In 1912–13, the 'Dogs won the NHA title with a 16–4 record, and Malone led the league with 43 goals. During the Stanley Cup challenge, he ripped nine goals in Game 1 as Quebec trounced Sydney 20–5 in their total-goals victory.

That performance was a harbinger of things to come. In 1916–17, his final year in the NHA, Malone ripped 41 goals, tying Ottawa's Frank Nighbor. One night against the Wanderers, Malone lit the lamp eight times.

With the birth of the NHL in 1917–18, Malone joined the Canadiens and united with former rivals Lalonde and Pitre. On the opening night of the season, he scored five goals. He enjoyed three five-goal games that year and victimized two future Hall of Famers by scoring five goals against Toronto's Hap Holmes on one occasion and humiliating Ottawa's Clint Benedict on two others.

Malone appeared in only eight games in 1918–19, notching but seven goals. In the playoffs, his Habs were embroiled in a heated battle for the Stanley Cup with Seattle of the PCHL when a flu epidemic broke out, afflicting players on both sides. The playoffs were suspended and, tragically, the Canadiens' "Bad Joe" Hall succumbed less than a week after falling ill.

Malone returned to Quebec in 1919–20 and led the NHL in goals (39) and points (48). On January 31, 1920, he ripped seven goals against Toronto goalie Ivan Mitchell, setting an NHL standard that has never been repeated. In 1920–21, Malone skated for lowly Hamilton and scored 30 goals in 20 games but couldn't keep the Tigers from a last-place finish. He added 25 goals the following season, but the Tigers again finished last.

Phantom Joe returned to the Canadiens in 1922–23, but his goal-scoring powers had all but disappeared. He retired following the 1923–24 season with 146 goals in just 125 NHL games.

## NHL STATISTICS

| GP | G | A | PTS | PIM |
|-----|-----|-----|-----|-----|
| 125 | 146 | 21 | 167 | 23 |

## LANNY McDONALD

**P**rofessional athletes are typically loath to let their fantasies of glory get the better of them, or to be distracted from the demands of the daily grind. Certainly no hockey player with two feet squarely planted in reality would dare dream up a script like the one that Hall of Fame right winger Lanny McDonald played out in his final NHL season, when he scored his 500th goal and captained the Calgary Flames to a Stanley Cup title, hoisting the coveted silver trophy overhead in the final game of his often brilliant 16-year career.

Before the Toronto Maple Leafs made McDonald the fourth overall pick in the 1973 amateur draft, the Alberta native recorded 112 goals and 253 points in two years at Medicine Hat of the Western League. As an NHL rookie in 1973–74, McDonald was a third-stringer behind Rick Kehoe and Ron Ellis and scored just 14 goals. After a 17-goal sophomore year, he teamed up with Darryl Sittler in 1975–76 and scored 37 goals. The addition of Tiger Williams to the unit in 1976–77 gave Sittler and McDonald extra operating room, and they made the most of it with Lanny ripping 46 goals (fifth overall) and tying Sittler in points (90).

A hard-shooting gunslinger with a blistering slap shot and the NHL's bushiest and most famous mustache, the charismatic McDonald scored 47 goals in 1977–78 and 43 more in 1978–79. During the 1978 Stanley Cup playoffs, the Leafs battled a heavily favored

Islanders team in the quarterfinals. It was McDonald who scored at 4:13 of sudden-death OT in Game 7 and allowed the Leafs to advance to the semifinals.

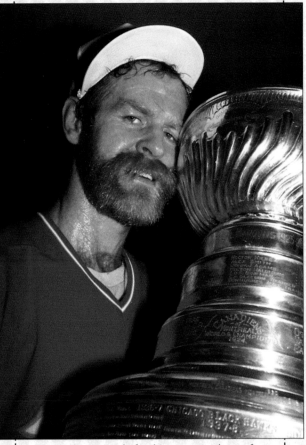

*Known as much for his moustache as for his blistering shot, McDonald accumulated 500 goals and one Stanley Cup.*

Midway through the 1979–80 season, McDonald was traded to the Colorado Rockies (who later became the New Jersey Devils). He finished the year with 40 goals, then dipped to 35 goals in 1980–81. Early the following year, he was traded to Calgary, where he would enjoy his finest hours. He finished the 1980–81 campaign with 40 goals, then exploded in 1982–83 with a career-best 66 goals, second only to Wayne Gretzky's 71. McDonald marked a career-high 98 points and, at 30, won the Masterton Trophy for perseverance and dedication.

McDonald spent seven and a half years in Calgary. In 492 games, he scored 215 goals, none bigger than the one he notched against Mark Fitzpatrick on March 21, 1989, during a 4–1 win over the Islanders, for it made him only the 14th man in NHL history to score 500 career goals. Just two weeks earlier, during a 9–5 blasting of Winnipeg, he had notched his 1,000th point.

The Flames went to the Stanley Cup Finals (unsuccessfully) in 1986, and again with better results in 1989. While McDonald scored only once in the 1989 playoffs, his goal against Montreal in the Finals put the Flames up for good in Game 6 and helped Calgary win its first-ever Stanley Cup. One of the most popular players in the league among teammates and opponents as well, McDonald hung up his skates following the 1989 playoffs, ending a Hall of Fame career that featured 500 goals and 1,006 points.

| NHL STATISTICS | | | | |
| --- | --- | --- | --- | --- |
| GP | G | A | PTS | PIM |
| 1,111 | 500 | 506 | 1,006 | 899 |

# MAURICE RICHARD

**K**nown as the "Rocket" for his fiery temper and explosive intensity, Maurice Richard was the dominant right winger in the NHL during the 1940s and 1950s, earning First or Second All-Star Team status 14 times from 1943–57. His illustrious career was dotted with milestone performances and moments of extreme high drama. And yet, through 18 years in the NHL, Richard won only a single Hart Trophy as league MVP (in 1946–47).

Born in Montreal, Richard was destined to and did in fact join the Canadiens, as a 21-year-old rookie in 1942–43 when he scored five goals in 16 games. As a sophomore, playing on the Punch Line with Elmer Lach at center and Toe Blake on the left side, the Rocket launched 32 goals and helped the team to a first-place finish. During that great season, Richard notched eight points in a single game. He then scored a dozen playoff goals (including five in a game against Toronto in the semifinals) as Montreal took the Stanley Cup in the spring of 1944.

A thrilling skater who could intimidate the opposition with his deep-set, glaring eyes, Richard attained heroic status in 1944–45 when he scored an unprecedented 50 goals in a single season, beating Boston's Harvey Bennett on the last night of the season to finish the deed. Two years later, he notched 45 goals—again leading the league—and earned his single Hart Trophy. He then led all playoff scorers with 11 points in 10 games, though the Habs lost to Toronto in the Cup Finals in six.

On November 8, 1952, Richard became the NHL's all-time leading goal-scorer when he scored the 325th goal of his career, surpassing Nels Stewart. The Rocket remained atop the goal-scoring chart for the next 11 years until Gordie Howe passed him on November 10, 1963.

Richard was a skilled puck-handler who could skate through the enemy and artfully elude all checkers, and he was also a tenacious bulldog who would battle if provoked. He sat out 1,285 penalty minutes in his career. In 1954–55, he was banned for the final three games of the season for fighting with Boston's Hal Laycoe and lost the chance to win his only scoring title when teammate Bernie Geoffrion edged him by one point.

On October 19, 1957, Richard scored against goalie Glenn Hall during a 3–1 win over Chicago, sending Montreal Forum fans into a frenzy. The goal was his 500th, making him the first NHLer to reach that hallowed mark. Richard retired in 1960 with 544 goals, although he was 35 points shy of the 1,000-point barrier. His chief rival, Howe, became the first to top the mark, doing so during Richard's first year of retirement.

In 15 trips to the playoffs, Richard put his name on eight Stanley Cups, including five straight from 1956–60, and potted the Cup-clinching goal in 1956. He still holds the record for most career overtime goals (six), is second all time to Wayne Gretzky for playoff hat tricks (seven), and shares the record for goals in a playoff game (five).

*The first to score 500 NHL goals, Richard was likely the most dangerous player ever from the blue line in.*

## NHL STATISTICS

| GP | G | A | PTS | PIM |
|----|----|----|----|----|
| 978 | 544 | 421 | 965 | 1,285 |

# SWEENEY SCHRINER

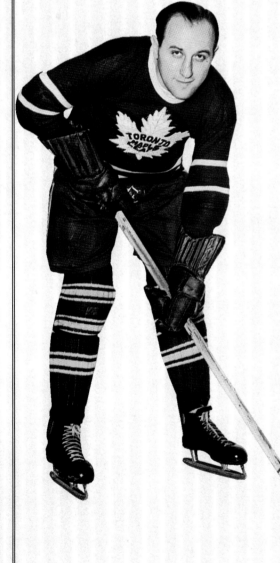

Round-faced and somber, David "Sweeney" Schriner looked more like a businessman than a professional athlete. And when it came to his hockey, Schriner was indeed all business. During 11 years in the NHL, he won two scoring titles and helped the Maple Leafs win two Stanley Cups.

Born in eastern Europe and raised in western Canada, Schriner debuted in the NHL during the 1934–35 season with Red Dutton's New York Americans. A solidly built left winger, Schriner wasted no time establishing his credentials, scoring 18 freshman goals and capturing the third-annual Calder Trophy as rookie of the year. Though the Americans' rivals, the New York Rangers, enjoyed more popularity, few could argue that Schriner was a highly skilled player worthy of note.

With the pressure of a sophomore jinx hanging over his head, Schriner calmly went about his business in 1935–36 and, teamed with Lorne Carr and Art Chapman, notched 45 points to lead the NHL and capture his first scoring championship. Unfortunately, his Americans won only 16 of their 48 games and finished third in the Canadian Division behind the Montreal Maroons and Toronto Maple Leafs. After a surprising 7–5 total-goals victory over Chicago in the quarterfinals, Schriner's Americans were eliminated in the semifinals by Toronto.

The 1936–37 season didn't bring any better fortune to the Americans, despite another stellar performance from Schriner. The classy winger scored 21 goals and took his second Art Ross Trophy with 46 points, narrowly edging Toronto's Syl Apps (45). But the Americans finished fourth, out of a playoff position, and nothing Schriner did could help the failing team resurrect its postseason dreams.

In 1939–40, after several more frustrating years, team boss Dutton finally made a move to improve his franchise's dwindling hopes, shipping Schriner to the Maple Leafs for Busher Jackson, Murray Armstrong, Buzz Boll, and Doc Romnes. In Toronto, Schriner began to regain the form that had eroded somewhat during his final campaigns with the struggling Americans. With a new lease on his NHL life, Schriner applied his great skills and put together three 20-goal seasons, including a career-high 27 goals in just 26 games in 1944–45 (the same year Rocket Richard scored 50 goals in 50 games).

The Maple Leafs went to the Stanley Cup Finals three times from 1940–45 and, with Schriner's help, won a pair of championships. In 1942, Schriner scored a pair of goals in Game 7 of the Leafs' Finals series against Detroit, capping the most dramatic comeback in playoff history; Toronto won the title after being down three games to none. In 1945, Toronto once again took on Detroit in a series that went the full seven-game limit. Schriner scored the only goal in Game 1, the final playoff point of his career. The Leafs held on to win the Cup. Schriner played one more year, scoring 13 goals in 1945–46, before calling it quits.

*Schriner won two scoring titles with the New York Americans before moving to Toronto in 1939–40.*

| NHL STATISTICS | | | | |
|---|---|---|---|---|
| GP | G | A | PTS | PIM |
| 484 | 201 | 204 | 405 | 148 |

## 15 BEST DEFENSEMEN

RAYMOND BOURQUE
KING CLANCY
SPRAGUE CLEGHORN
PAUL COFFEY
DOUG HARVEY
TIM HORTON
RED KELLY
BOBBY ORR
BRAD PARK
PIERRE PILOTE
DENIS POTVIN
BABE PRATT
LARRY ROBINSON
EDDIE SHORE
CYCLONE TAYLOR

Among NHL backliners, defense has meant different things to different people. Some, such as Doug Harvey, have brought their lunch buckets to work, preferring to play blue-collar hockey within their own zone. Others, such as Bobby Orr, have broken free from the backyard, energizing crowds with their mad rushes. Of the 44 Norris Trophies ever awarded, 32 were won by members of this exclusive group.

*Though overshadowed by Bobby Orr, Brad Park was one of the best defensemen of his era, finishing runner-up for the Norris Trophy six times.*

# RAYMOND BOURQUE

In the first 42 years in which the NHL presented the James Norris Trophy to the game's outstanding defenseman, Boston Bruins backliners took home the prize 13 times. More startling yet, just two men, Bobby Orr and Raymond Bourque, comprised the entire list of Boston defensemen to win this prestigious award. In 1993–94, Bourque won his fifth Norris Trophy, putting him third all time behind Orr (eight) and Doug Harvey (seven) in Norris wins.

Born in Montreal, Bourque played three outstanding years of hockey in the Quebec juniors before Boston made him the eighth pick overall in the 1979 entry draft. He immediately jumped to the NHL and recorded 65 points en route to a Calder Trophy as rookie of the year. He also earned first-team All-Star status for the first of 11 times (through 1996).

A hard-shooting, hard-hitting point man who combined great playmaking with clean, rugged defensive play, Bourque wasted no time in establishing himself as one of the game's premier defenders. In 1986–87, after twice being a runner-up, he finally won his first Norris Trophy when he scored 23 goals and 95 points. In his first 17 seasons, he reached or surpassed the 20-goal mark nine times, and in 1983–84 he scored a career-high 31 goals.

Bourque retained his Norris Trophy title in 1987–88, when he took the Bruins

all the way to the Stanley Cup Finals. Though Boston lost to Edmonton, Bourque's 21 points made him the top-scoring defenseman in the playoffs. In 1989–90, Bourque won his third Norris Trophy when he finished third among

*With five Norris Trophies, Bourque is the third-most decorated backliner in history behind Bobby Orr and Doug Harvey.*

NHL defensemen with 84 points and guided the Bruins to another first-place finish in the Adams Division. Boston squeaked past Hartford in seven games in the first round of Stanley Cup playoffs, then ripped Montreal in five before sweeping Washington in the semifinals. The Bruins took on Edmonton in the

Finals for the second time in three years, and once again they were humbled, this time surrendering in five games. Once more, however, Bourque was a bright light, leading defensemen in postseason scoring with 17 points in 17 games.

In 1990–91, Bourque recorded 94 points. His Bruins took the regular-season Adams Division title and seemed poised for another assault on the Stanley Cup. After harpooning the Whalers in the opening round, the Bruins took a hard-fought seven-game series from Montreal before facing Pittsburgh in the semifinals. But Mario Lemieux's Penguins were on a roll, and the Bruins were eliminated in six games. For his outstanding individual effort in the regular season, Bourque won his fourth Norris Trophy.

On February 29, 1992, Bourque became only the third defenseman in NHL history to reach the 1,000-point plateau, joining Denis Potvin and Paul Coffey on this elite list. And in 1993–94, he reached the 90-point plateau for the fourth time in his career and earned his fifth Norris Trophy. In 1995–96, he was runner-up for Norris honors to Chicago's Chris Chelios. The Hall of Fame awaits Bourque upon his retirement.

| NHL STATISTICS | | | | |
|---|---|---|---|---|
| GP | G | A | PTS | PIM |
| 1,290 | 352 | 1,001 | 1,363 | 953 |

# KING CLANCY

**F**ew players in the storied annals of pro hockey have been so well known for their enthusiasm as Frank "King" Clancy, who patrolled the blue line for Ottawa and Toronto during his 16 years as a player in the NHL. Though small in stature, standing only 5'9", Clancy had the proverbial heart of a lion and would often find resources within himself to succeed where players of lesser spirit would surrender. In a game in 1923, when his Ottawa Senators were battling Edmonton for the Stanley Cup, Clancy played every position on the ice—including goal after Clint Benedict was sent to the penalty box. Though crippled by injuries, the Senators held on, thanks to a single goal from Punch Broadbent and the virtuoso performance of Clancy, and beat the WCHL champion Eskimos of Alberta.

A native of Ottawa, Clancy debuted in the NHL in 1921 at the age of just 18 with his hometown Senators. In the course of nine seasons with Ottawa, he led the NHL in assists once (with eight, during his third campaign in 1922–23) and helped bring a pair of Stanley Cups to Ottawa. In 1924–25, his fourth season, he tied teammate George Boucher for most points by an NHL defenseman (19).

In 1926–27, Clancy topped the charts for points by a defender (19) and led the Senators to their final first-place regular-season finish. In the playoffs, Ottawa defeated Montreal in a total-goals semi-final series before taking on Boston for the Stanley Cup. After a scoreless Game 1 ended in double overtime when the ice was too rutted for play to continue,

Clancy got the Senators started in Game 2, scoring the opening goal in a 3–1 win. He assisted Cy Denneny's goal in Game 3, which ended in a 1–1 tie after ice conditions became intolerable. Ottawa won Game 4 and took the Cup, two games to none.

In his final season with the Senators, Clancy reached a pair of career-high

marks when he finished the 1929–30 campaign with 17 goals and 40 points, leading all of the league's defensemen yet again.

Toward the end of the 1920s, the Senators hit hard times, financially as well as on the ice, and on October 10, 1930, Clancy was sent to Toronto for two players and a bundle of cash. In a Maple Leafs jersey, Clancy became a legend, anchoring the club's defense while the Kid Line of Busher Jackson, Joe Primeau, and Charlie Conacher did the damage on offense. Clancy helped the Leafs to a Stanley Cup in 1931–32, his third, and continued to play until the 1936–37 season.

Clancy later coached the Montreal Maroons and then turned to a successful "second" career as an NHL referee, where his popularity as a player served him well. He coached Toronto from 1953 to 1956, but his teams never survived the first round of playoffs. He remained a member of the organization until his death in the 1980s. The King Clancy Memorial Trophy, first presented in 1988, is given to the NHL player who demonstrates extraordinary leadership and humanitarian contribution in the community.

*A player who'd do anything to win, Clancy once played goal for the Leafs in 1932–33.*

## NHL STATISTICS

| GP | G | A | PTS | PIM |
|-----|-----|-----|-----|-----|
| 592 | 137 | 143 | 280 | 904 |

# SPRAGUE CLEGHORN

A mean-edged defenseman with a penchant for violence and a talent for creating havoc, Sprague Cleghorn was a lot of things to a lot of people during his rambunctious decade in the NHL. He was a leader, a Stanley Cup champion, and an MVP candidate. He was also a hooligan worthy of jail time, whose many bloody assaults made him one of the NHL's original goons.

Born in Montreal, Cleghorn played in New York, Montreal, and Ontario during the pre–NHL era and joined the Ottawa Senators in 1918–19. He won his first Stanley Cup in 1919–20 when the Sens took a best-of-five series against Seattle, the PCHL champion. Sprague's Senators, led by the scoring prowess of Jack Darragh and Cy Denneny, successfully defended their playoff title in the spring of 1921, this time beating Vancouver of the PCHL in the Finals.

In 1921–22, Cleghorn was acquired by the Montreal Canadiens, where he reunited with his kid brother, Odie, the Habs' top center. A hostile player whose outbursts came quickly and with frightening force, Sprague showed no lingering measure of camaraderie toward his ex-mates in Ottawa. In his first year in Montreal, during a match against the Senators, he went into a frenzy, attacking Eddie Gerard, Frank Nighbor, and Cy Denneny, resulting in injuries that forced those superb players from the game. Police offered to arrest Cleghorn but were repelled by Montreal brass. Cleghorn was, as usual, unrepentant.

After all, this was not Cleghorn's first brush with the law. Many years earlier, he'd been involved in a nasty stick-swinging incident with Montreal ace Newsy Lalonde, cutting the Habs star for more than a dozen stitches over the eye. Facing incarceration, Cleghorn was saved by the pleas of his bosses, who kept the gendarmes out of the proceedings.

A talented player who could anchor a team with his intensity and will to win, Cleghorn was a runner-up for the first Hart Trophy in 1923–24. In a historic moment of true justice, Cleghorn was beaten out by Ottawa's Frank Nighbor, his ex-teammate and a gentlemanly player, for the MVP trophy. Cleghorn's MVP defeat was tempered with a third Stanley Cup, however, when the Canadiens, led by Howie Morenz and Aurel Joliat, pasted Vancouver of the PCHL in the semifinals, then trounced Calgary of the WCHL in two games. It was Cleghorn's third and last playoff championship.

In 1925–26, Cleghorn went to Boston, while brother Odie went to Pittsburgh. In Beantown, though he was again runner-up for the Hart Trophy in 1926 (to Nels Stewart), Sprague would soon be overshadowed by the emergence of Eddie Shore, whose truculence and scoring ability became, in very short order, as legendary as Cleghorn's had been.

*Though known for his toughness, Cleghorn once scored five goals in an NHA game.*

| NHL STATISTICS | | | | |
|---|---|---|---|---|
| GP | G | A | PTS | PIM |
| 256 | 84 | 39 | 123 | 489 |

# PAUL COFFEY

On December 13, 1995, in Detroit's Joe Louis Arena, Red Wings defenseman Paul Coffey went where no NHL defenseman had ever been before. When Igor Larionov tapped in Coffey's pass for a goal in the Wings' 3–1 win over visiting Chicago, Coffey became the first defender in the game's history to record 1,000 career assists. Among the first to congratulate him was his former teammate, Wayne Gretzky, the game's all-time assist leader, who phoned him in the locker room.

Considered by many to be the finest pure skater in the NHL (perhaps ever), Coffey is the NHL's all-time leading point-getter among defensemen.

Born in Ontario, Coffey began his brilliant career as an offensive juggernaut on the blue line with Sault Ste. Marie and Kitchener of the OHL, where he spent two years before Edmonton made him the sixth pick overall in the 1980 entry draft. He joined the Oilers in 1980–81, and after a modest rookie year (32 points) he exploded as a second-year man, notching 89 points.

In 1983–84, he reached the 100-point mark for the first time (126, most by a defenseman since Bobby Orr) and notched 22 points in the playoffs as the Oilers won their first Stanley Cup title. In 1984–85, he won his first Norris Trophy as the game's top defender when he recorded 37 goals and 121 points. He added a second Stanley Cup that year, then set a new NHL record in 1985–86 when he scored 48 goals, most ever by a defenseman. This compilation broke the 46-goal record of Hall of Fame defenseman Orr, the player with whom he has most often been compared. For setting a new goal-scoring mark, Coffey received his second straight Norris Trophy. On March 14, 1986, he notched six assists and eight points in a game against Detroit, tying the record set by Philadelphia's Tom Bladon in 1977.

After a one-year hiatus, the Oilers won their third Stanley Cup in 1986–87, Coffey's last year with Edmonton. After a contract dispute with Oilers boss Glen Sather, Coffey was traded to Pittsburgh, where he helped the Penguins win the first Stanley Cup in franchise history, in 1991. He was traded again, this time to Los Angeles midway through the 1991–92 season, rejoining Wayne Gretzky. His stay in southern California lasted only 60 games over two seasons, as he was then shipped to Detroit midway through the 1992–93 season.

With the up-and-coming Red Wings, Coffey added a third Norris Trophy in 1994–95, when he finished the lockout-shortened season with 58 points in 45 games and helped the Wings go to the Stanley Cup Finals before being swept by New Jersey. In 1996–97, Coffey was traded again, this time to the Hartford Whalers. Coffey's grace and artistry, to say nothing of his tremendous productivity, will put him in the Hockey Hall of Fame when he retires.

*Besides being the only defenseman to notch 1,000 helpers, Coffey is second to Wayne Gretzky on the all-time assists list.*

| NHL STATISTICS | | | | |
|---|---|---|---|---|
| GP | G | A | PTS | PIM |
| 1,211 | 381 | 1,063 | 1,444 | 1,674 |

# DOUG HARVEY

Misunderstood and largely unappreciated during his early years in the NHL, Hall of Fame defenseman Doug Harvey was nevertheless one of the most effective, efficient, and talented backliners the game has ever known. It's no accident he won seven Norris Trophies in eight years and is second only to Boston legend Bobby Orr (eight) for all-time defenseman-of-the-year awards.

Born in Montreal, Harvey climbed through the amateur and junior ranks until he was ready to try his luck in the NHL in 1947–48 at the age of 23. The Canadiens, a firebrand skating team with tons of talent, were not initially enamored with Harvey's laconic style of play. Not a proponent of the high-energy approach to hockey, he preferred to conserve his strength for moments of high drama. As a result, he often gave the impression of loafing on the ice. In fact, however, Harvey was a brilliant poke-checker, a confident and accomplished puck-handler, and an even better passer. His greatest gift was his ability to steal the puck from opposing players, hold on to the rubber biscuit while the enemy pursued him in vain, and then fire pinpoint passes to breaking teammates. Not a great goal-scorer, Harvey was, however, a tremendous assist-maker.

While he offered no apologies for his energy-saving style, after a few seasons it became clear that his skill and execution were well worth the anxiety caused by his apparent nonchalance. In 1952–53, he helped the Canadiens win their first

Stanley Cup in seven years, and he later was an integral part of the Montreal dynasty that won a record five consecu-

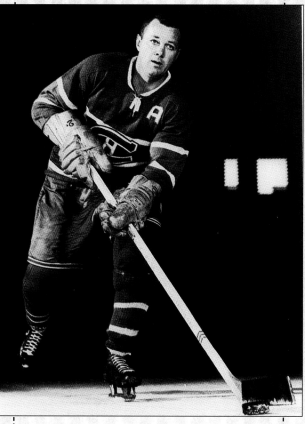

*During his tenure with the Rangers in the early 1960s, Harvey commuted between Manhattan and his Montreal home.*

tive championships from 1955–60. In 1952–53, he led all NHL defensemen in assists (30).

In 1954–55, the NHL presented the second annual James Norris Trophy, commemorating the finest performance by a defenseman. Following in the foot-

steps of Detroit rival Red Kelly, who won the inaugural sweepstakes, Harvey won his first Norris Trophy, then won it six of the next seven years. In 1954–55, he finished second overall in assists (43), trailing only teammate Bert Olmstead (48), and added the second Stanley Cup of his career. He'd be part of six Cup winners.

Intelligent and savvy, Harvey was also a no-nonsense player who'd protect his livelihood with extreme prejudice. In the mid–1950s, he was involved in a spearing incident with New York Ranger center Red Sullivan that landed the crimson-haired pivot in the hospital in critical condition. Harvey claimed Sullivan had kicked his skates—a hockey no-no—and made no other excuse for his violent outburst.

Harvey was traded to the same Rangers in 1961, where he served one year as New York's player-coach without much success. The Rangers sent him to the farm in 1963–64. He bounced around the minors for a couple of years until the expansion St. Louis Blues brought him back to the NHL for the 1967–68 playoffs. To the surprise of many, Harvey earned a spot in the Blues' lineup for the 1968–69 campaign, and he played well even at age 44. Harvey played 70 games that year, then hung up his skates for good.

### NHL STATISTICS

| GP | G | A | PTS | PIM |
|---|---|---|---|---|
| 1,113 | 88 | 452 | 540 | 1,216 |

# TIM HORTON

For 24 seasons, Tim Horton was a Rock of Gibraltar on the blue line, mostly with Toronto, combining raw physical strength with smart play on defense. Hard-nosed yet clean, Horton was vastly respected around the NHL. In the aftermath of his tragic death in a car accident midway through the 1973–74 season, Horton was honored posthumously for the great gusto he brought to hockey.

A native of Ontario, Horton broke into the NHL as a 19-year-old during the 1949–50 season when he suited up for one game with the Toronto Maple Leafs. He spent most of the next year in the minors, playing just four games in the NHL, then arrived for good in 1952–53. His 31 points in 1953–54 were tops among Leafs defenders and stood him fourth in the league among blue-liners. His offense lagged in 1954–55, and toward the end of the schedule he ran into Rangers defenseman Bill Gadsby. Horton came away with a broken leg and a busted jaw, which sidelined him for the first 35 games of the 1955–56 season.

Horton's great misfortune was to play in an era that featured Montreal's Doug Harvey, Chicago's Pierre Pilote, fellow Leaf Carl Brewer, and ex-Detroit blue-line ace Red Kelly; otherwise, he might have earned more votes for the Norris Trophy. Horton never won the prestigious trophy but was a runner-up to Pilote in 1963–64. By then he'd carved his name into another trophy—the Stanley Cup.

In 1961–62, Toronto finished second to Montreal in the regular-season standings. Horton was back in top form, reaching double figures in goals (10) for the first time in his career. In the playoffs, he was Toronto's leading scorer, with three goals and 16 points in 12 games. His assist on Dick Duff's goal at 14:14 of the third period in Game 6 against Chicago in the Finals unlocked a 1–1 tie and sent the Leafs to the championship, their first since the spring of 1951.

The Leafs were back in the Stanley Cup winner's circle in 1963 with a five-game triumph over Detroit in the Finals, and although Horton's offensive contribution (four points in 10 games) was more humble, his play on defense was, as usual, solid. Toronto continued its excellent play in 1963–64, and Horton concentrated on defense. Though the Leafs finished second, they rode the hot goaltending of Johnny Bower to a seven-game series win over Montreal in the semis before renewing hostilities with Detroit in the Finals. After a seesaw battle sent the teams to a seventh game, Toronto prevailed 4–0 in Game 7 to win its third straight Cup.

Horton put his name on a fourth Cup in 1966–67 with Toronto, then spent the remainder of his career traveling with the Rangers, Pittsburgh, and Buffalo. On February 21, 1974, at the age of 44, he was driving home to Toronto from Buffalo when his car went out of control and crashed. Horton's life and career came to a sudden and sorrowful end. Following a career characterized by his passion and sportsmanship, Horton was elected to the Hall of Fame just three years after his death.

*Though he was legendary for his defense, Horton had the puck-handling skill to play right wing, which he occasionally did.*

## NHL STATISTICS

| GP | G | A | PTS | PIM |
|-----|-----|-----|-----|-------|
| 1,446 | 115 | 403 | 518 | 1,611 |

# RED KELLY

One of the most versatile players ever, Red Kelly was a Norris Trophy-winning defenseman before switching to the forward line late in his career and becoming a respected center. In addition, during a sterling career spanning two decades with Detroit and Toronto, Kelly distinguished himself with his sportsmanship, winning the Lady Byng Trophy four times and twice finishing second in the voting.

An Ontario native, Kelly was a defenseman at Toronto's St. Michael's College, where he was scouted by Detroit and the Maple Leafs. The Leafs passed, and the Red Wings signed him in the mid–1940s. By 1947–48, Kelly was ready for prime time. After watching and learning the NHL game from his veteran backline mates, including Black Jack Stewart, Bill Quackenbush, and Leo Reise, he was the NHL's top scoring defenseman (40 points) during his third season (1949–50). In the next half-dozen years, he led all NHL defensemen in scoring five more times. In the spring of 1950, with Kelly leading the charge, Detroit won the Stanley Cup, its first in seven years, with a thrilling seven-game series victory over the Rangers.

In 1950–51, Kelly proved he was no flash in the pan, notching 54 points—a remarkable total for a defenseman—while sitting out just 24 minutes in penalties, earning his first Lady Byng Trophy. During the next five years, Detroit became the dominant team in the NHL, winning Stanley Cups in 1952, 1954, and 1955. Kelly was among the game's most outstanding backliners. During the 1952–53 campaign, he scored 19 goals and won his second Lady Byng Trophy with just eight penalty minutes. In 1953–54, the NHL presented a new postseason award to honor defensive excellence. The inaugural trophy, named for Detroit president and owner James

D. Norris, was given to Detroit's own Red Kelly.

Then the unthinkable occurred. Kelly ran into contract trouble with Detroit GM Jack Adams. On February 10, 1960, with only a few weeks left in the 1959–60 season, Kelly was shipped to Toronto for Marc Reaume, a comparative nobody who had scored eight goals in five years. Kelly joined the Leafs and moved to the front line, using his abundant skills as a playmaker to center a line with Bob Nevin and future Hall of Famer Frank Mahovlich. Skilled as a defenseman, Kelly proved equally adept as a pivot. Over the next three years, he scored 20, 22, and 22 goals—as well as a career-high 70 points in 1960–61.

In 1963–64, he was replaced on Toronto's top line by Dave Keon, but his influence was no less significant as the well-balanced Leafs won consecutive Stanley Cup championships in 1962, 1963, and 1964. Montreal knocked Toronto out of the playoffs in each of the next two years, but the Leafs were back in the winner's circle in 1966–67, Kelly's final season in the NHL, eliminating the Habs in six games and giving their classy veteran leader his eighth Stanley Cup ring.

*Gordie Howe once said, "The worst mistake Detroit ever made was trading Kelly. We never won anything without him."*

| NHL STATISTICS | | | | |
|---|---|---|---|---|
| GP | G | A | PTS | PIM |
| 1,316 | 281 | 542 | 823 | 327 |

# BOBBY ORR

Every once in a while, a player comes along who revolutionizes the sport of hockey. Goalie Jacques Plante did it by leaving his crease to handle the puck. Bobby Hull did it with his great slap shot. And in the late 1960s, a kid from Parry Sound, Ontario, turned the hockey world on its ear with brilliant skating, unparalleled playmaking, and laser-beam shooting. The fact that he was a defenseman made his offensive accomplishments all the more stunning.

Bobby Orr was an instant "impact player," scoring 13 goals and 41 points for the 1966–67 Bruins on his way to a Calder Trophy as top rookie. He quickly became the NHL's most dangerous player and Boston's best weapon in its assault on the Stanley Cup. In 1967–68, his second year, he notched 31 points in 46 games while battling a knee injury and earned his first of eight straight Norris Trophies. In 1969–70, he set an NHL mark with 87 assists (most by a defenseman) and won the Art Ross Trophy with 120 points, making him the first backliner ever to win a scoring title. He added the Hart Trophy as MVP and was called the greatest defenseman ever. He was 22 years old at the time. More than a quarter-century later, he continues to hold that title.

The Bruins won three Stanley Cups from 1929–41, then suffered through nearly three decades of playoff ineptitude. In 1969–70, Orr led a potent attack featuring Phil Esposito, and the Bruins charged to the Finals. They beat the Rangers in six and the Black Hawks in four, then swamped St. Louis. Just 40 seconds into sudden-death overtime in

*To this day, the majority of historians agree Orr was the single most dominant player of his era, and maybe any era.*

Game 4 of their sweep of the Blues, Orr took a pass from Derek Sanderson and beat Glenn Hall, leaping through the air with his stick held high in a famous moment of Stanley Cup history and ending Boston's long Stanley Cup drought with a dramatic 4–3 win. Bobby's winning goal and 20 playoff points earned him the Conn Smythe Trophy as playoff MVP.

In 1970–71, Orr notched 102 assists—the current record for helpers by a defenseman—and finished second in points (139) to Esposito (152). Though the Bruins were upset in the playoffs, Orr won his fourth Norris Trophy and his second Hart Trophy. In 1971–72, Boston dominated the regular season. Orr was second in points (117) and won his fifth Norris Trophy and third Hart Trophy. In the playoffs, his 19 assists topped the charts as Boston roared to its second Stanley Cup in three years. Orr tied Esposito in playoff points (24) and scored his second Cup-clinching goal, in Game 6 versus New York, to win another Conn Smythe Trophy.

Knee injuries plagued Orr and ultimately cut his career short. He won his second Art Ross with 135 points in 1974–75, his last full season in the NHL. After playing just 10 games in Boston in 1975–76, he signed a free-agent deal with Chicago, but his cranky knees wouldn't support him and he played only 26 games over two seasons before quitting in 1978–79 at just 31, the same year he entered the Hall of Fame. His eight Norris Trophies still hold up as the NHL record.

| NHL STATISTICS | | | | |
|---|---|---|---|---|
| GP | G | A | PTS | PIM |
| 657 | 270 | 645 | 915 | 953 |

# BRAD PARK

There's an indisputable if unscientific fact about Brad Park: No player in the history of the NHL ever faced the kind of persistent hard luck that dogged the talented and multi-faceted Park throughout his Hall of Fame career. He played 17 seasons in the NHL. He was a first- or second-team All-Star seven times, a Norris Trophy candidate six times (losing to Boston's Bobby Orr four times and Islander Denis Potvin twice), and a Stanley Cup winner . . . well, never. Hard luck, always hard luck, kept him from grabbing that brass ring.

An impressive NHL rookie when he debuted in 1968–69, Park, a baby-faced 20-year-old, notched 26 points and 70 penalty minutes in 54 games, but he was a distant also-ran to Calder Trophy winner Danny Grant of Minnesota. Solidly built and gifted with natural puck-handling ability, Park nevertheless quickly became a leader on the Rangers' blue line and gradually improved his numbers.

In 1971–72, the Rangers were favored to win the Stanley Cup with the GAG Line scoring at a rapid pace and "Fast Eddie" Giacomin in goal. Park, a four-year pro, recorded 24 goals and 73 points, setting team records for a defenseman. But Orr eclipsed him with 117 points. Worse, the Bruins added the proverbial insult by eliminating the Rangers in the Stanley Cup Finals, clinching the Cup on Madison Square Garden ice.

Undaunted, the hard-hitting Ontario native scored 25 goals in 1973–74 and crashed his way to a career-high 148 penalty minutes. But in the 1974 playoffs, the finesse-driven Rangers were chewed

*The son of a hockey coach, Park came to the NHL well educated in tactics, which he blended with great natural ability.*

up and spit out by a monster from Philadelphia called the Broad Street Bullies. In one game, defenseman Dale Rolfe was brutalized in a lopsided fight by Dave Schultz, and no Ranger, not even Park, could save him. After that, the Rangers, who hadn't won a Cup since 1940, were disassembled, and no players were awarded "untouchable" status.

Early in the 1975–76 season, Park was involved in perhaps the most shocking trade in Rangers history when he and Jean Ratelle were swapped to the rival Bruins for Boston's most-despised player (in New York, at least), Phil Esposito. Park and Ratelle went to Boston and helped revitalize the Bruins' playoff hopes, which had recently dwindled.

In 1976–77, Park's first full year in Beantown, the Bruins got to the Finals but couldn't get past Montreal, which swept the Bs. The same two teams faced each other in the 1978 Stanley Cup Finals, and Park—coming off a brilliant 22-goal, 79-point season—was poised for revenge. He led all Bruins in goals (nine) and points (20) and was third behind Canadiens Larry Robinson and Guy Lafleur, who had 21 points each, in playoff scoring. But the Bruins couldn't solve Habs goalie Ken Dryden, and Park's 11th year in the league ended in more frustration.

In 1983–84, Park, age 35, went to Detroit as a free agent. He played two years in Motown before retiring in 1985 with 213 goals and 896 points in 1,113 games. He never won a major NHL trophy, but in 1988 he was deservedly elected to the Hall of Fame.

### NHL STATISTICS

| GP | G | A | PTS | PIM |
|---|---|---|---|---|
| 1,113 | 213 | 683 | 896 | 1,429 |

# PIERRE PILOTE

In 1964–65, Pilote set a new league record for points by a defenseman (59), breaking the mark set by Babe Pratt (57).

Sometimes, the smaller the dog, the nastier the bite. Such was the case with Pierre Pilote, a slightly built defensive ace who patrolled the NHL for 14 years. Though he stood only 5'9" and carried comparatively little bulk, he was as tough as shoe leather and, at least early in his career, was willing to drop the gloves and fight anyone who had a notion to try him on for size.

But Pilote was also a vastly skilled player. Three times he was voted the top defenseman and awarded the Norris Trophy for his superb play.

A product of Quebec, where he came from a rugged mining town and learned how to take care of himself at an early age, Pilote came to the attention of the Chicago Black Hawks as a teenager and was assigned to the team's St. Catherines Junior A squad. After a lengthy minor-league stint, Pilote finally cracked the NHL in 1955–56, at the age of 24. His first year with the Black Hawks consisted of only 20 games, but he never looked back afterward.

The Hawks were a weak, last-place club in 1956–57, but they were tough, with two of the top penalty leaders—Gus Mortson (147 PIM) and Pilote (117)—on the squad. Pilote was still making his name as a rambunctious scrapper, but his play was also improving steadily. In 1957–58, the Hawks began to move up slightly in the standings, to fifth, then to third the following year. Pilote, who showed great skill as a playmaker and passer, notched 30 assists in 1958–59 and was the NHL's third-leading scorer among defensemen with 37 points, trailing only Ranger Bill Gadsby (51) and Montreal's Tom Johnson (39).

In 1959–60, the Black Hawks finished third and Pilote led all defensemen in points (45), but he could make no dent in the Norris Trophy domination of his rival and role model Doug Harvey. Even when Chicago won a playoff title, Pilote took a back seat. In 1960–61, the Hawks eliminated Montreal in the semifinals before challenging Detroit for the Stanley Cup. In a dozen playoff games, Pilote led his team in scoring with 15 points and was the top assist-maker in the postseason. He assisted the game-winning goals in Games 1, 3, and 4 and tied Red Wing Gordie Howe for the overall playoff point lead (15). That year, the Norris went to Harvey yet again.

In 1962–63, Pilote was finally recognized for his excellence. After finishing second in Norris Trophy voting the previous year, Pilote dethroned seven-time winner Doug Harvey and began a three-year reign of his own, winning the Norris in 1963, 1964, and 1965. Although his team managed only a pair of second-place finishes and one third-place finish during that span, and never again made it to the Stanley Cup winner's circle, Pilote was celebrated as the league's best defender, with excellent passing, solid skating, and that nasty edge.

In the summer of 1968, after 13 seasons with the Black Hawks, Pilote was traded to the Maple Leafs for Jim Pappin. He played only one year on fading legs before retiring at the end of the 1968–69 season.

## NHL STATISTICS

| GP | G | A | PTS | PIM |
| --- | --- | --- | --- | --- |
| 890 | 80 | 418 | 498 | 1,251 |

# DENIS POTVIN

Rarely does a player come along who combines as many characteristics as Denis Potvin boasted during his brilliant 15-year career with the New York Islanders. He was big and strong. He could skate and move the puck. He had a powerful shot and a nasty disposition on the ice that belied a thoughtful intelligence away from the rink. He was a thinking man's hockey player, even when he was putting the stick to someone or ramming him through the boards.

A native of Ontario, Potvin was a major star in Junior A hockey, earning raves during his five seasons with the Ottawa 67s. On May 15, 1973, following his fifth year in the OHA, he was the first player picked in the 1973 draft, by the Isles. Less than a year later, after recording 17 goals, 54 points, and 175 penalty minutes, he won the Calder Trophy as the NHL's top rookie.

Potvin wasn't just part of a building process for the Islanders in the late 1970s; he was the cornerstone on which the team built its championship. Potvin was a first-team All-Star five times and a second-team All-Star twice more. In 1975–76, his third season, he ripped 31 goals and earned the Norris Trophy, his first of three, as the game's best defenseman.

In New York, he was loved by Islanders fans and reviled by Rangers fans. He was blamed for breaking the leg of Rangers center Ulf Nilsson in 1978–79, effectively ruining the Rangers' playoff hopes (yet again!). Potvin played a rugged brand of hockey—not always the cleanest—but he was not the kind of skater who'd go out of his way to cause injury.

*Potvin was often alienated from teammates due to his intellectual off-ice pursuits, which were seen as affectations.*

As the Islanders grew into a dominant force, Potvin's leadership grew. In 1978–79, he scored 31 goals for the second time and notched his only 100-point season, finishing with 101 points and his third Norris Trophy (his second had come in 1977–78). Favored to go to the Stanley Cup Finals in the spring of 1979, the Isles were upset by the rival Rangers. But their day of reckoning was on the horizon.

In 1979–80, Potvin experienced the highest and lowest points of his career. Named team captain to start the year, he suffered a debilitating injury and played only 31 games in the regular season. However, he recovered for the playoff drive and recorded 19 points in 21 games as the Isles finally hoisted a Stanley Cup after defeating the Philadelphia Flyers in the Finals.

The Islanders won the next three Stanley Cups as well—and won 16 straight playoff series from 1980–83. In the Stanley Cup Finals, their killer's instinct emanated directly from Potvin. They beat the Minnesota North Stars in five games in 1981, swept the Vancouver Canucks in 1982, and put the broom to Wayne Gretzky's Edmonton Oilers in 1983. During those four championship seasons, Potvin scored 27 goals and 85 points in 78 playoff games.

On April 4, 1987, Potvin became the first defenseman in NHL history to reach the 1,000-point mark when he netted a goal against Buffalo. He retired following the 1987–88 season.

| NHL STATISTICS | | | | |
|---|---|---|---|---|
| GP | G | A | PTS | PIM |
| 1,060 | 310 | 742 | 1,052 | 1,356 |

# BABE PRATT

In 1943–44, playing in his ninth NHL season but just his first full year with the Toronto Maple Leafs, Walter "Babe" Pratt notched a career-high 57 points, by far the best point total of any defenseman in the league. His 40 assists tied him with Leafs scoring leader Gus Bodnar and earned him the Hart Trophy. Previously, Boston's Eddie Shore had been the only defenseman ever named MVP. In subsequent years, the only other defenseman to join Shore and Pratt in the MVP club was three-time winner Bobby Orr.

Pratt came into the NHL with Lester Patrick's New York Rangers in 1935, impressive with his great size (6'3" and 210 pounds) and puck skills. He quickly became known for his very big shot and ability to fire pinpoint passes to his teammates. Patrolling the back line with such NHL stalwarts as Ching Johnson, Ott Heller, and Art Coulter, Pratt soon lifted his status to that of team leader. By 1937–38, he was the team's top-scoring defender.

In 1939–40, the Rangers finished second to Boston in the regular-season standings. As the two top teams headed into the Stanley Cup playoffs, they were destined for a semifinal showdown. Down two games to one, the Rangers stormed back and won three straight contests, as goalie Dave Kerr pitched three shutouts in the series. Pratt's third playoff goal tied Game 2, won by the Rangers 6–2. The Leafs eventually tied the series at two games apiece before the Rangers eked out a pair of sudden-death victories, a double-overtime affair in

Game 5 and a single-OT thriller to win the Cup in Game 6—the Rangers' last Stanley Cup for more than 50 years.

Pratt continued to lead the Rangers' defensive corps in scoring, and he took the team to a first-place finish in 1941–42. But Toronto eliminated the

Blueshirts in the playoff semifinals. Early in the 1942–43 season, Pratt was shipped to the Maple Leafs for Dudley Garrett and Hank Goldup, and the Rangers tumbled all the way to the bottom of the NHL standings. It didn't take Pratt long to make the Rangers regret their decision. In 1943–44, teamed with tiny Moe Morris, Pratt had his finest year, finishing with 57 points, 22 ahead of former teammate Ott Heller, the second-highest scoring defenseman. But Pratt's best was yet to come.

In the 1945 playoffs, after dispatching Montreal in the semifinals, Toronto took on Detroit and jumped out to a three-games-to-none advantage before the Red Wings scored a single goal in the Finals. But the Wings fought back and tied the series, with Game 7 in Detroit. After Toronto's Mel "Sudden Death" Hill and Detroit's Murray Armstrong traded goals, Pratt converted a third-period pass from Nick Metz and deposited the puck behind Harry Lumley. Pratt's decisive goal held up for the final 7:46 of play, and the Leafs won the Cup.

Pratt finished his 12-year career in 1946–47 with the Boston Bruins, retiring with 83 goals and 292 points.

*Pratt won two Cups and a Hart Trophy, but he was also banned briefly from the NHL in 1946 for betting on games.*

## NHL STATISTICS

| GP | G | A | PTS | PIM |
|----|----|-----|-----|-----|
| 518 | 83 | 209 | 292 | 473 |

# LARRY ROBINSON

In a career marked by excellence and consistency, Larry Robinson won individual awards, won team championships, and was an idol to youngsters who wanted to be defensemen. Creative with the puck and punishing with a body check, Robinson could skate, shoot, make plays, and score goals. He was a fearless leader who always put his own goals second to those of the team—the Montreal Canadiens for 17 years, and the Los Angeles Kings for three more.

Robinson made his NHL debut in 1972–73 after playing junior hockey in his native Ontario and completing a two-year apprenticeship in Nova Scotia. The Habs' backline featured Serge Savard, Guy Lapointe, and Jacques Laperriere. But Larry played 36 games, plus 11 in the playoffs, and got his name on the Stanley Cup when the Habs beat Chicago in six games in the Cup Finals.

In 1973–74, his first full NHL season, Robinson notched six goals and 26 points. But over the next 13 years, he reached double figures in goals 12 times. He twice reached the 19-goal mark but never cracked 20. He won his second Stanley Cup in 1976 when Montreal swept Philadelphia in the Finals. During the championship round, Robinson took on and soundly thrashed Dave "The Hammer" Schultz, the Flyers' resident goon, and effectively gave his team the courage to win. In so doing, Robinson proved he could play as well as fight.

In 1976–77, the lanky defender chalked up a career-high 85 points, including 66 assists, which tied him with Toronto's Borje Salming for tops among NHL defensemen. For his work, he

*At the time of his retirement in 1992, Robinson had skated in 227 playoff games, more than any other NHLer.*

earned the Norris Trophy, to which he added his third Stanley Cup as Montreal took its second of four consecutive playoff titles in 1977, this time sweeping the Bruins in the Finals.

By now, Robinson had become known for his rock-solid play in the regular season, but in the spring of 1978 he proved he could also step to the fore and put on a blazing individual show. In the 1978 playoffs, the Habs crushed Detroit and Toronto en route to a rematch with the Bruins in the Finals. Ever the classy playmaker, Robinson led all players in assists during Montreal's 15-game march to a third straight Cup. He notched 17 assists (including the helper on Mario Tremblay's Cup-clinching goal in Game 6 of the Finals) and 21 points and was voted the Conn Smythe Trophy as the playoff MVP.

During his 17-year career in Montreal, Robinson never failed to get to the postseason, winning six championships (his fifth coming in 1979; the last one in 1986). In 1980, he added a second Norris Trophy to his collection of hardware.

In 1989–90, at the age of 38, Robinson left the Habs to play with Wayne Gretzky in Los Angeles. Although his skills were clearly on the downswing, his leadership and experience brought instant results as the Kings made three trips to the playoffs during Robinson's brief tenure, giving him a record 20 straight years in the postseason. He retired in 1992 with 208 goals and 958 points in 1,384 games.

## NHL STATISTICS

| GP | G | A | PTS | PIM |
| --- | --- | --- | --- | --- |
| 1,384 | 208 | 750 | 958 | 793 |

# EDDIE SHORE

You wouldn't go down a dark alley knowing an armed mugger was waiting for you. For 14 years, from 1926–40, players in the NHL approached Eddie Shore's side of the rink much as they would that dark alley—with genuine dread. And with genuine cause. Talented enough to win four MVP awards, Shore was also mean-spirited and dangerous enough to inspire fear and loathing among even his teammates.

In 1933, in the incident for which, sadly, he is perhaps best remembered, Shore nearly killed Toronto's Ace Bailey. Stories differ somewhat as to the brawl's origin, but either Red Horner or King Clancy had bodied Shore along the boards, lighting Eddie's short fuse. Upon regaining his feet and his faculties, Shore sought revenge and mistook Bailey for his attacker. He charged the unsuspecting Leaf, rammed him from behind, and flipped him head-first to the ice. Bailey was rushed to the hospital for life-saving brain surgery and never played again. Shore, who made only the slimmest of amends, continued his rampage for several more years.

A native of western Canada, Shore was 24 when he joined the Bruins in 1926. His rookie year featured 12 goals and 130 penalty minutes, evidence of his well-rounded play. As a second-year NHLer, he led the league in PIM (165) and tied Lionel Conacher for most points by a defenseman (17). As the decade progressed, Shore became the dominant backliner in the game, was regularly the top-scoring defenseman, and typically finished among the leaders in penalty minutes.

The Bruins won their first Stanley Cup in 1928–29, and Shore was Boston's backbone on defense while goalie Tiny Thompson kept the puck out of the net. In 1932–33, the Bruins were the top regular-season team. Shore had 35 points and won his first Hart Trophy. The Bruins flopped in the playoffs, however, as Toronto eliminated them in the semis.

Two years later, the 1934–35 Bruins finished atop the American Division, and Shore had another spectacular season. His 33 points were enough to earn him a second Hart Trophy. But again the Maple Leafs knocked the Bruins out of the playoffs, ending their season in more frustration.

Shore won two more Hart Trophies (1936 and 1938), but his crowning moment came in 1938–39, when the Bruins finally made it back to the Stanley Cup Finals for the first time since the spring of 1930. After squeaking past the Rangers in the semifinals, Boston got sweet revenge over Toronto in the Finals. Shore, nearing the end of his playing career, combined with Bill Cowley to set up Roy Conacher's Cup-clinching goal late in the second period of Game 5, and the Bruins went on to win 3–1 and take the championship.

After a brief stint with the New York Americans in 1939–40, Shore hung up his NHL skates with 105 goals, 284 points, and 1,047 PIM in 553 games, then went on to a storied career as a coach, manager, and team owner.

*Shore was the first Bruins player to be elected to the Hall of Fame and have his jersey number retired.*

| NHL STATISTICS | | | | |
|---|---|---|---|---|
| GP | G | A | PTS | PIM |
| 553 | 105 | 179 | 284 | 1,047 |

# CYCLONE TAYLOR

Though he's included here as one of the great defensemen of all time, Fred "Cyclone" Taylor was such a versatile performer that he might well have made the grade among forwards as well. At the turn of the 20th century, years before the NHL came into existence, Taylor was already dazzling hockey fans with his speed afoot. In fact, in an age when players struggled to keep pace with him in straight-ahead foot-races, Taylor was able to outskate many opponents while they sprinted forward and he skated backward! Legend has it, he even scored a goal this way.

Cyclone Taylor, born 34 years before the NHL coalesced in 1917–18, never played in the NHL, but that didn't stop him from becoming a legendary star of professional hockey. He got his start in eastern Canada, turned pro in 1908 with the Ottawa Senators of the Eastern Canada Hockey Association, and played alongside established stars Billy Gilmour and Marty Walsh. He scored regularly and helped the Senators to the Stanley Cup championship with a league-leading 10–2 record. In 1909–10, the ECHA changed its name to the CHA, but the Senators changed nothing, continuing to win and taking another Stanley Cup title. However, they did so without the help of Taylor, who signed a huge $5,000 contract to play for Renfrew in the newly established National Hockey Association.

Taylor stayed just two years in Renfrew before the team folded, and he traveled west in 1912 to try his luck in the Pacific Coast Hockey Association, spear-headed by hockey wizard Lester Patrick. In 1914–15, as a member of the Vancouver Millionaires, Taylor led a star-studded team in playoff competition against the NHA champion Ottawa Senators. The Millionaires were heavy underdogs, but with a roster containing names such as Taylor, Frank Nighbor, Hugh Lehman, and Mickey MacKay, no one could take Vancouver too lightly. And, in fact, they proved deadly, outscoring the Senators 26–8 in their three-game sweep and giving the PCHA its first Stanley Cup champion. Taylor's magnificent agility on the ice gave Vancouver a decided edge.

In 1915–16, Taylor had one of his greatest games, scoring six times against Victoria. He later led the PCHA in goals, during the 1917–18 season, with 32 tallies while appearing in just 18 games. Not only did he have great skating speed and deftness of shot, but he also wielded a rather peculiar stick, one that had its curve not in the blade but in the shaft, a characteristic that he claimed allowed greater stickhandling agility (as if he needed any extra advantage). With Taylor at the fore in 1918–19, leading the PCHA in goals with 23, the Millionaires captured yet another league title.

Though he left eastern Canada to find his fame and fortune in the West, Taylor survived the wrath of hometown fans who for a while accused him of everything up to and including treason. He eventually earned his place in the hearts of all hockey fans. He retired in 1923 at the age of 40 and was inducted into the Hall of Fame in 1947.

*Taylor was a star backliner in the East before switching to center during his 10 seasons in the PCHA.*

## NHL STATISTICS

No NHL Experience

# 15 BEST GOALIES

CLINT BENEDICT

JOHNNY BOWER

FRANK BRIMSEK

TURK BRODA

KEN DRYDEN

BILL DURNAN

GRANT FUHR

CHARLIE GARDINER

GLENN HALL

BERNIE PARENT

JACQUES PLANTE

PATRICK ROY

TERRY SAWCHUK

BILLY SMITH

GEORGES VEZINA

Some of these brilliant netminders proved dominant over many years (Glenn Hall and Terry Sawchuk). Others had short but extraordinary careers (Ken Dryden and Bill Durnan). Still others were called "money goalies" because of their uncanny playoff success (Turk Broda and Billy Smith). Whatever the case, each of these netminders lifted his team to a higher level, and each of their names is engraved on the Stanley Cup.

*No goalie in history has been more successful than Ken Dryden, whose lifetime record actually included more ties than losses (258–57–74).*

# CLINT BENEDICT

A hometown hero in Ottawa, Ontario, goaltending legend Clint Benedict starred for the Ottawa Senators when they were still part of the National Hockey Association, then took them to a handful of playoff championships once they entered the NHL. Throughout his 18-year pro career, he was one of hockey's most talented puck-stoppers.

Benedict was also a trailblazer, although his name does not always ring with the familiarity of some of his contemporaries. When he turned pro, it was against the rules of the game for a goaltender to leave his feet to make a save or smother the puck. Benedict defied this edict and regularly went down to stop a goal from being scored. He was penalized for his transgression, but he vowed to continue. In 1917–18, when Benedict first played in the NHL, the rule was changed, and "flopping" was born as a strategy for all goalies. They had Clint to thank.

Benedict made his professional debut with the Ottawa Senators in 1912–13, and two years later he led the NHA with the best goals-against average (3.30), as his Sens tied the Montreal Wanderers for first place. Benedict helped Ottawa defeat Montreal in the NHA playoffs, although he could not hold off the talented PCHA champion Vancouver Millionaires in the Stanley Cup challenge.

In 1917–18, after five years in the NHA, Benedict's Senators joined the NHL, and their star goalie began his 13-year NHL career. The Sens stumbled to a third-place finish with a 9–13 record in

their first NHL season, but their fortunes reversed in 1918–19, when Benedict led the league with a 2.94 goals-against average and was the league's winningest goalie (12 victories). He won a league-high 19 games in 1919–20, had the best goals-against average (2.67), and backstopped the Senators to their first NHL Stanley Cup with a five-game win over the PCHL champ, Seattle.

Benedict led the NHL in victories (14) and goals-against average (3.13) once again in 1920–21, and though the Senators finished second in the standings, they took on Vancouver of the PCHL for the Stanley Cup. They eked out a best-of-five victory when Benedict allowed just one goal in Game 5 and Jack Darragh's pair stood up for a 2–1 victory.

The Senators captured one last Stanley Cup during Benedict's watch, sweeping Edmonton (WCHL) in 1923 before their lanky goaltender moved on to play for the Montreal Maroons in 1924–25. The Maroons didn't even make the playoffs that year, but with Benedict in goal they quickly improved. In 1925–26, they finished second, then advanced to the Stanley Cup Finals and trounced Victoria of the WHL three games to one for their first Stanley Cup championship. Benedict had a microscopic 0.75 goals-against average in the postseason while sniper Nels Stewart filled the enemy goal.

Benedict retired in 1930. He had claimed a major role in four Stanley Cups, and in 1927 he was runner-up to George Hainsworth for the first-ever Vezina Trophy. Benedict's career 2.32 goals-against average is among the best in NHL history.

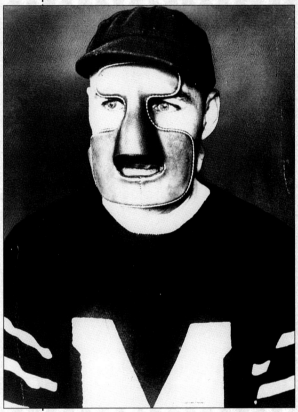

*A four-time Stanley Cup champ with Ottawa and the Montreal Maroons, Benedict is the all-time playoff shutout leader (15).*

| NHL CAREER STATISTICS | | | | |
|---|---|---|---|---|
| W | L | T | SO | GAA |
| 190 | 43 | 28 | 57 | 2.32 |

# JOHNNY BOWER

There are late-bloomers. Then there are *late bloomers!* Hall of Fame goalie Johnny Bower—who captured one Vezina Trophy outright, shared in a second one, and put his name on four Stanley Cups in Toronto—falls into the second category.

Born in western Canada, Bower was a soldier in World War II before he completed his junior hockey career at Prince Albert, Saskatchewan. In 1945, upon his return from military service, Bower took a job with the AHL's Cleveland Barons. He remained there for most of the next decade before the New York Rangers brought him to the NHL in 1953–54, at the age of 29. He led the NHL in minutes played (4,200), posted a 2.60 goals-against average, and played the entire season, yet he found himself back in the minors in 1954–55. From 1954–58, Bower played only seven games in the NHL.

Then the Maple Leafs acquired him. He was 34 years old but, to Toronto's way of thinking, far from over the hill. Little could they have known, however, that his greatest hockey was just around the corner. Bower's presence in nets didn't pay instant dividends, but his steady play allowed the Leafs to begin rebuilding, which became necessary when they bottomed out in the mid–1950s. By 1959–60, the Leafs were back up to second place, and Bower's 24 wins were second only to Jacques Plante's 40 wins for first-place Montreal.

In 1960–61, Bower led the NHL in victories (33) and goals-against average (2.50) and won his first Vezina Trophy. The following year, he was second in

*A brilliant stand-up goalie who notched 37 career shutouts, Bower earned the nickname "China Wall."*

wins (32) and goals-against average (2.58), but in the 1962 Stanley Cup playoffs he was unstoppable. After holding off the Rangers in six semifinal games, Bower carried the Leafs to the Finals against Chicago. Bower led all NHL

goalies in playoff goals-against average (2.20), although it was his goalmate, Don Simmons, who played the last two games of the Finals and held off the Black Hawks.

Bower was Toronto's man in nets in 1963, when the Leafs made a triumphant return to the Stanley Cup Finals against Detroit. He outdueled Terry Sawchuk, the Red Wings' star goalie, and allowed only 10 goals in five games during the championship round. He finished the playoffs with eight wins, two shutouts, and a 1.60 goals-against average.

The Leafs' dynasty extended to the 1964 playoffs, when they survived a seven-game tilt with Montreal in the semifinals and then took on their rivals from Detroit once more in the Finals. Bower, who'd won the regular-season goals-against average title (2.11), continued his superb play in the high-stress postseason. For the third straight year, he chalked up the most wins (eight) and most shutouts (two) and recorded the best goals-against average (2.14).

In 1964–65, Bower shared a second Vezina Trophy with former rival Sawchuk, now a teammate. And in 1966–67, the Bower-Sawchuk combo took the Leafs to their final Stanley Cup. Bower retired in 1970, at the age of 45.

## NHL CAREER STATISTICS

| W | L | T | SO | GAA |
|---|---|---|----|-----|
| 251 | 194 | 90 | 37 | 2.52 |

# FRANK BRIMSEK

It's tough enough breaking into the NHL without having to do so in goal, the last line of defense. In 1938–39, with hopes of maintaining the dominant place they'd built with Tiny Thompson as their stalwart backstop, the Boston Bruins installed in nets 23-year-old Frankie Brimsek from Eveleth, Minnesota.

Thompson, cut down by an eye injury, had been in goal for Boston's only Stanley Cup to date, back in 1928–29. Brimsek's task was to fill the void left by Thompson, and he did so magnificently, leading the league in wins (33), shutouts (10), and goals-against average (1.58). For his performance, he won not only the Vezina Trophy as top goalie but also the Calder Trophy as the game's best rookie. During one stretch, he played 212 minutes of shutout hockey.

Brimsek was the first American player to have a major role in the NHL. He'd played in Pittsburgh and Baltimore before landing his job in Boston in 1938. In Beantown, where Thompson was a king among the Bruins faithful, Brimsek faced a two-fold challenge: to win games and earn his keep, and to win fans and establish credibility. He succeeded on both counts.

In the 1939 playoffs, the first-place Bruins sneaked past the Rangers in the semifinals. Brimsek won three sudden-death overtime games, including a pair of triple-OT thrillers. In the Finals against Toronto, Brimsek allowed just six goals in five games to finish with a 1.50 goals-against average . . . plus a Stanley Cup championship in his first NHL season . . .

plus a new and highly descriptive nickname: "Mr. Zero."

During his second season, Brimsek shrugged off the sophomore jinx and led the NHL in wins (31) as his Bruins topped the standings again, although they were upset by New York in the playoff semifinals. Boston's powerful offense, led by scoring ace Bill Cowley, took the team to yet another first-place finish in 1940–41. And in the 1941 playoffs, Brimsek got hot again. He back-stopped the Bruins to a dramatic seven-game

series win over Toronto in the semis before slamming the door on Detroit in the Finals, holding the Red Wings to just six goals en route to a four-game sweep and a second Stanley Cup.

Brimsek won his second Vezina Trophy in 1941–42, when he boasted the NHL's best goals-against average (2.45),

then left the game in 1943 to join the U.S. Coast Guard. He served in the Pacific during World War II and didn't get back to the NHL until the 1945–46 season. By then, he had lost some of his polish. He played four more seasons with Boston, with limited success, then went to Chicago in 1949–50.

Brimsek retired in 1950 with a sterling career goals-against average of 2.70. His playoff goals-against average (2.56) was more proof of his ability to play at a high level in the clutch.

*Brimsek won two Stanley Cups in Boston and became the first NHL player from the U.S. elected to the Hall of Fame.*

## NHL CAREER STATISTICS

| W | L | T | SO | GAA |
|-----|-----|----|----|------|
| 251 | 194 | 90 | 37 | 2.52 |

# TURK BRODA

There's a story that Turk Broda once fell asleep in the dressing room while his coach gave the team its pregame "Gipper" talk. Now *that's* cool. Fact is, many historians agree it was Broda's poise and confidence (in other words, his ability *not* to worry) that made him a better playoff goalie than he was even during the regular season, when Broda was twice a Vezina Trophy winner.

Broda played 14 years in the NHL, all for the Toronto Maple Leafs. He was part of five Stanley Cup winners and was considered one of the game's greatest clutch performers—and one of its most colorful characters. On one occasion, Leafs boss Conn Smythe threatened to kick the chubby goalie off the team if he didn't lose some weight. Quick with a smile and a shrug, Broda—who stood only 5'9" and weighed close to 200 pounds—went on a crash diet and met Smythe's demands. That night, despite the fast he'd been on, Broda posted a shutout against the Rangers.

Born in Manitoba, Broda made his NHL debut in 1936–37 and won 22 games for the third-place Leafs. Fellow Leafs rookies Syl Apps and Gordie Drillon finished 1–2, respectively, in Calder Trophy voting, leaving Broda to take what solace he could in a 2.36 goals-against average.

In 1940–41, Broda led the NHL in wins (28) and goals-against average (2.06) as Toronto had the toughest defense in the league, giving up just 99 goals in 48 games. Broda earned his first Vezina Trophy that spring, beating out Boston's Frank Brimsek and Detroit's Johnny Mowers. He narrowly lost the

*Broda was the first goaltender in NHL history to back-stop his team to three consecutive Stanley Cup championships.*

Vezina to Brimsek in 1942 and to Mowers in 1943.

The Leafs rode the scoring of Apps and Drillon and the goaltending of Broda all the way to second place in 1941–42. In the Stanley Cup playoffs, Toronto earned a berth in the championship round by beating the Rangers in the semifinals, then staged the biggest comeback in hockey history, taking a seven-game series from Detroit after trailing three games to none. Broda outplayed his rival, Mowers, in the final four games, pitching a shutout in Game 6 and holding the Red Wings to just one goal in Game 7.

A year later, the Red Wings repaid the insult, knocking the Leafs out of the 1943 playoffs in six games. Broda missed the next two NHL seasons while he served in World War II, then made a triumphant return in 1946–47, finishing second in wins (31) and goals-against average (2.87). He then got hot in the playoffs as Toronto beat Detroit in five semifinals games before eliminating Montreal in the Finals in six games.

In 1947–48, Broda led the NHL in wins (32) and goals-against average (2.38), won his second Vezina Trophy, and carried the Leafs to their second of three consecutive Stanley Cups, sweeping Detroit. Toronto completed another sweep of Detroit in the 1949 Finals, with Broda in nets. He won his fifth Cup in 1950–51, sharing duties with Al Rollins, then retired following the 1951–52 season. His career goals-against average of 2.53 was terrific, but not as good as his playoff average of 1.98, the mark of a "money" goalie.

| NHL CAREER STATISTICS | | | | |
|---|---|---|---|---|
| W | L | T | SO | GAA |
| 302 | 224 | 101 | 62 | 2.53 |

# KEN DRYDEN

When you talk about filling big shoes—or in his case, big skates—few players came to the NHL with the pressure of expectations that faced the stoic, even placid, Ken Dryden. Tall, intense, highly intellectual, and supremely skilled, Dryden made a career of doing things his way, and doing them with a high degree of success, despite playing in the toughest hockey town in North America and following in the path of such Canadiens heroes as Vezina, Hainsworth, Durnan, Plante, et al.

Born in Hamilton, Ontario, Dryden rejected Canadian junior hockey for a scholarship to play and study at Cornell University. Upon graduation, he turned down a contract offer from Montreal in favor of the Canadian Nats. He eventually turned pro during the 1970–71 season, and after playing just six regular-season games—going 6–0–0 with a 1.65 goals-against average—Dryden was installed as Montreal's playoff goalie.

Dryden played every playoff game for the Canadiens as they struggled past Boston in seven and Minnesota in six to gain a berth in the Finals against Chicago. Dryden's implacable style kept the Habs alive through several taut moments, and when Henri Richard scored early in the third period against the Black Hawks in the championship's deciding game, Dryden had all the edge he needed. The Canadiens raised the Stanley Cup, and Dryden was voted the Conn Smythe Trophy as postseason MVP.

In 1971–72—his official rookie season!—Dryden used his 6'4", 210-pound frame and clever positional play to win a

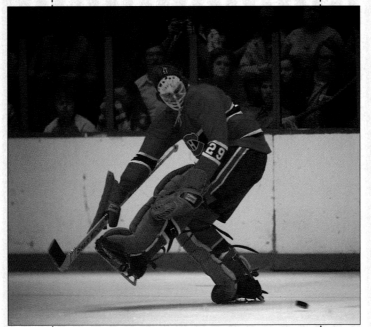

*Dryden was playoff MVP in 1971 before taking the Calder Trophy as rookie of the year in 1971–72.*

league-high 39 games, earning him the Calder Trophy as top rookie. He could not hold off the powerful Rangers in the quarterfinals, however, and the season ended on a mildly sour note.

But the Habs, with superb scoring and goaltending, were not a team to be taken lightly. In 1972–73, Dryden again led the NHL in wins (33) and earned his first Vezina Trophy with a league-best 2.26 goals-against average. In the 1973 playoffs, he led his team to an almost anticlimactic Stanley Cup victory, making it look so easy, before setting the hockey world on its ear.

A somewhat enigmatic person with a long view to his future in a complex world, Dryden abruptly quit hockey in 1973, returning to his "second love" of the law, spending the 1973–74 season as a clerk. But he was back in nets in 1974–75, taking his job back from Bunny Larocque and Wayne Thomas. The Canadiens made it to the Stanley Cup semifinals before a strong Buffalo team, led by the French Connection Line, pummeled them.

With Dryden still a force, the Habs returned to the Stanley Cup winner's circle in the spring of 1976, as their ace goalie won another Vezina Trophy after his 42 wins and 2.03 goals-against average led the league. During the next three years, from 1976–79, Dryden shared three more Vezina Trophies with Larocque and hoisted three more Stanley Cups, giving him six playoff titles in just eight seasons. In 1979, at just 31, Dryden quit permanently, giving in to a chronic back injury. Though his career was short, it was ever so sweet: Witness a 2.24 goals-against average and 258 wins in 397 games.

## NHL CAREER STATISTICS

| W | L | T | SO | GAA |
|-----|----|----|----|------|
| 258 | 57 | 74 | 46 | 2.24 |

# BILL DURNAN

The Montreal Canadiens have boasted some of the greatest goalies in NHL history—and some of the most short-lived. Georges Vezina played only eight NHL seasons; Ken Dryden played only eight campaigns; and Bill Durnan, who came between these two legends, played just seven. Like his prestigious colleagues in Habs history, Durnan accomplished a lot in a short period of time.

Born in Ontario, Durnan was 27 before he got to the NHL in 1943, but in the next seven seasons he was the game's top goalie, winning two Stanley Cups and leading Montreal to four first-place finishes. He also won the Vezina Trophy six times.

Durnan, the only ambidextrous goalie in the history of the NHL, first had a chance to play in the Toronto Maple Leafs' system in the 1930s, but he wasn't interested. Instead, he led the Sudbury Wolves to a Memorial Cup championship. Durnan later suffered a knee injury and was dropped by the Leafs, a development that disillusioned the talented goalie enough to make him quit the game. In the mid–1930s, he played softball and worked in a mine in Ontario, and he only returned to hockey when his mining company formed a team, the Blue Devils, which Durnan took to a national semipro championship in 1940.

In 1943, when Montreal goalie Paul Bibeault was conscripted to serve in World War II, the Habs offered Durnan a contract but couldn't get him to sign until the very brink of the 1943–44 season, when they assured him his NHL salary would make it worthwhile for him to quit his other two jobs, working as a clerk and playing semipro hockey.

Durnan won the Vezina Trophy as a rookie, leading the league in wins (38) and goals-against average (2.18), then capped off his brilliant debut by leading the Canadiens to a Stanley Cup, winning eight of nine playoff games. Durnan's 1.55 goals-against average in the postseason was every bit as impressive as Rocket Richard's dozen playoff goals. Durnan led the NHL in wins in each of his first four years, with 38, 38, 24, and 34 victories, and had the best goals-against average six times in his seven-year career. As a sophomore, he led the NHL with a 2.42 goals-against average, then followed up with averages of 2.60 and 2.30, adding his second, third, and fourth Vezina Trophies. In 1945–46, he won his second Stanley Cup title, with a 2.07 playoff average.

The high-strung Durnan had his only "bad" year in 1947–48, winning just 20 games while losing 28 for the fifth-place Canadiens. The team was offensively shallow and couldn't even get into the playoffs, and Durnan thought of quitting.

Montreal improved to third place in 1948–49, and Durnan won his fifth Vezina with a league-best 2.10 average and four straight shutouts. He quit after the 1949–50 season, with a career 2.36 average and his sixth Vezina Trophy,

giving in to bad nerves. Though brief, his career earned him Hall of Fame accolades.

*In 1948–49, Durnan led the NHL with 10 shutouts and enjoyed a streak of 309:21 in which he did not surrender a single goal.*

| NHL CAREER STATISTICS | | | | |
|---|---|---|---|---|
| W | L | T | SO | GAA |
| 208 | 112 | 62 | 34 | 2.36 |

# GRANT FUHR

**H**ockey dynasties are built around goaltending, after which the rest (i.e., the scoring) takes care of itself. Proof is in history. The Maple Leafs of the 1940s had Turk Broda; the Red Wings of the 1950s had Terry Sawchuk; the Canadiens of the late 1950s had Jacques Plante; and so on. In the mid–1980s, after a four-year dynasty by the New York Islanders (led by goalie Billy Smith), a new goaltending legend emerged in Edmonton, where Grant Fuhr became the latest in a long line of "money" goalies who could carry a team from excellence to greatness on the strength of their talent.

Fuhr came to the NHL from the Western juniors, where he had been an All-Star performer at Victoria (B.C.). The eighth pick overall in the 1981 entry draft, he joined the Oilers in 1981–82 and won 28 of 48 games. He was a Second All-Star Team selection as a rookie.

While names like Gretzky, Kurri, Messier, and Coffey dominated headlines with their outstanding offensive skills, Fuhr steadily developed into an icy-cool netminder who could—and often did—win as easily by a score of 8–7 as he would by a score of 2–1. He brought the attitude of "whatever it takes" and came through far more often than not.

In 1983–84, his third season in the NHL, Fuhr went 30–10–4 with a fairly inflated 3.91 goals-against average. But when the playoffs began, he became a brick wall, winning 11 of 16 games in which he appeared and carrying Edmonton to its first Stanley Cup championship.

In 1984–85, he shared regular-season goaltending duties with Andy Moog (who would become a fellow 300-game winner), then, as would become his custom, got red hot in the playoffs, leading all goalies in games played (18) and wins (15). The Oilers swept Los Angeles and Winnipeg in the first two rounds, then dismissed Chicago in six games in the semis. The Oilers trounced Philadelphia in five games in the Finals.

All roads seemed pointed toward a genuine dynasty in Edmonton, but it wasn't to be. Though they continued to dominate in the regular season, the 1986 playoffs ended in disaster when Calgary upset the Oilers in the second round. Fuhr took his share of the heat for the unacceptable defeat. However, he returned with a vengeance in 1986–87, winning 22 of 44 games and carrying the Oilers to a third Stanley Cup, culminating with a dramatic Game 7 win over the Flyers in the Finals.

Stanley Cup No. 4 came in 1987–88, when Fuhr led the NHL in games (75) and wins (40) and won his only Vezina Trophy. In the playoffs, he won 16 games—the limit—and won yet another Stanley Cup. Because he never had a dramatically low goals-against average, however, Fuhr was routinely passed over for Conn Smythe Trophy consideration.

After the 1990–91 season, Fuhr (who by then had lost his job to Bill Ranford) began a pilgrimage that would take him to four cities—Toronto, Buffalo, Los Angeles, and St. Louis—in five years. In 1995–96, he set an NHL record for games played (79), and only a late injury kept him from starting all 82 games. He won his 300th career game in 1995–96.

*Fuhr was the first to face two penalty shots in one Stanley Cup Finals series (vs. Philadelphia, 1985) and stop both.*

| NHL CAREER STATISTICS | | | | |
|---|---|---|---|---|
| W | L | T | SO | GAA |
| 353 | 250 | 93 | 20 | 3.48 |

# CHARLIE GARDINER

Charlie Gardiner is one of very few NHL goalies to make it to the Hall of Fame despite a career losing record (112–152–52). But when measured for his courage and ability to carry a team to its highest possible level, Gardiner was every bit the Hall of Famer.

A cherub-faced Scotsman who carried his stick in his left hand, Gardiner was born in Edinburgh and traveled with his family to Canada as a child, coming up through the hockey ranks in Winnipeg. In 1926, as a 21-year-old minor-leaguer stopping rubber for the Winnipeg Maroons, Gardiner came to the attention of the Chicago Black Hawks during their inaugural season. Hugh Lehman had backstopped the Hawks to a third-place finish in the American Division in 1926–27, but he was replaced by Gardiner the following season.

It was a rocky road for the goalie and his team during those early years. Gardiner was tagged with a league-high 32 losses as an NHL rookie. The Black Hawks finished last again in 1928–29, and once more Gardiner led in defeats (29) despite a 1.93 goals-against average. In a weak American Division, where only two of five teams finished with better than a .500 record, the 1929–30 Black Hawks (21–18–5) were a distant second to Boston (38–5–1), though Gardiner was third in the NHL in goals-against average (2.52) and finished second to Boston's Tiny Thompson in Vezina Trophy voting.

In 1930–31, the Hawks fell back to third place, though Gardiner won a career-high 24 games and notched a brilliant 1.77 goals-against mark. He threw a league-high dozen shutouts and narrowly lost the Vezina Trophy to Americans goalie Roy "Shrimp" Worters. He carried Chicago all the way to the Stanley Cup Finals for its first time ever, beating the Leafs and Rangers before losing to Montreal in the Finals.

Gardiner won his first Vezina Trophy in 1931–32 on the strength of his league-best 1.92 goals-against average, despite a record of 18–19–11. Toronto put Chicago out of the playoffs in the first round, however, and Gardiner's season ended badly. In 1932–33, he led the NHL in minutes played (3,010), but poor offensive play by his teammates landed the Hawks at the bottom of their division, out of the playoffs. In 1933–34, Gardiner had his best goals-against average (1.73) and recorded 10 shutouts to win his second Vezina Trophy. The Hawks rode Gardiner's shoulders to their second trip to the Stanley Cup Finals, against Detroit.

Unbeknownst to Gardiner or his teammates, the goalie was, by now, suffering from the effects of an infection, and his body was beginning to fail him. Racked with pain, the courageous goalie nevertheless stood tall in nets, holding off Detroit in Games 1 and 2 and putting the Hawks within a victory of their first Stanley Cup.

The weary Gardiner struggled in Game 3, however, losing 5–2. "Look," Gardiner said to his teammates, "all I want is one goal next game. Just one goal and I'll take care of the rest."

In Game 4, Gardiner shut the Red Wings out until Mush March scored in double OT to give Chicago the Cup. It was Gardiner's last game. He died two months later of a brain hemorrhage, at the age of 29.

*In 1928–29, Gardiner's 1.93 GAA was wasted as the Black Hawks managed just 33 goals in 44 games, an NHL record for nonsupport.*

### NHL CAREER STATISTICS

| W | L | T | SO | GAA |
|---|---|---|----|-----|
| 112 | 152 | 52 | 42 | 2.02 |

# GLENN HALL

*Hall took three teams to the Cup Finals, winning with Detroit and Chicago but losing three straight years with St. Louis.*

Most people who work a desk job don't report to work 502 days in a row without calling in sick at least a couple of times. So, consider Hall of Fame goalie Glenn Hall, who played in 502 consecutive games, beginning in 1955–56 with Detroit and extending into the 1962–63 season with the Chicago Black Hawks. But Hall paid a heavy price. He was among the most nervous of goalies, typically spending his pregame preparation time in the bathroom trying to settle his stomach.

Hall put his name on the Vezina Trophy three times during a brilliant career that spanned 18 seasons. He was named to 11 All-Star teams and was the playoff MVP in 1967–68, at age 37.

Born in western Canada, the man who would come to be known as "Mr. Goalie" made his NHL debut in 1952–53, after he was voted the MVP of the Ontario junior league in 1951. Stuck behind Terry Sawchuk, Hall spent several seasons in Detroit's farm system before he earned the starting job in 1955–56. As a rookie, he won 30 games, notched a 2.11 goals-against average, and led the league with 12 shutouts, which earned him the Calder Trophy.

Hall then led the NHL in wins in 1956–57, with 38, proving he was no flash in the pan. A less-than-stellar performance in the 1957 playoffs soured Red Wings management, which traded him to Chicago with aging Ted Lindsay for a handful of journeymen. Apparently feeling like a scapegoat for Detroit's playoff failure, Hall became a quiet, some say surly, man who had little to do with his colleagues, on or off the ice, merely going out and doing his job.

The 1957–58 Black Hawks were a rebuilding team that finished out of the playoffs. Hall, whose butterfly style helped revolutionize the way the position was played, led the NHL in losses (39), but he finished second in shutouts (seven). The next year, Hall carried Chicago to a third-place finish before Montreal eliminated the Black Hawks in the first round, a fate they would suffer yet again in 1959–60.

In 1960–61, the Hawks finished third for the third straight year. Hall led all goalies with six shutouts and was third in goals-against average (2.57); then he caught fire in the postseason. The Hawks began by avenging themselves against Montreal in the first round, then took on Detroit in the Finals. Certainly Hall was motivated by the chance to show his old team what a mistake it had made. In six Stanley Cup Finals games, Hall allowed just 12 goals, outplaying Sawchuk and finishing the playoffs with a 2.25 goals-against average and a Stanley Cup.

In 1962–63, Hall led the NHL in wins (30) and won his first Vezina Trophy. But the Hawks went to the Finals just twice more before his departure at the end of the 1966–67 season, when he won his second Vezina Trophy. Drafted by the expansion St. Louis Blues, Hall took the Blues to the Cup Finals in 1967–68 and was the playoff MVP in a losing effort. In 1968–69, he won his third Vezina, with Jacques Plante, after leading the NHL in goals-against average (2.18). He quit in 1971 with 407 wins (fourth all time) and 84 shutouts (third all time).

## NHL CAREER STATISTICS

| W | L | T | SO | GAA |
|-----|-----|-----|-----|------|
| 407 | 327 | 163 | 84 | 2.51 |

# BERNIE PARENT

Timing was everything for Bernie Parent during his 14 years in the NHL. Unfortunately, he was the victim of lots of bad timing; but he also made the most of his chances when he had them. His most successful stretch, certainly, came from 1973–75, when he carried the Philadelphia Flyers to a pair of Stanley Cup titles and won two Conn Smythe Trophies and two Vezina Trophies.

Born in Montreal, Parent first played in the NHL in 1965–66 with the lowly Boston Bruins. Despite playing reasonably well, he was soon displaced by the tandem of Ed Johnston and Gerry Cheevers. Drafted by expansion Philadelphia in 1967, Parent shared duties with Doug Favell. Parent helped the Flyers to a Western Division title in 1967–68 and had an impressive 2.48 goals-against average. Parent's Flyers dropped to third place in 1968–69 and to fifth in 1969–70. Parent's record in three years in Philly was 46–69–41, and during the 1970–71 season he was traded to Toronto, where he teamed with Jacques Plante in goal.

The World Hockey Association offered opportunities—and big salaries—for many NHL players, and in 1972–73 Parent signed with Philadelphia and led the WHA in wins (33). The Flyers reacquired his rights following that season, then sent Favell to the Maple Leafs and installed Parent as their No. 1 starter for the 1973–74 season.

Parent paid immediate dividends. While the Flyers—a team known as the Broad Street Bullies for its bruising use of

*Win or lose, Parent never removed his facemask until he was off the ice—so the opposition couldn't read his emotions.*

intimidation—dominated physically, Parent was a symbol of grace. He led the NHL in wins (47), goals-against average (1.89), and shutouts (12). His backup, Bobby Taylor, got into just eight of 78 games. In the Stanley Cup playoffs, Parent carried the Flyers past Atlanta

and the Rangers en route to the team's first trip to the Finals. In a hard-fought championship series, Parent outdueled Boston goalie Gilles Gilbert and finished with a 2.02 goals-against average, winning the Stanley Cup with a 1–0 shutout over the Bruins in Game 6. Parent completed the trifecta by winning the Vezina Trophy, the Conn Smythe as playoff MVP, and the Stanley Cup.

And he wasn't finished yet. The 1974–75 Flyers won the regular-season title with 51 victories, and Parent led all goalies with 44 wins, a 2.03 goals-against average, and 12 shutouts. After watching the first round of playoffs as division champs, the Flyers swept Toronto in the quarterfinals, then held off the Islanders in the semis to get back to the Stanley Cup Finals, this time facing Buffalo and the French Connection Line. Parent allowed just 12 goals in six games (five of them in a Game 3 overtime loss) and won his second straight Conn Smythe Trophy with a 1.89 playoff goals-against average. He also won his second Vezina Trophy and second Stanley Cup.

Midway through the 1978–79 season, Parent suffered an eye injury that ended his career. He remained with Philly as a goalie coach and went to the Hall of Fame in 1984.

| NHL CAREER STATISTICS | | | | |
|---|---|---|---|---|
| W | L | T | SO | GAA |
| 270 | 197 | 121 | 55 | 2.55 |

# JACQUES PLANTE

*To balance his intense nature in competition, Plante turned to reading and knitting for relaxation in his spare time.*

**T**railblazer Jacques Plante changed hockey in several very recognizable—and some less obvious—ways. Known respectfully as "Jake the Snake," thanks to his outstanding mobility in the crease and slot area, Plante was not only the first man to wear a mask on a regular basis in NHL games, but he was also the first goalie to make a custom of leaving his crease area to handle the puck to make passes to his teammates.

Plante was an innovator who understood the game as well as anyone ever to play and always was thinking about how to get even better. In a career that spanned 18 NHL seasons, Plante was good enough to win the Vezina Trophy seven times and to take a Hart Trophy as the NHL's most valuable player—a feat only three goalies (Roy Worters, Charlie Rayner, and Al Rollins) had ever accomplished before and none has repeated since. He also won six Stanley Cups during his 11 years with Montreal.

Plante was the oldest of 11 kids growing up on a farm in Quebec. He only became a goalie during his youth career when an asthmatic condition curtailed his skating ability. He was a natural between the pipes and soon caught the attention of the Habs, who brought him to the NHL as a starter in 1954–55, two years after he'd helped them win the 1952–53 Stanley Cup. In 1954–55, his first full season, he led the NHL in wins (31). The following year, he won a career-high 42 games and took the goals-against title (1.86) en route to his first Vezina Trophy. He then carried the Canadiens to the first of five consecutive Stanley Cup championships.

In 1956–57, Jake the Snake won his second of five straight Vezina Trophies when he finished the season with a 2.02 goals-against average, which he lowered to 1.75 in the playoffs as Montreal skated past the Rangers and Boston in 10 games to win another title. The Habs repeated as playoff champs in 1958 and 1959.

Early in the 1959–60 campaign, however, his good luck would change. Struck in the face by a slap shot from the stick of Rangers sniper Andy Bathgate, Plante retreated to the dressing room for stitches, and when he emerged he wore a plastic facemask he'd been experimenting with in practices. To the chagrin of his coach, Toe Blake, he insisted on wearing it in the game—and never played without it again. Any fears that it would curtail his ability were erased when he led the Habs to another Stanley Cup in the spring of 1960, with a 1.35 playoff goals-against average.

In 1961–62, Plante won 42 games for the second time in his career. He captured the Hart Trophy and the Vezina Trophy, becoming the only goalie ever to win both awards in a single year.

Plante went to the Rangers in 1963, then came out of a brief retirement to play for the St. Louis Blues from 1968–70 before moving to Toronto and Boston and ending his NHL career in 1973. He retired with 434 wins (second only to Terry Sawchuk), 82 shutouts (fourth all time), and a career 2.38 goals-against average.

| NHL CAREER STATISTICS | | | | |
| --- | --- | --- | --- | --- |
| W | L | T | SO | GAA |
| 434 | 246 | 147 | 82 | 2.38 |

# PATRICK ROY

On February 19, 1996, Patrick Roy survived a shootout in Denver. It came while he was tending goal for his new team, the Colorado Avalanche, to whom he'd been traded earlier in the year. The shootout, a 7–5 win over Edmonton, was no great work of art, not by the standards established by Roy in his first 10 years in the NHL. But it was still a huge victory, for it placed him in elite company, alongside such great names as Sawchuk, Plante, Esposito, Hall, Vachon, Worsley, Lumley, Moog, Smith, Broda, and Fuhr— the only other NHL goalies to reach the 300-win plateau.

Ever since he burst upon the NHL scene in 1985–86, Roy has been doing things in a rather spectacular fashion. Roy won 23 games as an NHL rookie, then stood the league on its ear in the Stanley Cup playoffs, taking Montreal all the way to the Finals, as Ken Dryden had done as a rookie in 1971. Winning 15 of 20 playoff games, Roy posted a 1.92 goals-against average, and Montreal captured its 22nd NHL playoff title. Roy earned the Conn Smythe Trophy for his work.

In each of the next three seasons, Roy shared the William Jennings Trophy as Montreal gave up the fewest goals in the NHL. In 1988–89, the Quebec City native earned his first Vezina Trophy with a league-best 2.47 goals-against average, although his Habs lost in the Stanley Cup Finals to Calgary and Roy was largely held to blame for not winning "the big one."

A butterfly goalie with tremendous poise and resolve, Roy won his second Vezina Trophy in 1989–90, leading the NHL in wins (31). He then won a third Vezina in 1991–92 with a career-high

*The superstitious Roy will not skate over any painted lines on the ice, hopping over them as he enters and leaves the rink.*

36 wins and a league-low 2.36 goals-against average.

The 1992–93 Canadiens were by no means favored to win the Stanley Cup. A third-place finish in the Adams Division sent them to a first-round tilt with arch rival Quebec. Roy, always a great playoff goalie, carried the Habs to a six-game win, taking Games 3 and 5 in sudden-death. Montreal then swept the Sabres,

winning Games 2, 3, and 4 in overtime. The Canadiens knocked off the Islanders in five semifinal games, adding two more sudden-death wins (in Games 2 and 3) to their streak. In the Finals, Roy's team faced a serious challenge from Wayne Gretzky's L.A. Kings. After the Kings stole Game 1 in Montreal, the Canadiens roared back with four straight wins, taking Games 2, 3, and 4 in sudden-death and setting a league record for consecutive overtime wins (10). Roy, now a two-time Stanley Cup champ, also earned his second Conn Smythe for his brilliant play in the most difficult setting.

In 1995–96, under coach Mario Tremblay, Roy experienced his first dark days in Montreal. On December 2, 1995, the Habs gave up 11 goals to Detroit. Roy was pulled after nine goals and vowed never to play for Montreal again. Four days later, he was traded to Colorado. Six months later, he carried Colorado to its first Stanley Cup title with 16 playoff wins and a 2.10 goals-against. He won the Cup on June 10, 1996, with a classic performance in Game 4 against Florida, a game that was tied 0–0 until Uwe Krupp won it for Colorado in triple overtime.

## NHL CAREER STATISTICS

| W | L | T | SO | GAA |
|-----|-----|-----|-----|------|
| 349 | 205 | 74 | 37 | 2.72 |

# TERRY SAWHCUK

More than anyone. That's the short story on Terry Sawchuk: more games played (971), more wins (447), and more shutouts (103) than any goalie in NHL history. And a lot more misery. Sawchuk arguably suffered more physical pain than any other goalie, including a broken arm that didn't heal properly in his youth, an eye injury that required surgery to save his vision, arthritis in his shoulder, neuritis in his legs, broken ribs and a collapsed lung suffered in an auto wreck, mononucleosis, and herniated discs in his back. And that's just a partial list.

Sawchuk was a teen star in junior hockey before turning pro at 17 with Omaha in the U.S. Hockey League. He quickly moved to the Red Wings' AHL affiliate in Indianapolis and was called up to the NHL in 1949–50 to spell injured Harry Lumley. In 1950–51, Sawchuk became the Red Wings' starter. He won 44 games, posted a 1.99 goals-against average, and won the Calder Trophy as the NHL's top rookie.

The following season, 1951–52, Sawchuk was virtually unbeatable. He won 44 games and had a 1.90 goals-against, good enough for the Vezina Trophy, and carried Detroit to a 22-point margin of victory over second-place Montreal in the standings. In the play-offs, Sawchuk won eight straight games, allowing Toronto just three goals and Montreal just two, finishing with four shutouts and an unparalleled 0.62 playoff goals-against average. (The Red Wings' eight-game sweep in 1952 gave birth to the octopus tradition in Detroit.)

In his first five seasons in the NHL, Sawchuk never had a goals-against average over 2.00 and won three Vezina Trophies, his second coming in 1952–53. He put his name on a second Stanley Cup in 1953–54, then added a third Vezina and a third Stanley Cup in 1954–55. But his future in Detroit was about to be interrupted. In 1955, he was traded to the Bruins, where he spent two seasons before returning to the Red Wings. Though he had won three Stanley Cups in his first five years, he wouldn't win another in Detroit.

After seven more seasons in the Motor City, Sawchuk was acquired by Toronto in 1964–65. He shared goaltending duties with Johnny Bower as the Leafs finished fourth in the standings. The Sawchuk-Bower tandem gave up the fewest goals in the league (173) and shared the Vezina Trophy. The Leafs climbed to third place in 1965–66 and maintained that station in 1966–67, though by now Bruce Gamble had turned the goalie duo into a trio. In the 1967 playoffs, the Leafs eliminated Chicago in the semifinals to earn a shot in the Finals against Montreal, the defending champs. With the Leafs leading the series two games to one after three, Sawchuk took over for the injured Bower and won two of the next three games to wrest the Stanley Cup away from Montreal, giving up just one goal in each of the final two games. Sawchuk called it a career highlight.

Considered the best goalie ever, Sawchuk left Toronto for stints in Los Angeles (1967–68), Detroit (1968–69), and New York (1969–70) before his untimely death in 1970 at age 40.

*Sawchuk notched shutouts in 10.6 percent of his games, second only to Ken Dryden (11.6) in the post–1950 era.*

## NHL CAREER STATISTICS

| W | L | T | SO | GAA |
|---|---|---|---|---|
| 447 | 330 | 173 | 103 | 2.52 |

# BILLY SMITH

**B**attlin' Billy Smith was as ornery about protecting his goal cage as he was stingy about letting the puck get past him into it. Quick to use his stick on the enemy and quicker to flash leather in a big save situation, Smith earned his rep as one of the game's all-time "money" goalies during a four-year stretch from 1979–83 when his Islanders simply owned the Stanley Cup.

An Ontario native, Smith came to the NHL through the Los Angeles Kings' system. Smith spent most of two years in Springfield (AHL) before the Islanders took him in the 1972 expansion draft. His early years in New York were tough. Smith went 16–47–15 in his first two years on the Island, then turned it around, as did the team. In 1974–75, he won 21 games. Over the next four years, his record reversed. He went 85–34–27 and transformed the Isles into genuine contenders.

The 1979–80 season saw Smith take a regular-season back seat to Chico Resch as the Isles finished second to Philly in the Patrick Division. In the playoffs, however, Smith was "the man," playing 20 of the team's 21 games. He carried the Isles past Los Angeles, Boston, and Buffalo en route to a grudge match with the Flyers in the Stanley Cup Finals. New York took a three-games-to-two lead and blew a 4–2 lead late in Game 6. Tied 4–4 after 60 minutes, it was up to Smith to hold off the Flyers until his team could make something happen. Bobby Nystrom's goal at 7:11 gave the Isles their first Stanley Cup.

In 1980–81, the Isles roared to a second Stanley Cup. Smith won 14 of 17 playoff games and led all goalies with a 2.54 goals-against average. With stars

*Smith earned his "Battlin' Billy" handle for his great work in the clutch as well as his 489 penalty minutes.*

such as Denis Potvin, Bryan Trottier, and Mike Bossy stealing the show on offense, Smith's play at times went almost unnoticed, except in New York. In 1981–82, Smith shared the goaltending duties with a new partner, young Rollie Melanson, and enjoyed his greatest season, with 32 wins and a league-leading 2.97 goals-against average. For his work, he was presented with the Vezina Trophy, which he added to a third Stanley Cup after going 15–3 in 18 playoff games.

In 1982–83, Smith narrowly relinquished the starting role to Melanson, who appeared in 44 games to Smith's 41, but once again, come playoffs, Smith got the nod. In 17 games, he chalked up 13 victories and peaked with a sound thrashing of Wayne Gretzky and the high-octane Edmonton Oilers in the Finals, not allowing the Great One a single goal and holding his teammates to just six tallies in a four-game sweep. Smith's 1.50 goals-against average in the Stanley Cup Finals (and NHL-best cumulative mark of 2.68 for the postseason) was enough to earn Smitty the Conn Smythe Trophy, making him only the fifth goalie ever to win the playoff MVP award.

Though the Isles faded in subsequent seasons, Smith continued to play effectively until he was 38 years old. On March 20, 1988, in Winnipeg, Smith faced 35 shots from the Jets, stopped every one of them, and notched his 22nd career shutout and his 300th victory. He retired after the 1988–89 season with 305 wins, four Stanley Cup rings, and, oh yes, 489 penalty minutes.

## NHL CAREER STATISTICS

| W | L | T | SO | GAA |
|-----|-----|-----|-----|------|
| 305 | 233 | 105 | 22 | 3.17 |

# GEORGES VEZINA

Even before there was an NHL, there was a growing legend in Montreal named Georges Vezina. Mild-mannered and poised in goal, Vezina, nicknamed the "Chicoutimi Cucumber," played a calm, cool style of goal that set a standard still felt throughout hockey nearly a century later.

Born in Chicoutimi, Quebec, Vezina was a local hero in amateur hockey when the Montreal Canadiens came through town in 1910 to play an exhibition game. After Vezina beat the Habs, he was immediately approached and offered a chance to play for money. In 1910–11, Vezina made his debut in what was still the National Hockey Association. Newsy Lalonde was Montreal's scoring leader. In the early years, the Quebec Bulldogs, led by Joe Malone, dominated the circuit.

A sturdy competitor, Vezina led Montreal to a tie with Toronto for the NHA title in 1913–14, but the Habs lost their total-goals playoff series when Toronto's Jack Walker notched a hat trick in Game 2. Vezina was overshadowed by Ottawa's Clint Benedict in 1914–15, and the Habs fell from contention. The Canadiens were back atop the NHA standings in 1915–16 and won their first Stanley Cup when Goldie Prodgers scored to win Game 5 against Portland, champs of the PCHA.

In its last pre–NHL season, Montreal won the 1916–17 NHA title but lost the Stanley Cup to Seattle (PCHA) as Vezina was outdueled by Harry Holmes.

In 1917–18, Vezina led the new NHL in wins (13) and goals-against (3.93).

The Canadiens made it to the Stanley Cup challenge in 1918–19, facing Seattle, but the series was suspended after an epidemic of flu broke out. The season ended on a sad note when Montreal Hall of Famer Joe Hall died in the hospital, and no champion was decided.

Despite a talented lineup that included the likes of Lalonde, Didier Pitre, Odie Cleghorn, and Vezina, the Habs failed to qualify for the Stanley Cup playoffs for five years, from 1919–23. Not until the arrival of Aurel Joliat in 1922–23 did the team show signs of deserving another Cup. In 1923–24, Vezina won 13 games and led the NHL with a 2.00 goals-against average. In 24 games, the Habs gave up just 48 goals. In the playoffs, they skated past PCHL champion Vancouver in two games, then took on Calgary of the WCHL for the Stanley Cup. Vezina allowed just one goal in Game 1 of the Finals, then shut out Calgary 3–0 in Game 2 to secure the title.

In 1924–25, Vezina had perhaps his greatest season, winning a career-high 17 games and winning a second goals-against title (1.87) with five shutouts. Though he was suffering from the effects of tuberculosis, Vezina gamely faced a tough challenge from the WCHL Victoria Cougars in the Stanley Cup Finals, but he could not hold off sniper Fred Frederickson or outplay rival goalie Holmes, as the Canadiens lost the best-of-five series in four games.

Though ravaged by tuberculosis, Vezina was back in uniform to start the 1925–26 season. But he collapsed on opening night and never played again.

He died less than a year later. In 1927, the NHL memorialized him with the annual Vezina Trophy for goaltending excellence.

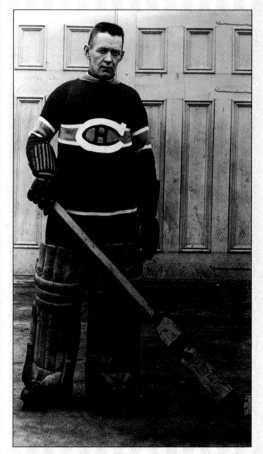

*Vezina, who spent his entire career with Montreal, never took a breather, playing in 328 consecutive regular-season games before his fatal illness.*

| NHL CAREER STATISTICS | | | | |
|---|---|---|---|---|
| W | L | T | SO | GAA |
| 105 | 80 | 5 | 13 | 3.28 |

# Chapter 2

# 10 BEST COACHES

They schooled their players in fundamentals, pushed them hard, and led them to ultimate glory. Behind the bench, they were like master chess players, always one move ahead of their opponents. These special individuals are the 10 best hockey coaches of all time.

Above: *Scotty Bowman led St. Louis, Montreal, Pittsburgh, and Detroit to the Stanley Cup Finals.* Opposite page: *Toe Blake won eight Cups as a coach before the pressures of the game pushed him into retirement.*

# JACK ADAMS

Jack Adams was a man known as much for his pugnacious temperament as for his cagey ability to build a team and inspire it to perform at its highest plane. He was a champion at every level of hockey, starting as a player, moving through more than two decades of coaching, and finishing as a general manager.

Born in Ontario in 1895, Adams was an outstanding player during his youth, skating for Toronto and Ottawa in the NHL and for the Vancouver Millionaires in the PCHL, where he was a scoring champion in 1921–22. Fearless despite a lack of physical brawn, he established his reputation as a battler early on. It was an image that followed him throughout his career. He quit playing in 1927 and took over as coach and general manager of the Detroit Falcons, who were just a year old at the time. He would remain as a team builder in Detroit for 35 years.

Adams initially needed time to organize a competitive team. In his first five years, Detroit finished out of the playoffs three times and twice was eliminated in the first round. Prior to the 1932–33 season, James D. Norris bought the team and renamed it the Red Wings. As if taking it as a good-luck charm, the club responded, finishing second in the American Division behind goalie Johnny Roach. Detroit won its first playoff series, a 5–2 total-goals win over the Maroons, before falling to the Rangers in the semifinals.

Adams added Cooney Weiland to the mix in 1933–34, and the Red Wings took their first division title. They roared to the Stanley Cup Finals before losing to Chicago. Adams continued to add talent

*Adams met his match when Red Kelly refused to report to the Rangers when Adams tried to trade him in 1960.*

to the lineup. Marty Barry led the team with 21 goals in 1935–36, and Detroit climbed to the top of the podium with a four-game thrashing of Toronto in the Stanley Cup Finals. With Norm Smith in goal and Larry Aurie sparking the attack,

Detroit gave Adams his second straight Stanley Cup in the spring of 1937 after defeating the New York Rangers in five tough games.

Circumstances worked against Detroit in ensuing years, and the club fell in the standings. However, after a fifth-place finish in 1941–42, the team gelled and advanced to the Stanley Cup Finals against Toronto, winning the first three games and all but ensuring a third Stanley Cup. However, during Game 4, won by Toronto, Adams became embroiled with referee Mel Harwood, whose calls against Detroit enraged the combative coach. At the game's conclusion, Adams attacked Harwood and had to be physically restrained by police. NHL boss Frank Calder suspended Adams indefinitely, and the Red Wings went on to drop the next three games and lose the Stanley Cup in the biggest choke job of all time.

The Red Wings did win a third playoff championship in 1943, the last for coach Adams, who retired with 423 career victories in 982 games. However, Adams continued as general manager, building dynasties with Gordie Howe, Alex Delvecchio, and others. Adams counted four more Stanley Cups before retiring as a manager in 1962.

| NHL CAREER STATISTICS | | | | |
|------|------|------|------|------|
| W | L | T | PCT | Cups |
| 423 | 397 | 162 | .513 | 3 |

# AL ARBOUR

Until Scotty Bowman passed him during the 1995–96 season, nobody in the history of the NHL had coached as many games as Al Arbour, the guiding force behind the design and development of the New York Islanders' dynasty of the late 1970s and early 1980s. Under Arbour's disciplined but fair leadership, such highly touted prospects as Denis Potvin, Bryan Trottier, Mike Bossy, and Billy Smith emerged as superstars.

Long before he arrived on Long Island as the successor to Phil Goyette and Earl Ingarfield, who worked the Isles' bench in the team's inaugural campaign (1972–73), Arbour learned a great deal about winning, playing for Jack Adams (Detroit), Rudy Pilous (Chicago), Punch Imlach (Toronto), and Bowman (St. Louis). As a player, Arbour was part of Stanley Cup winners in Chicago (1961) and Toronto (1962) and went to the Finals three times with the Blues (1968–70).

An average defenseman who was frequently shipped to the minors, Arbour distinguished himself more by the thick-rimmed glasses he wore on the ice than by anything he accomplished with his modest talent. But he was smart and insightful, and he quickly found his niche as a mentor once his playing days ended after 14 modest seasons. When Bowman left St. Louis for Montreal in 1971–72, Arbour—who had seen time behind the bench in 1970–71—was one of three men (with Sid Abel and Bill McCreary) who took turns coaching the Blues. However, after 13 games in 1972–73—and just two wins—Arbour was released by St. Louis. He wasn't out of work long.

The second-year Islanders jumped at Arbour. His reserved public persona, combined with a deep understanding of strategy and excellent communication skills, made him a logical choice to guide a young team long on promise but short on experience. Within a year, he had the Islanders playing .500-or-better hockey. And within five years, he had built the team into a Stanley Cup contender that was vilified in the newspapers when it did not win.

The Islanders were among the favorites to go all the way in 1977–78, only to have Toronto upset them in the quarterfinals. They were also a popular choice among the experts in 1978–79, when the Rangers upset them in the semifinals. Arbour was smart enough to stand up for his players and argue for keeping the team together, rather than hitting the panic button and agreeing to wholesale changes.

Key acquisitions put the Islanders over the top in 1979–80. They finished second in the Patrick Division and then marched to the Stanley Cup Finals, eliminating the Flyers when Bobby Nystrom scored in sudden-death of Game 6. Arbour pushed his troops harder than ever during the next three years, well aware that if winning once was difficult, repeating as champions would be next to impossible. Nobody mentioned the word "dynasty" until long after the fact.

Arbour did win three more Stanley Cups (1981–83) before turning over the reins to Terry Simpson in 1986. Forced out of retirement in 1988–89, he coached the Islanders back to respectability, then stepped down in 1993. His 781 career wins place him second all time behind mentor Bowman, the only man with more coaching experience than Arbour himself.

*Demanding and stern, Arbour nevertheless commanded respect and affection from his troops—a rare combination.*

### NHL CAREER STATISTICS

| W | L | T | PCT | Cups |
|---|---|---|-----|------|
| 781 | 577 | 248 | .564 | 4 |

# TOE BLAKE

Hector "Toe" Blake lived a charmed life in the NHL, first as a player, winning two Stanley Cups with the Montreal Canadiens as a member of the Punch Line with Elmer Lach and Rocket Richard, then as a coach, guiding the Habs to eight championships as the successor to Dick Irvin. A fiery bench boss who once punched a referee, Blake also had the invaluable capacity to keep the even-more-temperamental Maurice Richard in check, a characteristic that made him a brilliant choice to guide the Canadiens.

Unlike Irvin, Blake was known for administering his tongue-lashings in private instead of humiliating his players in public. This made Blake a favorite among his troops, who in turn would skate through the proverbial wall for their coach.

Under Blake's leadership, the Flying Frenchmen rewrote history, employing a relentless skating attack to wear the opposition down. In 1955–56, Blake's first year behind the Montreal bench after several years coaching in the minor leagues, the Habs thoroughly dominated the NHL, winning the regular-season title by 24 points over second-place Detroit. Led by the line of Jean Beliveau, Bert Olmstead, and Richard—and the goaltending of Jacques Plante—the team needed just five games to eliminate the Rangers in the semifinals and five more to dump Detroit and hoist the Stanley Cup. For Blake and the Canadiens, it was the beginning of a record-setting string.

From 1955–60, the Canadiens won five straight Stanley Cups, losing only nine playoff games along the way. In his first seven years as coach, Blake's Habs earned six first-place finishes and one second-place finish. In setting the record for consecutive championships, the Canadiens walloped Detroit (1956), Boston twice (1957, 1958), and Toronto twice (1959, 1960).

But the Habs fell from grace in 1960, starting a slump during which they were eliminated from the playoffs in the first round four years in a row. A third-place finish in 1962–63 sat poorly with Montreal fans, and some perceived a shift in Blake's style. Much of his easy-going manner was replaced by a more stern and unforgiving nature. And while it got results—the Habs won the Stanley Cup for Blake in 1964–65 and again in 1965–66—many of the players were no longer as willing to tolerate Blake's sometimes harsh treatment. While there was no mutiny among the players, Blake's popularity waned.

In 1966–67, the Canadiens battled Toronto in the Stanley Cup Finals but couldn't solve the goaltending of veterans Johnny Bower and Terry Sawchuk, ultimately losing in six games. Blake was nearly done as a coach. In the spring of 1968, his Canadiens made it to the Finals—their ninth trip in his 13-year tenure—and trounced expansion St. Louis in four games. However, citing the increase in tension between himself and the players, Blake somewhat reluctantly stepped down as coach. He took with him 500 wins in 914 games, eight Stanley Cups, and a well-deserved place in NHL history books.

*Blake (center) won more Stanley Cups as a coach (eight) than as a player (three), including five straight from 1956–60.*

| NHL CAREER STATISTICS | | | | |
|---|---|---|---|---|
| W | L | T | PCT | Cups |
| 500 | 255 | 159 | .634 | 8 |

# SCOTTY BOWMAN

Much has been said about Scotty Bowman during his quarter-century as an NHL coach. Lauded as a brilliant tactician, criticized as a cold fish who barely knows the names of his own players, and respected among his peers, he is one of the best motivators ever to step behind a bench to run a team. During the 1995–96 season, his 24th as an NHL coach, he surpassed Al Arbour as the all-time leader in games coached. By season's end, he added the new mark (1,654 games) to those he already owned, including most regular-season wins (975), most Stanley Cup games (263), and most Stanley Cup victories (162). He won his 1,000th game in 1996–97.

Born in Montreal, Bowman was a player of modest talent who never skated in the NHL. After a head injury curtailed his playing career, he applied his cerebral talents to coaching, cutting his teeth in Canadian juniors. In 1967, NHL expansion created new coaching opportunities, and Bowman was hired in St. Louis. The Blues, with Glenn Hall in nets and Red Berenson leading the attack, were quickly competitive. In his first three years, Bowman took the Blues to the Stanley Cup Finals three times. Destroyed twice by Montreal and once by Boston in those trips to the Finals, Bowman's résumé was nevertheless enhanced.

In 1971, Bowman left the Blues following a management dispute and was hired in Montreal, replacing Al MacNeil, who had just won the Cup. Inheriting a team that could fill the net with its awesome offensive skill, Bowman installed a defense similar to the one that had made the Blues a contender. Ironically, Bowman was not very popular in Montreal—particularly among his players, from whom he demanded total dedication and adherence to his policies. Nevertheless, his results were hard to dispute.

From 1972–79, Bowman's Canadiens won five Stanley Cups, including four straight (1976–79). And yet, when the exacting mentor opted to sign with Buffalo in 1979–80, his departure from the Province of Quebec, his homeland, was greeted with inexplicable merriment.

Bowman's seven-year tenure in Buffalo was not without tumult. In 1984–85, he sent Tom Barrasso to the AHL. Barrasso, only 19, had just won the Vezina and Calder Trophies as a rookie sensation in 1983–84. And though he was struggling at the time, the move caused a permanent rift between the goalie and his coach and left many players and observers bewildered. Bowman quit coaching after Buffalo failed to make the 1986 playoffs and got off to an awful start in 1986–87.

In 1991–92, Bowman (by now director of player development in Pittsburgh) stepped into the most difficult situation when he replaced beloved coach Bob Johnson, who had fallen ill with brain cancer just months after taking the Penguins to the 1991 Stanley Cup. With customary intensity, Bowman—who is credited with inventing the practice of juggling lines and using videotape as a coaching tool—guided the Pens to a repeat championship, his sixth. In 1993, he became coach of his fifth team, the Detroit Red Wings, and took them to the Stanley Cup Finals in 1995.

*On February 8, 1997, Bowman became the first coach in NHL history to win 1,000 regular-season games.*

### NHL CAREER STATISTICS

| W | L | T | PCT | Cups |
|---|---|---|-----|------|
| 1,013 | 460 | 263 | .659 | 6 |

# HAP DAY

Lost in the mayhem of the 1942 Stanley Cup Finals, during which the Detroit Red Wings took a presumably insurmountable three-games-to-none lead over the Toronto Maple Leafs before dropping four straight, was the cool, calm resolve of Maple Leafs coach Clarence "Hap" Day. A former NHL defenseman who had fought many seemingly losing battles in his career, Day endured vicious attacks from media and fans in Toronto.

Day had the audacity to bench two of his aces, Gordie Drillon and Bucko McDonald, as a tactic to get his team going. But when the smoke cleared and the Leafs had pulled off the greatest comeback in sports history, Day was celebrated as a hero, a master tactician, and a wily fox with demonstrable coaching talent.

Born in rural Ontario, Day made his NHL debut as a player for the Toronto St. Pats in 1924–25, skating alongside veteran center Jack Adams, who would later become a rival coach and Day's opposite number in the dramatic 1942 playoffs. In 1927–28, when Conn Smythe took over the team (renamed the Maple Leafs), Day was simultaneously moved from forward back to defense and given the team captaincy, which he would hold until 1937, when he left to play briefly for the New York Americans. Day won a Stanley Cup as a player in 1931–32, assisting Ace Bailey's Cup-clinching goal against the Rangers in Game 3 of their sweep.

Day returned to the Leafs in 1940, replacing coaching legend Dick Irvin,

*Day guided Toronto to five Stanley Cups and was the first coach ever to win three titles in a row (1947–49).*

who was on his way to the Montreal Canadiens. In 1941–42, just his second year behind the Leafs' bench, Day took Toronto to its most dramatic, if not its most dominating, championship. Trailing the Red Wings by three games, Day pulled out all the stops, even resorting to reading fan letters in the dressing room before games to charge up his troops. When the Leafs rebounded and won the Stanley Cup, many of his players credited Day's indomitable spirit with putting the team over the top.

But the best was yet to come. The Leafs finished third in 1944–45 but rode the goaltending of Frank McCool to a six-game win over Montreal in the semifinals and a seven-game squeaker over Detroit—without Syl Apps, who was off to war. As defending champs the next season, the club tumbled out of playoff contention despite Gaye Stewart's league-best 37 goals.

In 1946–47, Leafs boss Conn Smythe delivered a bunch of new players—including Howie Meeker and Harry Watson—as well as a stern mandate to coach Day: Win another Stanley Cup in three years or look elsewhere for work. Day set about the task immediately and turned the trick within one season, winning the Cup in 1947, then guiding the Leafs to two more in successive years, 1948 and 1949. This gave the Maple Leafs the first "dynasty" in modern hockey history, as no other team had ever won more than two straight titles.

Day retired after the 1949–50 season, with five Stanley Cups. Only Punch Imlach, with four Stanley Cups, could rival Day for achievement in Toronto.

## NHL CAREER STATISTICS

| W | L | T | PCT | Cups |
|---|---|---|-----|------|
| 259 | 206 | 81 | .549 | 5 |

# PUNCH IMLACH

After five-time Stanley Cup winner Hap Day retired and Joe Primeau guided the Maple Leafs to a Stanley Cup in 1950–51, Toronto went through a series of coaches, including King Clancy (1953–56), Howie Meeker (1956–57), and Billy Reay (1957–58) before George "Punch" Imlach arrived. Under Imlach, the Leafs regained their status as an NHL power, winning four Stanley Cups and making the ornery Imlach the second-winningest coach in Leafs history.

Born in Toronto, Imlach came up through minor pro hockey with the Quebec Aces, where he advanced from player to coach to manager before ultimately hiring on as manager-coach of the Boston Bruins' AHL affiliate in Springfield in 1957–58. One year later, he was brought to Toronto to replace Reay behind the Leafs' bench, a post he would hold for the next 11 years.

As a rookie NHL coach, Imlach enjoyed moderate success. The 1958–59 Leafs won just five of their first 20 games. Once Imlach came aboard, the team turned it around. Eventually they finished one point ahead of arch rival New York for the last playoff berth. In the playoffs, Imlach unleashed Frank Mahovlich, Dick Duff, and Bob Pulford, and the Leafs pulled off a shocking seven-game semifinal upset of Boston. For their trouble, they went to the Stanley Cup Finals against Montreal and were humbled in five games. But Imlach's influence had been felt.

In 1959–60, the Leafs climbed to second place and ripped Detroit in the semi-finals before taking another crack at Montreal in the Finals—with even worse results. Toronto lost in four games, sending Imlach home fuming.

Seeing his team eliminated in the first round of the 1961 playoffs, Imlach's burning desire to bring a Stanley Cup to

*Though he never played in the NHL, Imlach enjoyed monumental success as a coach, winning four Cups in Toronto.*

Toronto was further stoked. In 1961–62, the Leafs, led by Frank Mahovlich's 71 points, finished second. With stellar performances from unlikely heroes George Armstrong and Tim Horton (who led the team in goals and points, respectively), the Leafs roared through the playoffs, with six-game victories over New York and Chicago to hoist the Cup, Imlach's first. Vastly talented and confident, the Leafs won the league title in 1962–63 (by one point over Chicago), then dispatched Montreal in five games to get back to the Stanley Cup Finals against Detroit. The Red Wings were no match, going down in five games.

A hard-nosed boss who conducted business in a my-way-or-the-highway fashion, Imlach never rested on his laurels, played any favorites, or offered any guarantees. Late in the 1963–64 season, he traded a handful of talented youngsters to New York for Andy Bathgate. The deal, at first criticized, proved a stroke of genius as Bathgate finished the year well, helped the two-time defending Cup champs get back to the Finals against Detroit, and scored the Cup-clinching goal in Game 7 to give the Leafs a "three-peat" and Imlach his fourth title.

Imlach left Toronto for expansion Buffalo in 1970, then left hockey after a heart attack in 1972. He returned briefly in 1979–80 to manage the Leafs.

| NHL CAREER STATISTICS | | | | |
|---|---|---|---|---|
| W | L | T | PCT | Cups |
| 395 | 336 | 148 | .534 | 4 |

# DICK IRVIN

While Dick Irvin made his name—and earned his place in the Hockey Hall of Fame—as a coach, he might have done the trick as a player if not for an injury that forced him to quit prematurely. Playing for the Chicago Black Hawks in 1926–27, the rookie NHLer led the league in assists (18) and lost the Art Ross Trophy to New York's Bill Cook by one point, 37 to 36. Midway through the 1927–28 season, he was rammed by Montreal Maroons defenseman Red Dutton and suffered a fractured skull in the fall. While a promising playing career was cut short, Irvin soon took over the coaching reins in Chicago, and for the next 26 years he was one of the best coaches in the game.

Crafty and ruthless, Irvin expected a lot from his men and would use dirty tricks and battlefield psychology to get results. He once dressed a pair of injured players, then sat them on the bench until a moment presented itself for him to send them out. By hitting the ice, the players received automatic one-game suspensions and sat out games they would have been unable to play in anyway. Once when a player came off the ice after scoring a goal, Irvin leaned over and, instead of congratulating him, told the young man he had to lose some weight if he wanted to keep his job.

In Chicago, it took Irvin only one year to put his imprint on the team, leading the Black Hawks to the 1931 Stanley Cup Finals before losing to Montreal. But that wasn't good enough for Chicago owner Major Frederic McLaughlin, so Irvin left for Toronto, replacing Art Duncan as Leafs coach five games into the 1931–32 season. With the Kid Line of Joe Primeau, Charlie Conacher, and Busher Jackson tearing up the league, Irvin guided Toronto to its first Stanley Cup, sweeping the Rangers in the Finals in the spring of 1932.

Over the next eight years, Irvin's Leafs finished atop the NHL regular-season standings three more times and advanced—unsuccessfully—to the Stanley Cup Finals six times, losing twice to the Rangers and once each to the Maroons, Detroit, Chicago, and Boston.

In 1940, Irvin left the Maple Leafs to coach the one team that had not victimized him in the playoffs, the Montreal Canadiens. When he got to the Habs in 1940–41, the team was in a world of trouble, having finished dead last the previous year. Without much talent to work with, Irvin had his hands full. And after a sixth-place finish his first year, the Canadiens lost Elmer Lach for most of the 1941–42 season and again finished near the bottom of the league. But in 1942–43, the Habs added a young man named Maurice Richard to the lineup, and the team climbed to fourth place and back into the playoff hunt. In 1943–44, the Punch Line was created with Lach centering Toe Blake and Richard, and Montreal finished first overall and won the Stanley Cup. A powerhouse was born.

Irvin's gruff personality was seen as a perfect fit for Richard, who was equally fiery. Over the next 10 years, the Habs won two more Stanley Cups and lost in the Finals five other times. With his health failing, Irvin left Montreal to coach once more in Chicago in 1955–56. He died of cancer in 1957, having won 690 NHL games and four Stanley Cup championships.

*Irvin's go-for-broke Canadiens teams of 1943–44 and 1944–45 scored goals by the bunches and had a combined record of 76–13–11.*

## NHL CAREER STATISTICS

| W | L | T | PCT | Cups |
|---|---|---|---|---|
| 690 | 521 | 226 | .559 | 4 |

# MIKE KEENAN

When Mike Keenan held the Stanley Cup over his head at Madison Square Garden on June 14, 1994, one Rangers fan lofted a placard that read, "Now I Can Die In Peace." The same was not true for Keenan. Only weeks after reaching the pinnacle, he left the Rangers to forge a playoff contender in St. Louis. With Keenan, winning isn't the only thing; doing things on his own terms is.

Born in Ontario, Keenan played hockey at both St. Lawrence University and the University of Toronto, where he earned a master's degree in education. Insightful and analytical, Keenan began his coaching career with the Junior B Oshawa Legionnaires in 1978 and won a pair of metro titles. He moved up to the Peterborough Petes in 1979 and won the OHL title before guiding the Petes to the Memorial Cup Finals, Canada's junior hockey championship.

In 1980–81, Keenan was hired by the Rochester Americans of the AHL, a job he held for three years. In his third season, his Amerks won the Calder Trophy as playoff champs. He then took his title-winning ways back to the University of Toronto, where he coached the varsity team to a Canadian collegiate championship in the spring of 1984.

Keenan arrived in the NHL in 1984–85, when the Flyers installed him behind the bench. In his first year, Philadelphia topped the NHL with a team-record 53 wins and went to the Stanley Cup Finals, losing to the Oilers in five. From 1984–87, the Flyers won two division titles, and Keenan became the first NHL coach ever to win at least 45 games in each of his first three years.

*In a career of highs and lows, Keenan won a Stanley Cup in New York but was fired in Philly, Chicago, and St. Louis.*

The Flyers made it back to the Stanley Cup Finals in 1987 but lost to Edmonton again, in seven games. In 1987–88, his team was knocked out of the playoffs in the first round, and Keenan—whose style had made him unpopular with many players—left the Flyers.

Without missing a beat, Keenan hired on with Chicago, which had gone 16 years without a trip to the Stanley Cup Finals. Keenan, now armed with GM duties, again clashed with some of his players, most notably Denis Savard, whom he tried to convert from a free-wheeling scoring threat to a more defensive two-way player. In Keenan's defense, the change he forced on Savard, and the resultant feud that led to Savvy's trade to Montreal, later served Savard well when he returned to the Windy City in 1995 as an aging but more valuable veteran. Under Keenan, the Blackhawks became playoff contenders, finishing atop their division twice. In 1991–92, the Hawks went to the Stanley Cup Finals, but Mario Lemieux and the Pittsburgh Penguins trounced them.

In 1993, Keenan joined the Rangers. In one season, he assembled a hard-working team that displayed few defects. When the team ended its 54-year Stanley Cup drought, he was among the heroes on Broadway. However, he soon became a villain when he left for St. Louis, where he irked Blues fans by trading several favorites and feuding with Brett Hull, the Blues superstar. Keenan has never apologized for nor threatened to alter his style. And with nearly 500 NHL victories and a Stanley Cup to his credit, why should he?

## NHL CAREER STATISTICS

| W | L | T | PCT | Cups |
|---|---|---|-----|------|
| 491 | 336 | 109 | .583 | 1 |

# LESTER PATRICK

According to those who knew him best, Hall of Fame coach and general manager Lester Patrick, builder of the New York Rangers in their early years, had such great intelligence and dramatic flair that he could easily have carved out a successful career as an actor. Long before he made his mark as a two-time Stanley Cup coach in the NHL, Patrick was a highly respected hockey genius. Co-creator of the Pacific Coast Hockey Association in 1911, he operated in direct competition with the NHL and lured many if its best skaters to play in his league.

A native of Quebec, Patrick was a defenseman in his playing days, an offense-minded puck-handler. He made his professional debut with the 1903 Montreal Wanderers. In 1906, he scored the goals that gave Montreal a total-goals victory over Ottawa to win the Stanley Cup, then repeated in 1907.

When their father moved the family to British Columbia to open a logging business, the young Patrick brothers—Lester and Frank—built a chain of rinks and started the PCHA, with teams in Victoria, Vancouver, Seattle, Edmonton, Calgary, Regina, and Saskatoon. Lester did it all, playing for, coaching, and managing his own team. For 13 years, the Patrick brothers gave the NHL all the trouble it could take. In 1924–25, Patrick's own team, the Victoria

Cougars, took on and beat the Montreal Canadiens in the Stanley Cup Finals, winning three games to one. It was the first of several crowning moments for Patrick.

In 1926–27, Conn Smythe was assembling a team in New York City, but things were not going well for Smythe. At the last minute, with the entire operation in

They called Patrick (behind Cup) "The Silver Fox" not only for his elegant mane of hair but for his wily tactics.

jeopardy, Lester Patrick was called in. With smooth business savvy and an almost aristocratic air, Patrick saved the day and the Rangers franchise was launched.

Just two years later, with a team led by the line of Bill Cook, Frank Boucher, and Bun Cook, the 1927–28 Rangers won their first Stanley Cup. At 44 years of age, Patrick had a direct hand in the outcome. During Game 2 of the Finals, Rangers goalie Lorne Chabot was badly cut from a shot. When the Rangers could not find a substitute, Patrick donned the pads himself and went in to play goal. Although he surrendered Nels Stewart's game-tying goal with only 1:09 to play, Boucher scored in sudden-death. The Rangers, with Joe Miller of the rival New York Americans in goal, went on to win the best-of-five series three games to two.

Patrick, who ran his team with intellect rather than a drill instructor's bark, coached and managed the Rangers until 1939, winning a second Stanley Cup in 1933 before hiring Boucher as his successor. He quit coaching with 281 wins in 604 NHL games and remained as GM until 1946.

A tremendous innovator, Patrick is credited with inventing the penalty shot, the assist as a recorded stat, the forward pass, and the rule allowing goalies to leave their feet to stop the puck. More than any other figure, the "Silver Fox" was responsible for thrusting forward the development of hockey in the 20th century.

| NHL CAREER STATISTICS | | | | |
|---|---|---|---|---|
| W | L | T | PCT | Cups |
| 281 | 216 | 107 | .554 | 2 |

## ANATOLI TARASOV

Through 1996, only two former Soviets were in the Hockey Hall of Fame—goaltender Vladislav Tretiak and the man credited with creating him, Anatoli Tarasov, one of the most inventive hockey minds the world has ever known.

Tarasov was supreme architect of the Soviet Red Army and Soviet national teams that dominated hockey in the USSR and Europe throughout the 1960s and early 1970s. During his distinguished 29-year career, Tarasov won seven world titles and three Olympic gold medals (1964, 1968, and 1972). In a moment of great tongue-in-cheek humor following the USA's "miracle" win at Lake Placid in 1980, Tarasov allowed that the Soviets let the Americans win every 20 years to maintain good relations between the two countries (the Americans had last won gold in 1960 at Squaw Valley). He also counted 18 Soviet League titles among his highlights.

In 1946, Tarasov introduced "Canadian style" hockey to the Soviet Union for the first time. Just eight years later, in 1954, he guided the Soviet team to an international amateur hockey championship. As time stretched on, he moved away from North American methods and, with a "showdown" against Canada vividly in his imagination, created what became the Soviet style of hockey. He concentrated on puck control, speed afoot, and an amazing tolerance for physical abuse, which his players were trained to absorb without retaliating. Tarasov's version of hockey looked, to many, like soccer on ice. But his results were impressive.

His imagination and foresight were his greatest gifts. For example, Tarasov calculated that an average hockey player

*Without the inventiveness of Tarasov (center), hockey in the USSR might never have gained international acclaim.*

would skate about four miles in a game, and so he made sure his players could skate eight miles without running out of gas. And although he once referred to North American hockey as "primitive," he also knew that to be among the world's elite, he would have to beat the Canadians. In so doing, he revolutionized the way the game itself was played. And coaches from around the world—including the United States and Canada—traveled to Moscow to learn from the master.

To his mind, success depended upon imagination, hard work, discipline, and dedication to achieving the goal. He said a hockey player must have the wisdom of a chess player, the accuracy of a sniper, and the rhythm of a musician. But most of all, he must be a superb athlete, which Tarasov made sure his players were. Tarasov insisted that the great netminder Tretiak carry a tennis ball wherever he went to help improve his reflexes, and he even made the goaltender swim with a tennis ball sewn into his trunks.

Harsh at times and always demanding, Tarasov once sent star center Valeri Kharlamov to the minors for a year, and yet the player anxiously returned to his beloved coach at first chance—such was the respect and admiration Tarasov commanded. The "godfather" of Soviet hockey was inducted into the Hockey Hall of Fame in 1974.

| NHL CAREER STATISTICS | | | | |
|---|---|---|---|---|
| W | L | T | PCT | Cups |
| No NHL Experience | | | | |

# Chapter 3

# 10 BEST TEAMS

One team (1973–75 Flyers) bullied its way to supremacy. Another club (1984–88 Oilers) relied on relentless offensive firepower. Though their styles differed, each of the following teams won multiple Stanley Cups. Together, they comprise the 10 best hockey clubs ever assembled.

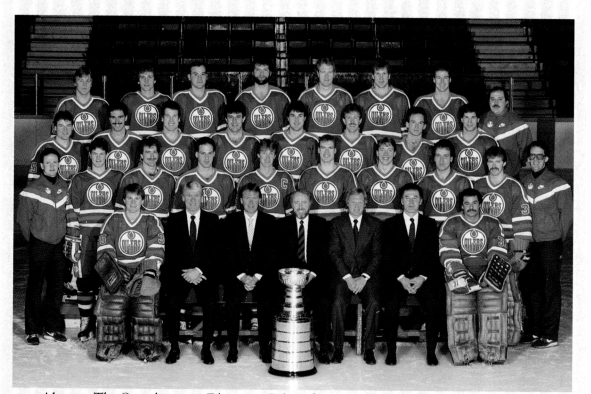

Above: *The Cup-champion Edmonton Oilers of 1983–84 exploded for 446 goals, a number never approached before or since. Opposite page: Ted Kennedy captained Toronto to the 1949 Stanley Cup, the Leafs' third straight.*

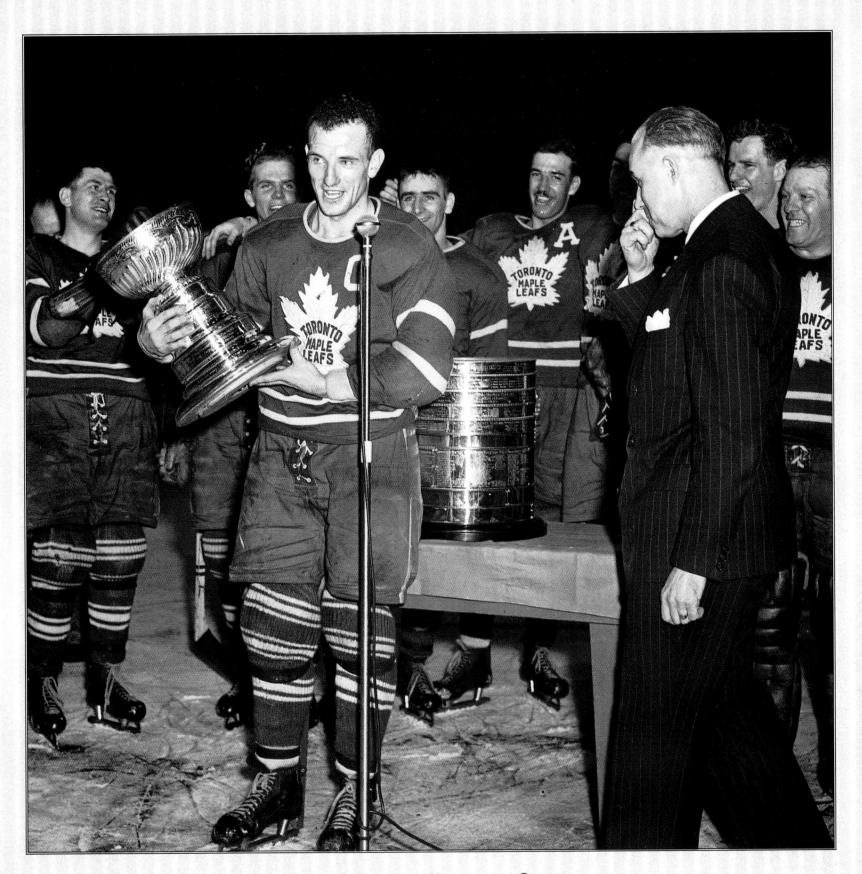

# OTTAWA SENATORS, 1903–05

**M**ore than a decade before the National Hockey League dropped the puck for its first official season, the Ottawa Senators, nicknamed the Silver Seven, had already made their mark as one of the most dominant hockey teams ever (although at the time, "ever" wasn't a very lengthy span). Nearly a century later, however, the Silver Seven remain one the greatest units of all time.

In 1902–03, the Senators, who played seven-man hockey with a "rover" as the seventh skater on the ice, featured three Gilmours—Dave, Suddy, and Billy—as a forward line. They teamed with ever-dangerous rover Frank McGee, who was one of the pre–NHL superstars of hockey. McGee, who once scored 14 goals in a single game, was the second-leading scorer in the Canadian Amateur Hockey League in 1902–03, netting 14 goals in eight games. After tying Winnipeg for the regular-season title with a 6–2 record in the comparatively short season, the Silver Seven watched Montreal AAA defend its 1902 Stanley Cup title by whipping Winnipeg in four games. However, Montreal was no match for the speed and artistry of Ottawa, and the Senators skated past Montreal and the Rat Portage Thistles to win their first-ever Stanley Cup.

Clearly the star of the team was McGee, who possessed dashing speed and unparalleled puck-handling ability. His skill and finesse were all the more

sensational in light of the fact that he had sight in only one eye, thus lacking full peripheral vision. Nevertheless, he

*Ottawa was led by Frank McGee, a sensational skater and stick-handler who often scored two or three goals a game.*

was able to dart around the rink and create endless chaos for the opposition. McGee averaged nearly three goals per game during his career. Tragically, he was killed while serving in France during World War I.

During their heyday, the Silver Seven had an embarrassment of riches where players were concerned, with McGee leading a lineup that featured Harry Westwick, Harvey Pulford, and J. B. Hutton, all stars of their era. Another was Alf Smith, the eldest of seven hockey-playing brothers. Alfie was the team's "hatchet man," but he was also a fine player. His brother Tommy, a tiny player who stood just 5'4", starred in the Federal Amateur Hockey League with the Ottawa Vics, and was later a leading scorer in two other leagues.

In 1904, the Ottawa Senators left the CAHL and joined the FAHL. Although the Montreal Wanderers took the league title, the Senators—as defending Stanley Cup champs—earned the right to compete in what was called the Stanley Cup "challenge." They first dispatched the Winnipeg Rowing Club's hockey team, then whipped Toronto of the Ontario league. The Silver Seven then took on the Wanderers in a showdown for the Cup. A dispute arose regarding sites for the games. After Game 1 ended in a tie and no agreement could be reached as to where Game 2 should be played, the series was canceled. The Senators turned their attention to their adversaries from Brandon, Manitoba, whom Ottawa ultimately beat to retain the Cup.

Another star emerged on the powerful Silver Seven squad in 1905, as Harry "Rat" Westwick, a former goaltender, scored 24 goals in 13 games (including playoffs) as the Senators' ace rover. With the goal-scoring wizardry of Westwick and McGee, who led the regular-season scoring race with 17 goals, the Senators went 7–1 and captured the FAHL title. Once more they would face the difficult challenge of defending their Stanley Cup title.

That year, the first challenge came from far, far away, as a team from Dawson City, in the Yukon Territory, traveled 4,000 miles to play against Ottawa. According to legend, the team made its way to Ottawa by train, ship, and even dogsled and had to shell out $3,000 for expenses along the way—a huge expenditure in those days. For their trouble, the Dawson City skaters soon found themselves on the bad end of a record-setting avalanche. As a "warm-up" to the series finale, the Silver Seven pumped nine goals past Dawson City in Game 1 and took a decisive 9–2 victory. But the best—or worst—was yet to come. In Game 2, they pummeled the poor Yukonites 23–2. It was in this contest that McGee etched his name in the history books with a 14-goal explosion. From there, the Silver Seven went on to hand their old rivals from Rat Portage

*Billy Gilmour was the best of Ottawa's three Gilmour brothers, making the Hall of Fame in 1962.*

another beating to win their third straight Stanley Cup.

In March 1906, the Silver Seven finally lost their grip on the Cup. After switching leagues to the Eastern Canada Amateur Hockey Association, the Senators, led by Harry Smith's 38 goals (eight in one game against the Montreal Shamrocks), thwarted Stanley Cup challenges from Queens University and Smiths Falls (FAHL). But the Silver Seven were eventually dethroned by the Wanderers by the score of 12–10 in a total-goals series, and the original hockey dynasty came to an end.

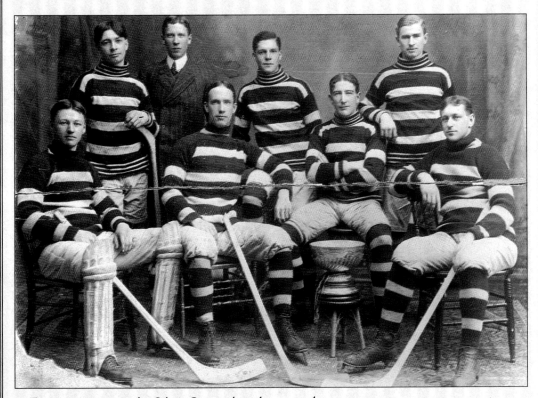

*From 1903–05, the Silver Seven played 24 regular-season games, winning 17 times. What's more impressive is that they went 13–2–2 in Stanley Cup competition.*

# TORONTO MAPLE LEAFS, 1946–49

**P**rior to the 1946–47 season, only two NHL teams had ever won and then successfully defended a Stanley Cup championship. Howie Morenz's Montreal Canadiens had won successive playoff titles in 1930 and 1931, while the Detroit Red Wings had linked a pair of Stanley Cups in 1936 and 1937. No team had ever succeeded in putting together three consecutive championships—that is, until the Toronto Maple Leafs came along in 1946–47. With a powerful offensive attack, led by scoring superstars Ted Kennedy and Syl Apps, and the outstanding Walter "Turk" Broda in goal, the Leafs were a quick-footed, hard-shooting team that could win the big game.

But the Leafs weren't only deadly because they could fill the net. With bangers like Gus Mortson, Bill Barilko, and "Wild Bill" Ezinicki around, they could win in the alley as well as on the ice. And their team confidence surpassed normal levels. Only a few short seasons earlier, the 1942 Leafs had been down three games to none in the Stanley Cup Finals against Detroit. In the greatest comeback in sports history, the Leafs scratched their way back, forced a seventh game, and won the decisive match on the strength of Broda's superb goaltending. Five years after their collective imitation of Lazarus rising from the dead, the Leafs—with Apps and Broda back from World War II—were poised to resume their dominance.

In 1946–47, the Leafs had to chase Montreal all year while league MVP Rocket Richard was the toast of the NHL with 45 goals. But Toronto regularly neutralized him with physical aggression, usually from Ezinicki and Vic Lynn, who would haunt the Rocket in the playoffs. The Leafs also boasted a hotshot rookie, Howie Meeker, who blasted 27 goals and edged Detroit freshman Gordie Howe for the Calder Trophy as rookie of the year. After finishing second to the Habs, the Maple Leafs made short order of the Red Wings in the playoffs, eliminating Detroit in five games and setting up their long-awaited showdown with the defending-champion Canadiens.

As the series progressed, Ezinicki and Lynn continued to harass Richard, who finally blew a gasket and used his stick to open bloody gashes on *both* players. NHL boss Clarence Campbell, whose run-ins with Richard were legendary, lowered the boom, fining him $250 and suspending him for Game 3 of the Finals. The Leafs rolled to a 4–2 win, then added a 2–1 sudden-death heartbreaker in Game 4 to take a three-games-to-one lead. Montreal won Game 5 as Richard scored twice, but Toronto won Game 6 as Kennedy, its leader all year, netted the winner.

*NHL boss Clarence Campbell (right) congratulates Leafs coach Hap Day after Toronto's third straight Cup title, in 1949. The Leafs swept the Red Wings in the Finals.*

*It wasn't until Max Bentley (left, with "A") left Chicago and his brother Doug for Toronto that he and the Leafs became dominant NHL figures.*

Riding high from their Stanley Cup victory, the Leafs won the 1947–48 league title by five points over Detroit, while Montreal fell to fifth place. With an eye on another Cup, the Leafs pulled off a blockbuster trade on November 2, 1947, that put them over the top. Sending Gus Bodnar, Gaye Stewart (who had led the NHL in goals in 1945–46), and Bud Poile to Chicago, the Leafs picked up the magnificent Max Bentley, who'd been toiling away on a defensively feeble Black Hawks team. Bentley added enthusiasm and a third prong to Toronto's attack, and the Leafs finished first while Broda, with a 2.38 goals-against average, won the Vezina Trophy.

Returning to the postseason, the Leafs were favorites to win another Stanley Cup, despite the inherent difficulties of repeating. After whipping Boston in five semifinal games, the Leafs took on Detroit and the Production Line of Ted Lindsay, Sid Abel, and Howe. Ever confident, Leafs GM Conn Smythe called this Toronto assembly "the best team I ever had." And the Leafs responded, sweeping Detroit.

In 1948–49, Detroit's Production Line took the Red Wings to a league title while Toronto, the target of revenge-seekers around the circuit, adopted a more physical brand of play. Without retired heroes Apps and Nick Metz, Toronto dropped to fourth place and sent shock waves through the NHL when it reportedly tried to purchase Rocket Richard from Montreal.

When the playoffs began, many concluded that Toronto's heyday was over and that Detroit would power its way to a Stanley Cup title. But when the two met in the Finals, having dispatched Boston and Montreal, respectively, the NHL was in for a jolt. While Broda earned his reputation as the game's premier money goalie, allowing the Red Wings just five goals in four games, the Leafs outchecked, outskated, outbattled, and outscored their rivals to pull off another stunning four-game sweep. In so doing, they became the first team in NHL history to win three consecutive Stanley Cups, thus redefining the concept of a hockey dynasty.

| 1947–48 Maple Leafs 32–15–13 | | | | |
|---|---|---|---|---|
| Skaters | G | A | PTS | PIM |
| M. Bentley | 26 | 28 | 54 | 10 |
| S. Apps | 26 | 27 | 53 | 12 |
| T. Kennedy | 25 | 21 | 46 | 32 |
| H. Watson | 21 | 20 | 41 | 16 |
| V. Lynn | 12 | 22 | 34 | 53 |
| H. Meeker | 14 | 20 | 34 | 62 |
| B. Ezinicki | 11 | 20 | 31 | 97 |
| J. Klukay | 15 | 15 | 30 | 28 |
| J. Thomson | 0 | 29 | 29 | 82 |
| G. Mortson | 7 | 11 | 18 | 118 |
| S. Smith | 7 | 10 | 17 | 10 |
| B. Barilko | 5 | 9 | 14 | 147 |
| W. Stanowski | 2 | 11 | 13 | 12 |
| N. Metz | 4 | 8 | 12 | 8 |
| D. Metz | 4 | 6 | 10 | 2 |
| G. Boesch | 2 | 7 | 9 | 52 |
| | | | | |
| Goalie | W | L | T | GAA |
| T. Broda | 32 | 15 | 13 | 2.38 |

# DETROIT RED WINGS, 1948–55

Great teams have always been more than just the sum of their parts. But the Detroit Red Wings teams that dominated the NHL from 1948–55 and won four of seven possible Stanley Cups had some of the greatest parts any team could hope for. Manager Jack Adams and coach Tommy Ivan steered the ship, skaters Gordie Howe, Sid Abel, and Ted Lindsay poured in the goals, and goalie Terry Sawchuk and defenseman Red Kelly shut down the opposition.

Beginning in 1948–49, the Red Wings were the NHL's team to beat. Their Production Line (Lindsay, Abel, and Howe) was in place, and—led by Abel's league-high 28 goals—the Wings finished in first place by nine points. Picked to win the 1949 Stanley Cup, they beat arch rival Montreal but stumbled in the Finals, losing to Toronto in a humiliating four-game sweep.

Detroit lost only 19 games in 1949–50 and beat Montreal by 11 points for first place. Lindsay, the Production Line's truculent left winger, showed remarkable diversity when he led the league in assists (55) and points (78) and was third in penalty minutes (141). Abel (69 points) and Howe (68) were second and third overall. A 20-year-old Sawchuk made his NHL debut in goal, but Harry Lumley remained the starter. Lumley had been the youngest goalie in NHL history (at 17) when he made his debut in 1943–44. Now a veteran, he was poised to take Detroit to the top.

*The Wings combined style, brawn, and grit with (left to right) Red Kelly, Ted Lindsay, Metro Prystai, and Gordie Howe.*

Detroit was flying high as the 1950 playoffs began, but its hopes were dashed when Howe tried to check Toronto's Teeder Kennedy and fell to the boards, fracturing his skull. While Howe lay near death in a Detroit hospital, his mates carried on. However, not until Leo Reise scored at 8:34 of sudden-death in Game 7 did the Wings advance to the Finals. Against New York, Lumley outdueled Rangers goalie Chuck Rayner for seven grueling games, and it took another sud-den-death marker, in double OT from Pete Babando, to earn the Wings their Stanley Cup.

During these years, the Red Wings relied on role players as much as they did on their stars. Babando, for example, played only one year in Detroit during an otherwise modest career. Doc Couture was another hero of the 1950 playoffs whose career was a roller-coaster of ups and downs. George Gee scored steadily throughout his career but never received much press. Crafty manager Adams knew exactly when to tinker and when to leave well enough alone. Despite several playoff disappointments, Adams made precious few changes to his club between 1948 and 1955.

Howe, his life saved by emergency surgery, made a dramatic recovery in 1950–51, regaining both his health and his scoring touch. He won hockey's triple crown by leading in goals (43), assists (43), and points (86) and earned his first of four straight Art Ross Trophies as the league's scoring champion. Over the next five years, he won four scoring titles and a pair of Hart Trophies as MVP. Lindsay, who took the 1950 Art Ross Trophy, finished second in points in 1952 and 1953. Abel, winner of the 1949 Hart Trophy, remained the glue of the line without adding any hardware to his trophy case.

In 1950–51, Sawchuk took the Calder Trophy after setting a league record with 44 wins. Over the next five years, he was the NHL's dominant goalie, earning three Vezina Trophies (1952, 1953, and 1955) and finishing second twice (1951 and 1954). When the dust settled in 1950–51, the Red Wings had set a new NHL record with 44 wins and 101 points.

From top to bottom, the Red Wings ruled. While Howe dethroned Rocket Richard as king of right wingers, Kelly established his place as the game's top defenseman. In 1954, he won the first-ever Norris Trophy, and he and Bill Quackenbush set high standards of excellence and sportsmanship with four Lady Byng Trophies between them (1949, 1951, 1953, and 1954).

The Red Wings lost to the Canadiens in the 1951 playoffs, but they took the Stanley Cup in 1952, 1954, and 1955. The 1952 playoffs were a show-case of Sawchuk's brilliance in goal. He allowed a total of five goals (an 0.63 goals-against average) and won eight straight games, giving rise to the tradition in the Motor City of throwing an octopus on the ice. In 1954, the first-place Red Wings went to the Stanley Cup Finals against Montreal. A new-comer named Alex Delvecchio led them in assists while Sawchuk stood the Canadiens on

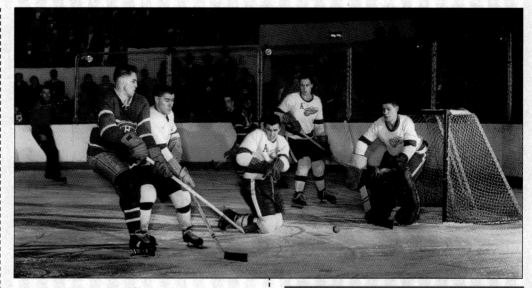

*In the 1952 playoffs, Detroit outscored its opposition 24–5, as goalie Terry Sawchuk pitched four shutouts.*

*Terry Sawchuk (left) and Sid Abel demonstrate the oldest tradition in hockey— kissing the Cup.*

their collective ear, winning the series in seven dramatic games.

Detroit won its fourth Stanley Cup with yet another seven-game nail-biter over Montreal in 1955. Howe notched 20 points in 11 playoff games and scored the Cup-clinching goal in Game 7. The Red Wings saw their string of regular-season titles end in 1955–56. Although they made it back to the Stanley Cup Finals that year, they could not hold off the Canadiens, and their dynasty slowly but steadily dwindled and ended. Still, this club remains one of the greatest ever.

| 1951–52 RED WINGS 44–14–12 | | | | |
|---|---|---|---|---|
| Skaters | G | A | PTS | PIM |
| G. Howe | 47 | 39 | 86 | 78 |
| T. Lindsay | 30 | 39 | 69 | 123 |
| S. Abel | 17 | 36 | 53 | 32 |
| R. Kelly | 16 | 31 | 47 | 16 |
| M. Prystai | 21 | 22 | 43 | 16 |
| A. Delvecchio | 15 | 22 | 37 | 22 |
| M. Pavelich | 17 | 19 | 36 | 54 |
| G. Skov | 12 | 14 | 26 | 48 |
| T. Leswick | 9 | 10 | 19 | 93 |
| M. Pronovost | 7 | 11 | 18 | 50 |
| B. Goldham | 0 | 14 | 14 | 24 |
| V. Stasiuk | 5 | 9 | 14 | 19 |
| L. Reise | 0 | 11 | 11 | 34 |
| B. Woit | 3 | 8 | 11 | 20 |
| J. Wilson | 4 | 5 | 9 | 18 |
| Goalie | W | L | T | GAA |
| T. Sawchuk | 44 | 14 | 12 | 1.90 |

# MONTREAL CANADIENS, 1955–60

Of all the dynasties to emerge and dominate in the NHL, perhaps no team was more frightening to behold than the Montreal Canadiens from 1955–56 through 1959–60. During this five-year span, the Habs simply had no weaknesses and boasted the best players at every position. They were virtually unbeatable for the duration, losing an average of only 18.2 games per year while playing a 70-game schedule. On their home ice at the fabled Montreal Forum, they were almost guaranteed to beat you, putting together a five-year regular-season home-ice record of 119–31–25.

With speed, playmaking, solid defense, and the best goaltender in hockey, the Canadiens finished first four times during this reign. And when they finished second, in 1956–57, it was by just six points to Detroit. Behind the bench, replacing the irascible Dick Irvin, who had built the team, was former Canadiens scoring star Toe Blake, the former left winger on the Punch Line with Elmer Lach and Rocket Richard. By 1955–56, Richard was 34 years old and beginning to slow down. But there was still some fire in the Rocket, and Blake was just the man to harness the fury without letting it burn out of control. Other players liked and respected the down-to-earth Blake.

The Canadiens were the ultimate juggernaut during these five seasons of glory. They outscored their opponents 1,195 to 780, averaging 3.41 goals per

*Maurice Richard scored the Cup-winning goal in 1956, while brother Henri (right) led the Habs in playoff points in 1960.*

game while allowing just 2.23 goals against. Their new star center, Jean Beliveau, captured both the Art Ross and Hart Trophies in 1955–56 (and was the team leader in penalty minutes with 148). The following year, he was the MVP runner-up. In 1957–58, Dickie Moore won the first of his two straight Art Ross Trophies, while teammates Henri "Pocket Rocket" Richard and Beliveau were runners-up.

Of course, no man in the NHL could match the year-by-year excellence of Jacques Plante, the Habs' extraordinary netminder. Plante won the Vezina Trophy seven times in his great career. From 1955–56 through 1959–60, he won it each year. During this stretch, he won 185 of 318 games in which he appeared and posted 37 shutouts, leading the league three times in that category.

Meanwhile, defenseman Doug Harvey also took hold of a piece of impressive hardware—the Norris Trophy—which he won a total of seven times, four of them during the Habs' five years as NHL champs. Teammate Tom Johnson won it in 1958–59, but controversy tarnished the selection. Harvey, the game's first true rushing defenseman, finished second in the voting.

Montreal won 45 games in 1955–56, dethroning the powerful Red Wings and setting a new league mark for single-season victories. While youngsters such as Beliveau were emerging as the new superstars, veterans such as Bert Olmstead, who led the league in assists, showed they too had some gas left in the tank. A new arrival in Montreal during the 1955–56 season was Henri Richard, kid brother of the Rocket. Henri would go on to win 11 Stanley Cups in his 20-year career. As a capper on a tremendous season, it was the Rocket himself who scored the Cup-clinching goal against Detroit in the 1956 Stanley Cup Finals.

The Canadiens were so offensively dominant, a major rule change was made to the start of the 1956–57 season, allowing players to return from minor penalties if a power-play goal was scored. The team still led the league in goals (210). It finished second to the Red Wings in the regular season but was not to be denied come playoff time. Montreal needed only five games against Detroit and five against Boston to retain its Stanley Cup.

During this era of mastery, the Canadiens were rarely better than in Stanley Cup action. In five years, they played 49 playoff games and won 40. Their awesome firepower accounted for 185 goals (3.78 per game) while their equally impressive defense and goaltending gave up just 95 goals (1.94 per game). Teams traveling to the Montreal Forum for a playoff game knew deep in their hearts that it was hopeless, as Montreal amassed a 24–2 home record from 1956–60.

The Habs beat Boston in the 1958 Stanley Cup Finals, taking six games to complete the series and hoist their third straight Cup. In the 1959 Finals, they became the first team ever to win four straight Cups when they trounced Toronto in five games. They added an exclamation point in the 1960 championship round by sweeping the Leafs for title No. 5.

Winning five straight Stanley Cups put this Canadiens squad at the top of the list of great teams; its achievement has only been challenged on rare occasions. This franchise won four straight Cups from 1976–79 and the New York Islanders won four straight from 1980–83. Some say the magic "five" will never be duplicated.

*Montreal goalie Jacques Plante shows his intense nature, putting his stick in the face of Detroit's Alex Delvecchio as Rocket Richard backchecks.*

### 1955–56 CANADIENS
### 45–15–10

| Skaters | G | A | PTS | PIM |
| --- | --- | --- | --- | --- |
| J. Beliveau | 47 | 41 | 88 | 143 |
| M. Richard | 38 | 33 | 71 | 89 |
| B. Olmstead | 14 | 56 | 70 | 94 |
| B. Geoffrion | 29 | 33 | 62 | 66 |
| D. Moore | 11 | 39 | 50 | 55 |
| D. Harvey | 5 | 39 | 44 | 60 |
| H. Richard | 19 | 21 | 40 | 46 |
| F. Curry | 14 | 18 | 32 | 10 |
| K. Mosdell | 13 | 17 | 30 | 48 |
| C. Provost | 13 | 16 | 29 | 30 |
| J. Leclair | 6 | 8 | 14 | 30 |
| J.G. Talbot | 1 | 13 | 14 | 80 |
| T. Johnson | 3 | 10 | 13 | 75 |
| D. St. Laurent | 4 | 9 | 13 | 58 |
| D. Marshall | 4 | 1 | 5 | 10 |
| B. Turner | 1 | 4 | 5 | 35 |

| Goalies | W | L | T | GAA |
| --- | --- | --- | --- | --- |
| J. Plante | 42 | 12 | 10 | 1.86 |
| R. Perreault | 3 | 3 | 0 | 2.00 |

# TORONTO MAPLE LEAFS, 1961–64

**R**eflecting the colorful nature of their coach, Punch Imlach, the Toronto Maple Leafs of the early 1960s played hard-nosed hockey—confident, beat-you-in-the-alley hockey. And if they didn't have the most talent, man for man, in the league, they were rarely outworked. The demanding Imlach wouldn't allow it. Whether you were scoring ace Frank Mahovlich or checking for Mahovlich. Veteran Dick Duff was still scoring well. Dave Keon and George Armstrong played tough, classy hockey. Keon won the Lady Byng Trophy in 1962 and 1963 and was runner-up in 1964. The Leafs' defense had a little bit of everything, from the strength and intelligence of Tim Horton and Allan Stanley to the tough, mean-edged play of Carl Brewer and Bobby Baun. A young, career minor-leaguer, finally earned a real chance in the NHL in 1958–59 (at the age of 34) and was still going strong through the 1960s. Even if Toronto did not win the regular-season title (which it managed only once during its three-year reign as Stanley Cup champ), it was lethal in the playoffs, relying on a will to win that emanated from its leader, Imlach.

*Coach Punch Imlach and nine of the 1962 Maple Leafs pictured here would be inducted into the Hockey Hall of Fame.*

expert Ron Stewart, you had a role; and when you performed as required, the team won. From 1961–62 to 1963–64, Toronto won three straight Stanley Cups, none by accident, all from hard work.

The 1961–62 Maple Leafs were not without a cluster of skilled skaters. Red Kelly had been obtained from Detroit and converted into a magnificent center

bespectacled Al Arbour also saw action on the Leafs' blue line and learned a lot about what it takes to make a championship team.

The Leafs were also quite stingy about giving up goals. Goalie Johnny Bower, a

The Leafs were successful because of their collective effort. They didn't have a scoring champion or a league MVP in any of their championship seasons. However, Bower was twice a runner-up for the Vezina Trophy. Keon, scrappy but clean inasmuch as he took very few penalties, was a Lady Byng Trophy winner. Brewer and Horton were runners-up for the Norris Trophy in 1962–63 and

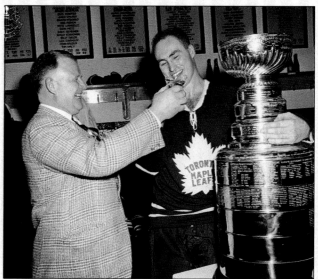

*Leafs owner Harold Ballard toasts center Red Kelly, who contributed brilliant two-way play and veteran leadership.*

1963–64, respectively. And in 1962–63, big defenseman Kent Douglas made a sterling debut and won the Calder Trophy as top rookie.

During this Leaf dominance, Toronto put a player on the NHL's list of top-five scorers three years running—twice with Mahovlich (1962 and '63) and once with Andy Bathgate (1964). Imlach wasn't only a tough-minded coach, he was also an exacting manager who would make a deal if it would help the club, regardless of the egos involved. Getting Bathgate from the Rangers midway through the 1963–64 campaign raised eyebrows in Toronto because the Leafs had to give up five talented players (Arnie Brown, Bill Collins, Duff, Bob Nevin, and Rod Seiling) to get him. Imlach took the heat but was eventually vindicated.

The 1961–62 Leafs finished 13 points behind Montreal in the regular season, then rode the goaltending of Bower and his sidekick, Don Simmons, past the Rangers and defending-champion Black Hawks, prevailing in the Stanley Cup Finals in six games. While the battle was hard-fought, the Leafs developed new strength and unity that they rode in 1962–63, when they captured their first regular-season title in 15 years.

The 1962–63 Leafs won 35 games and had the second-best offense in the NHL. Mahovlich, who was third overall in goals (36) and fourth in points (73), led the charge. Toronto edged Chicago by one point to take the regular-season title. In the Stanley Cup Finals against Detroit, the Leafs jumped all over the Wings when the dangerous Duff scored twice in the first 1:08 of Game 1. Toronto whipped Detroit in five games, with an unlikely scoring hero, Eddie Shack, netting the Cup-clinching goal. Shack's goal brought a joyous end to a season that began sadly with the June discovery of the 1951 plane crash that killed Leafs playoff hero Bill Barilko.

Although the Leafs were virtually unchallenged for their second straight Stanley Cup, the NHL took the Leafs' measure in 1963–64 and smacked them down to a third-place finish behind Montreal and Chicago. Mahovlich, a brooding superstar, saw his stats fall dramatically—which ultimately led Imlach

to acquire Bathgate. In his new surroundings, Bathgate finished well, first overall in assists (58) and fourth in points (77). If Imlach was initially skewered for trading away so much raw talent and potential for an aging star, Bathgate bailed him out in the playoffs.

After the Leafs narrowly escaped a seven-game series with Montreal in the semifinals, they renewed old acquaintances with Detroit in the Stanley Cup Finals. After a seesaw battle, Bathgate emerged as the ultimate hero when he scored the Cup-clinching goal in Game 7, capping three years of playoff magic.

### 1962–63 MAPLE LEAFS
### 35–23–12

| Skaters | G | A | PTS | PIM |
|---|---|---|---|---|
| F. Mahovlich | 36 | 37 | 73 | 56 |
| R. Kelly | 20 | 40 | 60 | 8 |
| D. Keon | 28 | 28 | 56 | 2 |
| B. Pulford | 19 | 25 | 44 | 49 |
| G. Armstrong | 19 | 24 | 43 | 27 |
| D. Duff | 16 | 19 | 35 | 56 |
| B. Nevin | 12 | 21 | 33 | 4 |
| B. Harris | 8 | 24 | 32 | 22 |
| R. Stewart | 16 | 16 | 32 | 26 |
| C. Brewer | 2 | 23 | 25 | 168 |
| T. Horton | 6 | 19 | 25 | 69 |
| E. Shack | 16 | 9 | 25 | 97 |
| K. Douglas | 7 | 15 | 22 | 105 |
| A. Stanley | 4 | 15 | 19 | 22 |
| E. Litzenberger | 5 | 13 | 18 | 10 |
| B. Baun | 4 | 8 | 12 | 65 |

| Goalies | W | L | T | GAA |
|---|---|---|---|---|
| J. Bower | 20 | 15 | 7 | 2.62 |
| D. Simmons | 15 | 8 | 5 | 2.50 |

# MONTREAL CANADIENS, 1964–69

In the mid–1960s, after a "lengthy" Stanley Cup drought (actually a mere four years), Montreal fans were growing increasingly restless. Following five years of champagne and bragging rights, the Habs had failed to get past the semifinals four years running, from 1961–64.

Coach Toe Blake, who had won Stanley Cups in each of his first five seasons behind Montreal's bench, knew he had to turn things around. Jacques Plante was gone, Rocket Richard and Boom Boom Geoffrion had retired, and Doug Harvey had long since moved on to the Rangers. The core of his previous dynasty was just a memory. However, thanks to the crafty management skills of Frank Selke and Sam Pollock (who took over in 1964–65), the Canadiens made quick work of their reorganization.

From 1964–65 through 1968–69, a period of history that included a dramatic doubling of the NHL from six teams to 12, the Habs took three regular-season titles and finished second twice. Yet their road was often rocky. For example, after taking the 1965–66 season title by eight points over Chicago, the Habs finished second to the Hawks the very next year, trailing them by a whopping 17 points. A new cast of characters was clearly needed to forge the next "dynasty" in Montreal.

Jean Beliveau was Montreal's new leader, taking the reins from Richard.

His classy, finesse-driven style (toned down considerably from his aggressive youth) gave the team its character and identity. He continued to vie for MVP honors and three times finished as a runner-up for the Hart Trophy (1966, 1968, and 1969).

*Henri Richard and Montreal swept St. Louis in both the 1968 and '69 Finals. The '68 affairs were all one-goal games.*

Beliveau had help from assorted Flying Frenchmen, such as Bobby Rousseau, the 1966 Lady Byng runner-up, who was third overall in scoring in 1965–66. Claude Provost led the Habs in points in 1964–65 and became the inaugural winner of the Bill Masterton Memorial Trophy in 1967–68, commemorating his dedication to the game.

In the absence of Plante, the Habs turned to Charlie Hodge, Gump Worsley, and Rogie Vachon. Hodge and Worsley won Vezina honors in 1965–66, Hodge alone was runner-up in 1966–67, and Worsley and Vachon combined to win it in 1967–68, the first year of expansion.

With Harvey gone, the team looked for new defensive leadership from 1964 rookie of the year Jacques Laperriere, who was a Norris Trophy runner-up in 1965 before winning it in 1966. Montreal backliner J. C. Tremblay finished second in Norris voting in 1967–68.

Throughout their transition, the Habs remained quite skilled at every position and continued to dominate many of their adversaries—despite the four years of playoff ruin. In 1964–65, all the new pieces fell into place and the Habs returned to the winners' circle so familiar to them.

After trailing Detroit by four points in the standings at season's end, the Canadiens entered the 1965 playoffs with one objective: to get past the first round. The reigning-champion Maple Leafs had other ideas and gave Montreal all it could handle, stretching the series to six games. But Provost lifted the Habs with a Game 6 sudden-death goal that ended the Leafs' season and broke their hold on the Stanley Cup. But the Black Hawks were no pushovers, either. In the Finals, the Habs and Hawks battled to seven games before Worsley pitched a home-ice shutout in Game 7 to give Montreal fans their Stanley Cup back. Beliveau notched 16 points, scored the Cup-winning goal, and was awarded the first-ever Conn Smythe Trophy as playoff MVP.

Riding high, the Habs excelled in 1965–66, finishing eight points ahead of Chicago and taking only four games to erase Toronto and return to the Finals. Detroit offered a worthy challenge in the championship round, winning the first two games, but the Canadiens rallied to win four straight contests to protect their playoff title.

Montreal finished second in 1966–67 and could not stop the upstart Maple Leafs, who shocked first-place Chicago in the semifinals. The Habs departed in the Stanley Cup Finals in six games and prepared for the start of 12-team league play in 1967–68, when the NHL's original six teams were clustered in the East Division.

*Jean Beliveau's 15 points in the 1969 playoffs led the Canadiens and earned him his ninth of 10 Stanley Cup rings.*

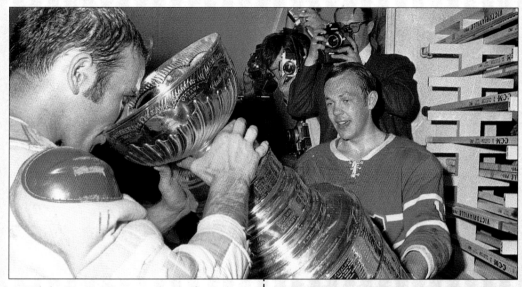

*While Jacques Lemaire drinks from the Cup, Yvan Cournoyer—Montreal's top playoff scorer in '68—waits his turn.*

After a first-place finish, the Habs whipped Boston and Chicago en route to the Stanley Cup Finals against first-year St. Louis, winner of the West playoffs. The Habs swept the overmatched Blues (winning twice in sudden-death OT), then grabbed another league title in 1968–69 with new coach Claude Ruel running the bench. The Rangers and Boston could not stop Montreal, as the Canadiens roared to another championship, clobbering the Blues in the Finals yet again in four games. Sophomore defenseman Serge Savard won the Conn Smythe Trophy.

Montreal remained a prominent team in the early 1970s, winning Cups in 1971 and '73. In the late 1970s, they would reach even greater heights.

| 1965–66 CANADIENS 41–21–8 | | | | |
|---|---|---|---|---|
| Skaters | G | A | PTS | PIM |
| B. Rousseau | 30 | 48 | 78 | 20 |
| J. Beliveau | 29 | 48 | 77 | 50 |
| H. Richard | 22 | 39 | 61 | 47 |
| C. Provost | 19 | 36 | 55 | 38 |
| G. Tremblay | 27 | 21 | 48 | 24 |
| D. Duff | 21 | 24 | 45 | 78 |
| R. Backstrom | 22 | 20 | 42 | 10 |
| J.C. Tremblay | 6 | 29 | 35 | 8 |
| C. Larose | 15 | 18 | 33 | 67 |
| J. Laperriere | 6 | 25 | 31 | 85 |
| Y. Cournoyer | 18 | 11 | 29 | 8 |
| J. Ferguson | 11 | 14 | 25 | 153 |
| J.G. Talbot | 1 | 14 | 15 | 50 |
| T. Harris | 0 | 13 | 13 | 81 |
| T. Harper | 1 | 11 | 12 | 91 |
| D. Balon | 3 | 7 | 10 | 24 |
| | | | | |
| Goalies | W | L | T | GAA |
| G. Worsley | 29 | 14 | 6 | 2.36 |
| C. Hodge | 12 | 7 | 2 | 2.58 |

# PHILADELPHIA FLYERS, 1973–75

*Bernie Parent stymied the Rangers in the 1974 semifinals en route to taking the Flyers to their first Cup title. Parent's 2.02 playoff GAA earned him the Conn Smythe Trophy.*

Judging by the belligerent style employed by the Philadelphia Flyers in the 1970s, when they grew from patsies into Stanley Cup contenders and won two titles, it's hard to believe that when they first came into the NHL in 1967–68 they were a small, finesse-driven team routinely pushed around. The Flyers of the mid–1970s, whose coach, Fred Shero, had grown up on blood-and-guts hockey in the minors, earned the nickname "Broad Street Bullies" because they wielded a purposeful brand of intimidation. Their team motto was: "Take a straight line to the puck and arrive in ill humor."

Players like Dave Schultz, Don Saleski, Bob Kelly, Gary Dornhoefer, Moose Dupont, Ed Van Impe, and, of course, Bobby Clarke gave the team its nasty character, while snipers Rick MacLeish, Reg Leach (who set a record for goals by a right winger in 1975–76), Bill Barber, and Ross Lonsberry bent the twine behind enemy goalies.

Ironically, while this team was built on the willingness of its core players to engage in large-scale brawls, the man largely responsible for bringing two Stanley Cups to Philadelphia was its classy goaltender, Bernie Parent, a comparatively mild veteran who exhibited grace and artistry in nets. In the mid–1970s, Parent was serving his second tour

*Without Dave "The Hammer" Schultz (No. 8), the Flyers might not have won two Cups.*

with the Flyers. He had spent four years in Philly as an expansion pick before playing briefly in Toronto and then for the World Hockey Association. The Flyers reclaimed him in 1973–74, and he paid huge dividends, leading the NHL with a record 47 victories, a dozen shutouts, and a sparkling 1.89 goals-against average, earning him his first Vezina Trophy. He took another Vezina in 1974–75 when he won 44 more games with another dozen shutouts and a league-best 2.03 average.

If Parent was the quiet backbone in goal, the team's fiery spiritual leader was Clarke, a diabetic who came to the NHL in 1969–70 and immediately set about proving he was tough enough—and talented enough—to play and thrive. In 1972–73, he was appointed team captain. A great playmaker who twice led the NHL with 89 assists (1975 and 1976), Clarke won three Hart Trophies during his heyday (1973, 1975, and 1976) as well as a Masterton Trophy (1972) and later a Selke Trophy as the game's top defensive forward (1983). Intense in his desire to win, Clarke inspired the whole team. Under his command, the Flyers adopted the philosophy that any team in their path would have to be conquered.

To achieve their goals of intimidation and destruction, Schultz, known as "The Hammer," was unleashed. As a rookie in 1972–73, he led the league in penalty minutes (259). He then topped the charts the next two years as well with 348 and a league-record 472 in Philly's two championship seasons.

To their credit, the Flyers made no apologies for their tactics. Instead, they relied on the ends to justify their means. When, during the 1974 Stanley Cup semifinals, Schultz attacked and thrashed Rangers defenseman Dale Rolfe—a lanky, placid veteran not known for fighting—and no teammate came to Rolfe's aid, the Flyers pinpointed the Rangers' lack of team unity as a chief cause of their playoff demise. Even purists had to allow that the Flyers were correct on that score.

And the Flyers enjoyed very successful ends, even if their means were dubious.

After going to the playoff semifinals in 1973, the Flyers finished atop the Western Division in 1973–74, then crushed Atlanta and humiliated the favored Rangers in the playoffs. In their first trip to the Stanley Cup Finals, a rugged, high-scoring Bruins team awaited them, but Parent slammed the door on Boston, finishing the playoffs with a 2.02 goals-against average and posting a Stanley Cup-winning shutout in Game 6 of the Finals, earning the Conn Smythe Trophy as playoff MVP.

To many, the Flyers represented a step backward in the evolution of the NHL, and seemingly everyone wanted them to lose in 1974–75. However, Clarke won his second Hart Trophy and Parent took his second Vezina. The team earned a

franchise-record 113 points. With impressive wins over Toronto and the Isles, the Flyers went back to the Finals, this time against Buffalo. With a blanket defense and hard-hitting forechecking, Philadelphia took the series in six games. Parent surrendered just 12 goals in the Finals, finishing with a 1.89 goals-against average and a second Conn Smythe.

Like them or hate them—and nobody was neutral about these Flyers—the Broad Street Bullies were legitimate champions, winning big games, taking their lumps, and remaining near the top of the league for many years.

*Wrapped in the arms of Rick MacLeish is Flyers goalie Bernie Parent, who shut out the Bruins 1–0 in Game 6 of the 1974 Stanley Cup Finals.*

### 1974–75 FLYERS
### 51–18–11

| Skaters | G | A | PTS | PIM |
|---|---|---|---|---|
| B. Clarke | 27 | 89 | 116 | 125 |
| R. MacLeish | 38 | 41 | 79 | 50 |
| R. Leach | 45 | 33 | 78 | 63 |
| B. Barber | 34 | 37 | 71 | 66 |
| R. Lonsberry | 24 | 25 | 49 | 99 |
| G. Dornhoefer | 17 | 27 | 44 | 102 |
| B. Clement | 21 | 16 | 37 | 42 |
| O. Kindrachuk | 10 | 21 | 31 | 72 |
| A. Dupont | 11 | 21 | 32 | 276 |
| T. Bladon | 9 | 20 | 29 | 54 |
| B. Kelly | 11 | 18 | 29 | 99 |
| D. Saleski | 10 | 18 | 28 | 107 |
| T. Crisp | 8 | 19 | 27 | 20 |
| D. Schultz | 9 | 17 | 26 | 472 |
| Jim Watson | 7 | 18 | 25 | 72 |
| Joe Watson | 6 | 17 | 23 | 42 |
| E. Van Impe | 1 | 17 | 18 | 109 |

| Goalies | W | L | T | GAA |
|---|---|---|---|---|
| B. Parent | 44 | 14 | 10 | 2.03 |
| W. Stephenson | 7 | 2 | 1 | 2.72 |

# MONTREAL CANADIENS, 1975–79

The ghosts at the Montreal Forum were as legendary as the teams and players for whom those spirits live on. The dressing room at the Forum, with the faces of past heroes looking over the shoulders of present warriors, served as a constant reminder that anything less than a Stanley Cup championship was a failure. The Canadiens weren't the most successful playoff team in NHL history by accident. Hard work and great talent were key.

In 1975–76, the Habs began what would become their third major dynasty, in which they would win four straight Stanley Cups. With new coach Scotty

*From 1976–79, Ken Dryden went 48–10 with a 1.98 GAA in playoff action.*

*One of the most talented assemblies in NHL history, the Habs of the late 1970s ruled the NHL with speed and toughness. Their record from 1975–79: 229–46–45.*

Bowman (who came from St. Louis in 1971–72), a devastating arsenal led by top gun Guy Lafleur, the superb goaltending of perennial Vezina Trophy winner Ken Dryden, and a cast of star-quality role players, the Canadiens could do everything. With this new cast of characters at the forefront, the team carried huge expectations; but like teams that came before them, they ascended to greatness and took their place among the forefathers in the *bleu, blanc, et rouge*.

From 1975–76 through 1978–79, the Canadiens won 229 of 320 regular-season games. Scoring an average of 4.44 goals per game while surrendering just 2.29 goals, these high-powered Canadiens were a juggernaut that could intimidate the opposition by the sheer volume of their talent. Lafleur combined breakaway speed with a huge slap shot and terrific puck-handling skills. He won three Art Ross Trophies, two Hart Trophies, three Lester B. Pearson Awards (the MVP voted by the players), and the 1977 Conn Smythe Trophy during these four seasons. With his hair sailing in the wind behind him, Lafleur was the ultimate Flying Frenchman, and he rarely failed to deliver.

In goal was the unflappable Dryden, who had made his NHL debut with a Conn Smythe Trophy performance in the 1971 Stanley Cup playoffs. The slender, cerebral netminder with the cranky back and pretzel facemask won four of his five Vezina Trophies during this championship tenure, amassing a personal record of 150–33–30 and a 2.12 goals-against average.

The big, mobile defense corps was led by veteran squad leader Serge Savard and rising star Larry Robinson, who won the Norris Trophy in 1976–77, took the Smythe Trophy in the 1978 playoffs, and was runner-up for a second Norris in 1978–79. Robinson also thrashed Flyers hitman Dave Schultz in a fight during the 1976 Finals, a one-sided decision that helped launch the Habs past the defending champs and initiate their latest dynasty. And as if the defensemen weren't tough enough, the club also played a smothering defensive style that was perfected by Bob Gainey, who won the first four Frank Selke Trophies for best defensive forward (1978–81) and was MVP of the 1979 playoffs.

Even the second-fiddle players were virtuosos. Steve Shutt, a sleek left winger on Lafleur's line, scored 191 goals during this span (including a league-high 60 in 1976–77). Jacques Lemaire, who won eight Stanley Cups in 11 trips to the play-

*Brilliant checking forward Bob Gainey was MVP of the 1979 playoffs.*

offs, had a "career" year in 1977–78, with 97 points (fourth in the NHL). Yvan Cournoyer, Reggie Houle, and Mario Tremblay added speed, scoring depth, and toughness and helped make this team virtually unbeatable.

Historically, teams venturing into Montreal to face the Habs knew their chances of victory were extremely slim. From 1975–79, the Canadiens treated their hometown fans to an almost ridiculous diet of winning hockey. In 160 home games, Montreal won 126 and lost only 14, fewer than one in 10. To make the insult more painful, the Habs also boasted a 103–32–25 road record—the kind of numbers most teams would pray for at home. In 1976–77, the team won 60 of 80 regular-season games, dropping just eight decisions en route to a 132-point first-place finish, 20 points ahead of the league's second-best Flyers.

And if their regular-season domination didn't impress critics who cited over-expansion and viewed the NHL as a watered-down circuit, the Habs simply turned up the heat when the playoffs began, putting up even better numbers.

During their four-year Stanley Cup reign of terror, the Habs played 58 playoff games and won all but 10 of them. They outscored their opponents 219–108. In 30 playoff games held at the Montreal Forum, the Canadiens lost just

three times: in sudden-death to the Islanders in Game 5 of the 1977 semifinals, a series the Habs won in six games; to Detroit in Game 2 of the 1978 quarterfinals, a series won by Montreal in five; and finally to the Rangers in Game 1 of the 1979 Finals, which the Habs came back to win in five games.

With their dismissal of the Rangers in 1979, the Canadiens claimed their 21st Stanley Cup title since joining the NHL in 1917, a remarkable feat for a truly remarkable franchise.

| 1976–77 CANADIENS 60–8–12 | | | | |
|---|---|---|---|---|
| Skaters | G | A | PTS | PIM |
| G. LaFleur | 56 | 80 | 136 | 20 |
| S. Shutt | 60 | 45 | 105 | 28 |
| L. Robinson | 19 | 66 | 85 | 45 |
| G. LaPointe | 25 | 51 | 76 | 53 |
| J. Lemaire | 34 | 41 | 75 | 22 |
| P. Mahovlich | 15 | 47 | 62 | 45 |
| D. Risebrough | 22 | 38 | 60 | 132 |
| Y. Cournoyer | 25 | 28 | 53 | 8 |
| R. Houle | 22 | 30 | 52 | 24 |
| Y. Lambert | 24 | 28 | 52 | 50 |
| M. Tremblay | 18 | 28 | 46 | 61 |
| S. Savard | 9 | 33 | 42 | 35 |
| D. Jarvis | 16 | 22 | 38 | 14 |
| B. Gainey | 14 | 19 | 33 | 41 |
| M. Wilson | 13 | 14 | 27 | 26 |
| B. Nyrop | 3 | 19 | 22 | 21 |
| J. Roberts | 5 | 14 | 19 | 18 |
| P. Bouchard | 4 | 11 | 15 | 52 |
| R. Chartraw | 3 | 4 | 7 | 59 |
| | | | | |
| Goalies | W | L | T | GAA |
| K. Dryden | 41 | 6 | 8 | 2.14 |
| M. Larocque | 19 | 2 | 4 | 2.09 |

# NEW YORK ISLANDERS, 1979–83

Patience isn't only a virtue, it's an absolute necessity if you're trying to build a hockey team with staying power. The New York Islanders, born in 1972–73, were lucky to have as their chief architect one of the most patient and intelligent managers in NHL history. Bill Torrey knew the Isles might suffer in the early going. But, instead of trading away the future—his draft picks—for temporary success, he held his course. In his first six draft years, Torrey acquired Billy Harris, Bob

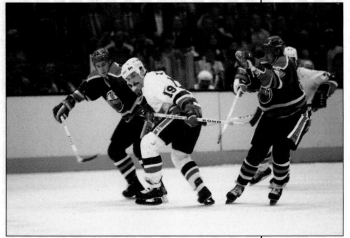

*In 1983, the last year of their four-year dynasty, Bryan Trottier and the Islanders swept the Oilers in the Finals.*

Nystrom, Denis Potvin, Clark Gillies, Bryan Trottier, Mike Bossy, and John Tonelli. In years to come, he proved to be a master at adding the right player at the right time.

Thanks to good management, the Isles experienced a relatively short prelude to success. In 1974–75, with their first play-off berth, they pulled off a huge upset of the Rangers in the first round, then staged an epic comeback from three games down to eliminate the Penguins in the quarterfinals. They nearly repeated the task in the semifinals before the Cup-bound Flyers put down the insurrection in seven games.

Torrey also had the insight to hire a coach with a keen sense of how to balance strategy, preparation, and execution; a man who knew when to turn his naturally talented players loose to do their thing. Al Arbour, who became one of the most successful coaches ever, taught his players team defense and created brilliant line combinations with the talent Torrey fed him each year. Soon he had a squad worthy of a run at the Stanley Cup.

But the Islanders didn't do with it smoke and mirrors. Though they enjoyed a Cinderella performance in 1975, they suffered hardships as well. In 1978, after three trips to the semifinals, the Isles were touted as a team that could go all the way. When they were upset by a nasty, physical Toronto club in the quarterfinals, they were labeled as choke artists and chickens. In 1979, after another first-place division finish, the Isles lost to the arch-rival Rangers in the semifinals and were lambasted in the local press and booed by their fans.

But the defeated protagonists swallowed their pride and chalked it up as yet another painful learning experience. They knew they had the horses to win the race; they simply couldn't afford to stumble. In 1979–80, they found a way to finish the ultimate race ahead of the pack.

Though fast, offensively lethal, and defensively sound, the Isles nevertheless faced a major challenge from Philadelphia, finishing 25 points behind the Flyers in the standings. After each team worked its way methodically through the playoffs, their high noon came in the Finals. The Isles took a three-games-to-one lead before the Flyers won Game 5. Leading 4–2 in Game 6 at home, the Isles faltered, allowing Philly to tie the game. But in the sudden-death session, the Isles attacked. With seven minutes gone, Tonelli carried into the Flyers' zone and centered the puck across the slot. Cruising down the wing, Nystrom knocked the rubber past Pete Peeters and

*On the Islanders' backline, Denis Potvin's take-no-prisoners attitude set the mood.*

*One of the great "money" goalies of all time, Billy Smith carried New York past Minnesota in the 1981 Finals for Cup No. 2. He won 57 playoff games from 1980–83.*

and Boston, the wily Isles gave Wayne Gretzky's high-powered but inexperienced Oilers a spanking, sweeping Edmonton to win their fourth Cup. Smith won 13 playoff games, had a 2.68 average, and took the Conn Smythe.

The Isles made it back to the Finals in 1984, but the Oilers were having none of New York's "Strive For Five," ending the Isles' domination and ringing in the dawn of their own supremacy.

sent the entire tri-state metro area into an uproar. The Islanders, in just their eighth season, had done what the Rangers hadn't been able to do in the previous 40 years—win a Stanley Cup. Trottier, a former Art Ross and Hart Trophy winner, won the Conn Smythe.

In coming years, the Islanders established themselves as a classic high-pressure team, and Billy Smith confirmed he was one of the best "money" goalies of all time. With three-time Norris Trophy defenseman Potvin providing offense and punishing body work, the Isles took the league title in 1980–81 and charged through the playoffs, losing only three games. Sniper Bossy led with 17 goals and 35 points, but it was Butch Goring,

with seven points against Minnesota in the Finals (including a hat trick in Game 3), who won the Conn Smythe Trophy.

Not to be outdone, Bossy won the Smythe Trophy in 1982 with another 17-goal playoff. Winning another league title on Smith's Vezina Trophy puck-stopping, the Isles lost only four games en route to the 1982 Finals. They swept the towel-waving Canucks, whose efforts were spoiled by the antics of Dave "Tiger" Williams, who savaged the Islanders, specifically Bossy and his own childhood pal, Trottier.

Smith carried the Islanders through the 1983 playoffs after the team fell to fifth overall in the regular season. After dispatching Washington, the Rangers,

| 1981–82 ISLANDERS 54–16–10 | | | | |
|---|---|---|---|---|
| Skaters | G | A | PTS | PIM |
| M. Bossy | 64 | 83 | 147 | 22 |
| B. Trottier | 50 | 79 | 129 | 88 |
| J. Tonelli | 35 | 58 | 93 | 57 |
| C. Gillies | 38 | 39 | 77 | 75 |
| D. Potvin | 24 | 37 | 61 | 83 |
| B. Bourne | 27 | 26 | 53 | 77 |
| D. Sutter | 18 | 35 | 53 | 100 |
| M. McEwen | 10 | 39 | 49 | 50 |
| B. Nystrom | 22 | 25 | 47 | 103 |
| S. Persson | 6 | 37 | 43 | 99 |
| B. Sutter | 21 | 22 | 43 | 114 |
| A. Kallur | 18 | 22 | 40 | 18 |
| W. Merrick | 12 | 27 | 39 | 20 |
| T. Jonsson | 9 | 25 | 34 | 51 |
| B. Goring | 15 | 17 | 32 | 10 |
| B. Carroll | 9 | 20 | 29 | 32 |
| D. Langevin | 1 | 20 | 21 | 82 |
| K. Morrow | 1 | 18 | 19 | 56 |
| G. Lane | 0 | 13 | 13 | 98 |
| H. Marini | 4 | 9 | 13 | 53 |
| | | | | |
| Goalies | W | L | T | GAA |
| B. Smith | 32 | 9 | 4 | 2.97 |
| R. Melanson | 22 | 7 | 6 | 3.23 |

# EDMONTON OILERS, 1984–88

The Edmonton Coliseum on 118th Avenue should have been called the O.K. Corral. During the 1980s, when gunslinger Wayne Gretzky ruled the West—as well as the East, North, and South—shootouts were typical, with most won by the Oilers. Gretzky and his band of crack marksmen shattered every standard for offense. From 1983–84 to 1987–88, the Oilers won four of five Stanley Cups, and only the worst kind of misfortune—a rare "own" goal in the 1986 playoffs—kept them from challenging Montreal's record of five titles running.

The Gretzky saga is a tale of puck tyranny. The NHL's all-time leader in goals, assists, and points, he won four of his 10 Art Ross Trophies during this five-year stretch—not to mention four of his nine Hart Trophies and three of his five Lester B. Pearson Awards. He added Conn Smythe Trophies in 1985 and 1987.

With the Great One at the helm, the Oilers became the first—and so far only—team ever to score 400 goals in a season, and they did it five years in a row (1981–86). Gretzky had a lot of help. Jari Kurri was a two-time Ross Trophy runner-up who set a record for goals by a right winger while playing on Gretzky's wing. Paul Coffey won two Norris Trophies while setting new standards for scoring by a defenseman. He was a Ross Trophy runner-up in 1983–84. And, of course, Mark Messier was the NHL's best second-line center. From 1983–84 to 1987–88, Gretzky, Kurri, Coffey, and Messier made the NHL's top-10 scoring list 14 times collectively. The Oilers were

*While Wayne Gretzky, Mark Messier, and others stole the headlines with goal-scoring, defensive ace Kevin Lowe (No. 4) provided muscle in front of Grant Fuhr.*

both willing and able to play wide-open "river" hockey, knowing goalies Grant Fuhr and Andy Moog would do whatever it took to win.

During this five-year span, the team scored 2,008 goals (more than five per game), though it didn't have the tightest defense, allowing nearly 3.75 goals per night. Yet the Oilers won nearly 70 percent of their games. In five seasons, they won 256 times. At home, where most teams had good reason to fear the inevitable Gretzky-led blitzkrieg, the Oilers were 146–32–22. Their road record (110–72–18) was better than many teams could manage on home ice.

The Oilers whipped the Islanders in the 1984 Stanley Cup Finals, just a year

after being swept by the Isles. The torch wasn't so much passed along as ripped from the weakening grip of an aging champ. The Oilers were bigger, stronger, faster, and hungrier. And it showed in the way Gretzky, Kurri, Coffey, Messier, and Fuhr attacked, thrashing the Isles by scores of 7–2, 7–2, and 5–2 in the last three games of the series, going for the jugular and finding it.

The Oilers dominated the 1985 playoffs, appearing almost to shrug off the mythological pressure of defending a Stanley Cup title. They didn't lose a game until Game 3 of the semifinals: After humiliating the Black Hawks by scores of 11–2 and 7–3, they suffered a brief letdown but ultimately cruised to

*Jari Kurri, aided by pinpoint passes from Wayne Gretzky, perfected the one-timer and became an awesome scoring threat.*

the Finals. In the title round, they spotted Philadelphia a win in Game 1 before winning four straight, outscoring the Flyers 20–10.

After taking the 1985–86 regular-season title, the Oilers were poised to continue their march to NHL immortality. After sweeping Vancouver in the prelims, they faced arch rival Calgary in a series that seesawed back and forth. With Game 7 on home ice, the Oilers had the perceived advantage, but after fighting back from 2–0 to tie the game in the middle stanza, they saw the roof cave in. Five minutes into the third period, Calgary dumped the puck behind the Oilers' net. Defenseman Steve Smith retreated to fire the puck back up ice. But it never got there. Instead, it struck the back of Grant Fuhr's leg and caromed into the Oilers' net, giving Calgary its

margin of victory and sending the shocked Oilers and their "dynasty" packing.

Humbled, the Oilers stormed through the 1987 playoffs. In the first three rounds, they lost only twice before facing the Flyers for the championship. In one of the great Stanley Cup Finals, the teams matched up perfectly. The Oilers attacked relentlessly while the defense-minded Flyers waited to counterpunch. The series lasted seven games and was tied 1–1 late in Game 7 when Edmonton's Glenn Anderson beat rookie goalie Ron Hextall to give Edmonton its third Cup.

To suggest the 1988 playoffs were a mere formality would disparage the other teams, but in retrospect the Oilers

*What made Wayne Gretzky great was his ability to analyze the play before others could figure it out, then capitalize.*

made it seem so, losing only twice in 18 games. In his final game with the team, Gretzky scored the Cup-clinching goal against the Bruins in the Finals—a five-game "sweep" that included a canceled game in Boston—and restored the Oilers to their place atop the NHL as four-time Stanley Cup champs.

Ironically, it was Gretzky's new team, the Los Angeles Kings, who dethroned Edmonton in the first round of the 1989 playoffs. But his contributions in Alberta had been mammoth.

### 1983–84 OILERS
### 57–18–5

| Skaters | G | A | PTS | PIM |
|---|---|---|---|---|
| W. Gretzky | 87 | 118 | 205 | 39 |
| P. Coffey | 40 | 86 | 126 | 104 |
| J. Kurri | 52 | 61 | 113 | 14 |
| M. Messier | 37 | 64 | 101 | 165 |
| G. Anderson | 54 | 45 | 99 | 65 |
| K. Linseman | 18 | 49 | 67 | 119 |
| P. Hughes | 27 | 28 | 55 | 61 |
| D. Hunter | 22 | 26 | 48 | 90 |
| K. Lowe | 4 | 42 | 46 | 59 |
| C. Huddy | 8 | 34 | 42 | 43 |
| R. Gregg | 13 | 27 | 40 | 56 |
| W. Lindstrom | 22 | 16 | 38 | 38 |
| K. McClelland | 10 | 24 | 34 | 189 |
| J. Pouzar | 13 | 19 | 32 | 44 |
| L. Fogolin | 5 | 16 | 21 | 125 |
| D. Lumley | 6 | 15 | 21 | 68 |
| D. Jackson | 8 | 12 | 20 | 120 |
| D. Semenko | 6 | 11 | 17 | 118 |
| P. Conacher | 2 | 8 | 10 | 31 |

| Goalies | W | L | T | GAA |
|---|---|---|---|---|
| G. Fuhr | 30 | 10 | 4 | 3.91 |
| A. Moog | 27 | 8 | 1 | 3.77 |

# Chapter 4

# 10 BEST PLAYOFF SERIES

What comprises a great playoff series? One that goes the limit. Games that enter sudden-death. Fierce competition, a miraculous comeback, and a stunning twist of fate. Each of these dramatic elements can be found in this section, which relives the 10 best playoff series ever played.

Above: *The Rangers defeated the Maple Leafs in the 1940 Stanley Cup Finals; three of their four wins came in sudden-death. Opposite page: Goalie Kelly Hrudey and Wayne Gretzky stunned the Great One's former team, the Edmonton Oilers, in the 1989 playoffs.*

# SENATORS 2, KLONDIKES 0

### 1905 STANLEY CUP CHALLENGE

Never in the history of Stanley Cup playoff action has a team traveled so far, at such great personal expense and over such difficult terrain, and come up so dreadfully short in its final test. Such was the fate of the courageous but vastly overmatched Dawson City Klondikes, who challenged the Ottawa Senators for the Stanley Cup in 1905. While the series lasted only two games, it must have seemed much longer for Dawson City, particularly its beleaguered goalie, 17-year-old Albert Forest, who surrendered enough goals to fill a net for 10 games.

The Senators, nicknamed the Silver Seven, were a powerful club with several scoring aces. One of which was Frank McGee, who despite having sight in only one eye managed to wheel around the ice in spectacular fashion and regularly place himself at or near the top of the scoring charts. In his heyday with Ottawa, McGee's cast of supporting players included Harvey Pulford, Harry "Rat" Westwick, Hamby Shore, Bones Allen, and the Gilmour Brothers—Billy, Dave, and Suddy. Alf Smith was a legitimate scoring threat who was equally prominent for his rough-and-ready style, which ensured that the Senators' best players would not be taken advantage of by opposing hooligans.

The Senators dominated Stanley Cup play for several years, winning a Cup in 1903 by beating the Rat Portage Thistles in the Finals and retaining it in 1904 by strafing Brandon in the title round. By 1905, they had departed the Canadian

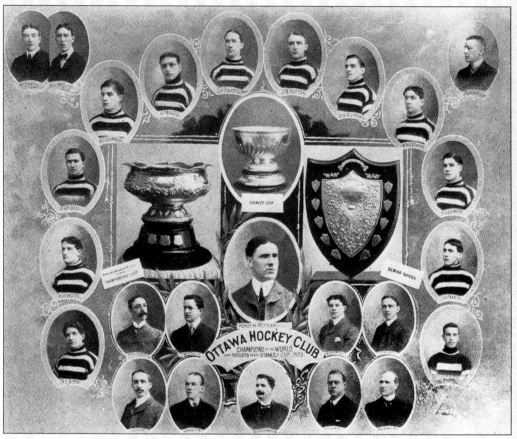

The Senators defeated nine consecutive challangers for the Stanley Cup, punctuated by their two-game, 32–4 humiliation of Dawson City in 1905.

Amateur Hockey League and joined the Federal Amateur Hockey League.

On December 12, 1904, three weeks before the start of its eight-game regular-season schedule, the FAHL held an executive meeting, during which it authorized the Silver Seven to accept a challenge from the Yukon champions from Dawson City for the Stanley Cup. The series was to be held during the season, in mid-January 1905. The Klondikes left

Dawson City on December 19 for the long journey. They eventually covered nearly 4,000 miles to reach Ottawa, paying their own way at a cost of nearly $3,000. The players' only hope for reimbursement was box-office receipts. Along the way, they crossed Canada by bicycle, train, boat, and even dogsled before reaching their destination.

The Senators played only one regular-season game, a 9–3 thrashing of the arch-rival Montreal Wanderers, before facing Dawson City. The Senators would lose only one game in 1905, to Brockville on January 23, their first game after the Dawson City series. Eventually, they would win the league title with seven wins in eight games. McGee led the league with 17 goals, tying Montreal's Jack Marshall, while Westwick (15) and Smith (13) followed.

On January 13, 1905, before a crowd of about 2,200, the Senators and Klondikes clashed in the first game of their Stanley Cup series. With precious few skilled players, the Yukonites had to scratch and claw for every chance. Former Ottawan Weldy Young was slated to join Dawson City, but business concerns kept him in the Yukon. His place on the roster was filled by Lorne Hanna, a Brandon star whose claim to fame was his role as Lester Patrick's first defense partner in Quebec. The only player in Dawson City's lineup with any Stanley Cup experience was forward Doc McLennan, who had skated for Queens University against the Montreal Victorias in the 1895 championship (in a losing cause). The Klondikes needed a superb effort from every member of their feisty group, but the challenge would prove too difficult.

**HARRY WESTWICK**

*The Senators' Harry Westwick, who began his career as a goalie, had his greatest game ever against Dawson City in Game 2, with five goals.*

In Game 1, McLennan managed a goal against Ottawa's spry netminder, Dave Finney, who would finish the 1905 season with an FAHL-best 2.40 goals-against average. But the Senators poured goal after goal past Al Forest. Smith led the assault, with and without the puck, as Ottawa netted nine goals. Smith alone had four. McGee was quiet, with just one goal. Dawson City added a second goal, but the Silver Seven skated to an almost effortless 9–2 victory.

Had they known what was yet to come, the Klondikes might never have made the arduous journey to Ontario. In Game 2, the Senators completely embarrassed their "guests," scoring 23 times. McGee went ballistic, scoring 14 goals of his own, a Stanley Cup record that has never been approached. While McGee was personally annihilating the Klondikes, his mates were chipping in with their own fun. Westwick's five-goal performance was hugely overshadowed, and Smith's paltry three-goal hat trick was practically mundane. Needless to say, Dawson City made a hasty retreat out of town.

As a postscript, Ottawa accepted another challenge from the Rat Portage Thistles in March 1905. After dropping the first game, the Senators won the next two amid accusations of ice-tampering, and they thus remained Stanley Cup champs for the third straight year.

*Frank McGee, who tallied 17 goals in the eight-game regular season, scored 15 times in the two Dawson City games.*

| 1905 STANLEY CUP CHALLENGE | | | |
| --- | --- | --- | --- |
| Game 1 | January 13 | @ Ottawa | Ottawa 9, Dawson City 2 |
| Game 2 | January 16 | @ Ottawa | Ottawa 23, Dawson City 2 |

# RANGERS 3, MAROONS 2

## 1928 STANLEY CUP FINALS

Four of the 10 teams comprising the NHL in 1927–28 had better records than the New York Rangers, who finished second in the American Division. Among those teams was the Montreal Maroons. But, as so often is the case in Stanley Cup history, the best regular-season team isn't always the one to raise the Cup.

When the playoffs began, the Rangers—led by the Bread Line of Frank Boucher and the Cook brothers, Bill and Bun—skated past Pittsburgh and Boston. The Maroons, led by Nels Stewart and goalie Clint Benedict, beat Ottawa and the Canadiens, winning Game 2 of their semifinal series against the Habs on a sudden-death OT goal from Russ Oatman, who had scored just seven goals all year.

The best-of-five Stanley Cup Finals featured a matchup of superior lines: the explosive Bread Line and the equally dangerous S Line of the Maroons (Stewart, Babe Siebert, and Hooley Smith). It was also a showdown of stellar goalies. At one end of the rink stood Benedict, a 34-year-old winner of three Stanley Cups with the Ottawa Senators and one with the Maroons, exhibiting the skills that earned him a 1.73 goals-against average in the regular season. At the other end was Rangers second-year man Lorne Chabot, 27, with an equally impressive 1.80 average, poised to prove he could outduel the old master. As if the Rangers didn't face a difficult enough challenge, the unavailability of ice at Madison Square Garden required that the series be played—in its entirety—at the Montreal Forum, giving the Maroons a distinct if quantitatively immeasurable edge.

With their home crowd encouraging them, the Maroons took Game 1 behind Benedict's 14th career playoff shutout. A goal by Red Dutton, the only playoff tally of his career, was all Montreal needed, although tiny Bill Phillips added an insurance marker with 14 minutes to play. The real drama didn't come until Game 2, however.

The scene unfolded when Stewart ripped one of his patented bullets into the left eye of Chabot, knocking the Rangers goalie out of the game. New York had only the one goalie and could find no substitute, so Rangers GM-coach Lester Patrick—a man respected throughout the hockey world as a master innovator and risk-taker—did the inconceivable. He inserted himself into the lineup as the Rangers' goalie. At 45 years of age, he strapped on the pads and took Chabot's place between the pipes. Bill Cook scored 30 seconds into the third period, and Patrick was nothing short of brilliant, stopping everything the Maroons threw at him—that is, until Stewart converted a Smith relay and fired the puck past Patrick to tie the game

*New York Mayor Jimmy Walker (center) congratulates coach Lester Patrick and the Cup-champion Rangers, who overcame the loss of their goalie to defeat the Maroons.*

with just 1:09 left in regulation time.

At first feeling he had failed his team, Patrick nevertheless persevered. In the heart-stopping sudden-death session, his star player, Boucher, bailed him out with the game-winning goal. This not only tied the series but also bought the Rangers a much-needed opportunity to regroup.

Ever the wizard of personnel management, Patrick hung up his goalie pads while the sports world reveled in his Herculean audacity, and he went about finding a *real* goalie. The answer to his problem came in the form of Joe Miller, who had spent the recent season tending goal for the arch-rival New York Americans. In the only playoff action of his brief career, Miller took on the task of filling Chabot's sizable skates and making sure the Rangers' season didn't go up in smoke.

Game 3, with Miller in goal, featured the final playoff shutout of Benedict's Hall of Fame career, a 2–0 affair decided by Stewart midway through the middle period, with Siebert adding late insurance. But if the Rangers were down, they were certainly not out. In Game 4, it was Miller's turn to shine. While the Maroons went for the Cup-winning vic-

*In Game 2, goalie Lorne Chabot was injured, forcing 45-year-old Lester Patrick into the nets.*

tory, Miller stopped every shot they could muster. When Boucher slipped the puck past Benedict at 13:13 of period two, the Rangers had their margin of victory, forcing the series to a climactic fifth game.

If there had been a vote to determine who was the series' biggest hero, the leading candidates would have been Patrick, Miller, and Boucher. Patrick's Game 2 exploits saved New York from devastation, while Miller plugged a giant hole laudably. But it was Boucher who scored just 5:32 into Game 5 to put the Rangers on a winning path. He sealed the victory—and the Stanley Cup—with his second goal early in the third period, writing a triumphant final chapter to one of the most amazing Stanley Cup tales ever told.

*A heroic effort by Montreal goalie Clint Benedict, who finished with a 0.89 playoff GAA, went for naught.*

| 1928 STANLEY CUP FINALS | | | | |
|---|---|---|---|---|
| Game 1 | April 5 | @Montreal | Montreal 2, New York 0 | GWG Dutton |
| Game 2 | April 7 | @Montreal | New York 2, Montreal 1 (OT) | GWG Boucher |
| Game 3 | April 10 | @Montreal | Montreal 2, New York 0 | GWG Stewart |
| Game 4 | April 12 | @Montreal | New York 1, Montreal 0 | GWG Boucher |
| Game 5 | April 14 | @Montreal | New York 2, Montreal 1 | GWG Boucher |

# MAPLE LEAFS 3, BRUINS 2

## 1933 STANLEY CUP SEMIFINALS

For everyone but the New York Rangers and their loyal fans, the 1933 Stanley Cup Finals were anticlimactic, particularly coming on the heels of one of the most thrilling semifinal series ever played, between Boston and Toronto. This five-game clash featured four overtime games, with the finale going into six sudden-death periods before a winner emerged. When compared to the almost-mechanical defoliation of the Leafs by New York in the Finals, the Toronto-Boston series was a proving ground for heroes, a setting where Stanley Cup action lived up to its reputation for bringing out the best in players.

Bolstered by the Kid Line of Joe Primeau, Busher Jackson, and Charlie Conacher, the Leafs won 24 games in 1932–33. The Bruins, with Nels Stewart up front, Eddie Shore on defense, and Vezina Trophy goaltender Tiny Thompson in nets, won 25. Thompson led the NHL in victories (25), shutouts (11), and goals-against average (1.83).

As the semifinals began, historians did not miss the irony of Leafs goalie Lorne Chabot standing between Boston and a shot at the Stanley Cup. In the 1928 Finals, while playing for the Rangers, Chabot was knocked out of Game 2 by Stewart, then a Montreal Maroon. New York won the Cup without Chabot. Now, it seemed, Chabot was back to haunt Stewart—or was it to be the other way around? In this best-of-five series, the team with the hotter goaltender would have the edge.

Little could anyone imagine that both Chabot and Thompson would blow the mercury out of the thermometer with their spectacular play. In Game 1 at Boston Garden, the Bruins and Maple Leafs traded goals and quit after 60 minutes of play tied 1–1. Chabot and Thompson were brilliant, each man keeping his team in the game. The first "break" of the series came in the 15th

*In Game 5 of the series, Leafs goalie Lorne Chabot held Boston scoreless for more than eight periods of play.*

minute of sudden-death, when Marty Barry—the Bruins' leading regular-season goal-scorer (24)—beat Chabot to secure the win.

The Leafs were a resilient team, however, and Chabot was at the top of his game as the teams rejoined the battle three nights later. Thompson, on the other hand, was equally stingy, and once more the teams rested after three periods without a winner. This night, regulation ended at 0–0. But Toronto's Jackson, whose 27 regular-season tallies had ranked for the league lead, delivered the Leafs to victory when he found a tiny chink in Thompson's armor at 15:03 of sudden-death, tying the series 1–1.

Heading to Toronto for the next three games, the Leafs were brimming with confidence, even though the series so far had proven to be emotionally and physically exhausting. Were it not for the goalies, either of the first two games could have ended with lopsided scores—such was the nature of the talent on both sides.

The Bruins were unfazed by the partisan support shown the Leafs in Game 3. After all, they had arguably the most intense player in hockey, Shore, on their side. Nothing ever got to Shore. After the teams completed regulation play tied 1–1, it was Shore who engineered a hard-fought victory when he slipped a shot past Chabot 4:23 into OT, ending the third straight sudden-death game. Despite home-ice advantage and the stellar play of Chabot, Toronto suddenly found itself on the brink of elimination.

Leafs coach Dick Irvin was a harsh disciplinarian, severe in temperament, pitiless in his judgments. But he was also a superior motivator. If anyone could get the Leafs to focus on the challenge at hand, he could. After three defensive

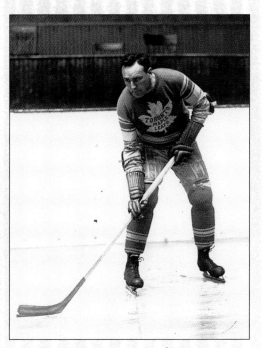

*In Game 5, part-time Leaf Ken Doraty ended the second-longest NHL game ever, scoring at 4:46 into the sixth OT.*

gems, Game 4 was proverbial river hockey, with the teams combining for eight goals—one more than they'd scored collectively in the first three games. The Leafs rolled to a decisive 5–3 win, knotting the series at 2–2 and giving their goalie, Chabot, one more chance to be a hero.

Game 5 was one for the ages. Scoreless after regulation, the teams battled back and forth through one sudden-death period and then another . . . and another . . . and another. Chabot and Thompson turned aside everything the weary shooters could produce. Through five full sudden-death periods, the teams dueled,

with the ice deteriorating steadily and the players nearing exhaustion.

Before the season began, Toronto had signed tiny Ken Doraty, a winger of minor repute. Doraty had scored just five goals in 38 games in 1932–33. In the playoffs, however, he equaled that total. His most important tally came 4:46 into the sixth period of sudden-death, when he broke Thompson's heart and ended the longest game in NHL history— 164 minutes and 46 seconds.

*Game 4 notwithstanding, Boston goalie Tiny Thompson allowed just four goals in 21 periods of play during the series.*

## 1933 STANLEY CUP SEMIFINALS

| Game 1 | March 25 | @Boston | Boston 2, Toronto 1 (OT) | GWG Barry |
| Game 2 | March 28 | @Boston | Toronto 1, Boston 0 (OT) | GWG Jackson |
| Game 3 | March 30 | @Toronto | Boston 2, Toronto 1 (OT) | GWG Shore |
| Game 4 | April 1 | @Toronto | Toronto 5, Boston 3 | GWG Jackson |
| Game 5 | April 3 | @Toronto | Toronto 1, Boston 0 (6OT) | GWG Doraty |

# RANGERS 4, MAPLE LEAFS 2

## 1940 STANLEY CUP FINALS

History has shown that without good—make that *great*—goaltending, a team cannot win a championship. In 1940, two of the best goaltenders in the NHL carried their teams to the Stanley Cup Finals for a thrilling confrontation.

New York Rangers goalie Dave Kerr was coming off a brilliant year in which he had led the league in shutouts (eight) and goals-against average (1.60), earning his only Vezina Trophy. At 30, Kerr was at the peak of his career. Meanwhile, the Toronto Maple Leafs' husky netminder, Turk Broda, playing in only the fourth season of his 14-year career, was a mere 12 months away from winning his first Vezina Trophy (1941).

*The Rangers won this battle on the ice and in the alley, taking Game 2 of the Finals at Madison Square Garden 6–2.*

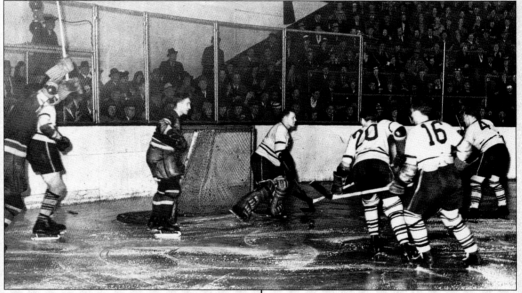

The Rangers and Leafs finished the regular season second and third, respectively, behind the Boston Bruins. While the Leafs eliminated Chicago and Detroit in total-goals series, the Rangers

*Turk Broda posted a 1.90 GAA in the 1940 playoffs, but this goal, by Bryan Hextall, won the Cup for New York.*

and Bruins met in a best-of-seven semifinal. With Kerr holding the fort against Boston's formidable Kraut Line, the Rangers upset the Bruins in six games. Kerr was the difference, posting shutouts in Games 1, 4, and 5.

During the regular season, the Rangers had won four of their eight meetings with the Leafs, losing just once. Led by Bryan Hextall, Neil Colville, and fiery Phil Watson, New York had a decided edge in scoring. Toronto was rugged, with three of the NHL's top five penalty leaders in its lineup (Red Horner, Murph Chamberlain, and Jack Church), but they didn't scare anyone offensively. Gordie Drillon led the team with 21 goals. Syl Apps was next with just 13.

As the Finals began, the Rangers jumped ahead, taking Game 1 at Madison Square Garden on Alf Pike's sudden-death winner. Two nights later, they bombed the Leafs 6–2. Hextall fired a hat trick against Broda. With the circus invading Manhattan for its annual visit, the series switched to Toronto for its duration, eliminating the Rangers' home-ice advantage. It didn't take long for the Leafs to exploit the change in scenery.

Before the home fans, Toronto overcame a first-period goal by Watson with a pair of late tallies from Drillon and rookie Hank Goldup to win Game 3 2–1. Broda, who had four shutouts during the regular season, stood the Rangers on their ears in Game 4, stopping every shot they unleashed. Journeyman Gus Marker scored his only goal of the playoffs with 40 seconds left in the first period, and the Leafs rolled to a surprising 3–0 win to tie the series.

But the Rangers were not a team prone to fits of panic. Neil Colville, playing with kid brother Mac and left winger Alex Shibicky, scored 12 minutes into Game 5 before Apps answered in the middle period. After a scoreless third period, the game went into sudden-death overtime. Once more, Kerr and Broda were brick walls. Nothing got through them. When no winner was declared following the first period of overtime, a second session was staged. Not until the midway point in the period did the tide finally turn, when Neil Colville relayed the puck to Muzz Patrick (son of GM

Lester Patrick), who found a small opening and fired the winning goal past Broda, putting his team within one victory of the Stanley Cup.

*Goalie Davey Kerr, flanked by Bryan Hextall (left) and coach Frank Boucher, won three OT games in the Finals.*

But if they were outmanned and outclassed offensively, the Leafs proved beyond doubt that they did not lack heart. Though they teetered perilously on the brink of extinction, they refused to submit to the Rangers' will. In Game 6, the Leafs worked methodically, shutting down the Rangers' attack and patiently waiting for their chance to counter. Over the first 25 minutes of action, they picked away at the Rangers and forged a 2–0 lead on goals from Apps and Nick Metz. Following the second period, the Blueshirts were visited in their dressing room by GM Patrick, who instructed them, effectively, to quit fooling around and get busy. By some accounts, Patrick had already arranged a victory party in Toronto and was not about to leave town with egg on his face.

Thus inspired, the Rangers tied the game with goals from Neil Colville and Pike and forced one last foray into overtime. Hextall, who had led the league in goals (24), emerged as the hero of the night when his line—with Watson and Dutch Hiller—attacked in the first two minutes of OT. In a neat three-way passing play, Hiller dished to Watson, who found Hextall alone. Broda could not stop Hextall's Cup-winning goal, and the Broadway Blueshirts wrested their third Stanley Cup.

| 1940 STANLEY CUP FINALS | | | | |
|---|---|---|---|---|
| Game 1 | April 2 | @New York | New York 2, Toronto 1 (OT) | GWG Pike |
| Game 2 | April 3 | @New York | New York 6, Toronto 2 | GWG Hextall |
| Game 3 | April 6 | @Toronto | Toronto 2, New York 1 | GWG Goldup |
| Game 4 | April 9 | @Toronto | Toronto 3, New York 0 | GWG Marker |
| Game 5 | April 11 | @Toronto | New York 2, Toronto 1 (2OT) | GWG Patrick |
| Game 6 | April 13 | @Toronto | New York 3, Toronto 2 (OT) | GWG Hextall |

# MAPLE LEAFS 4, RED WINGS 3

## 1942 STANLEY CUP FINALS

**W**hether a glass is half empty or half full is a question of perspective and attitude. Some will argue that the 1942 Red Wings were guilty of the biggest choke job in the history of Stanley Cup hockey. Others, equally sure, will insist the 1942 Maple Leafs simply staged the greatest playoff comeback of all time. Either way, the 1942 Stanley Cup Finals were a hotbed of high drama and intrigue as Detroit took a seemingly overwhelming advantage—up three games to none in the best-of-seven series—and squandered it while Toronto lost battle after battle before finally winning the war.

In their defense, the Red Wings didn't bring huge expectations into the postseason. After five years of finishing no better than third in the standings (three times placing fifth), they backed into the playoffs—with a 19–25–4 record—by virtue of the league's generous playoff format, which allowed six of seven teams to participate. Conversely, Toronto had very high hopes after a second-place finish, not to mention six trips to the Finals in the previous nine years. Yet the Leafs were a decade removed from their last Stanley Cup (1932), and the natives were restless.

Detroit, led by Don Grosso, began its unlikely march by first skating past Montreal in the best-of-three quarterfinals. Then as Toronto, led by Syl Apps and Gordie Drillon, upset the Rangers in their best-of-seven semifinal, Detroit gathered momentum with a two-game sweep of the Bruins. Still a heavy underdog, the Red Wings invaded Maple Leaf Gardens on April 4, 1942, to fight for the Stanley Cup.

*Pete Langelle (No. 8), author of just five career playoff goals, netted this 1942 Cup-winner as Toronto beat Detroit 3–1 in Game 7.*

Aware of his team's unfavorable odds, Detroit coach Jack Adams instructed his players to thwart Toronto's speed by playing "dump and chase" hockey, firing the puck deep and hustling to retrieve it. Taking its enemies by surprise, Detroit stunned the Leafs 3–2 in Game 1, with two goals from Grosso (who notched eight of his 14 career playoff goals in 1942). Grosso scored twice in Game 2, and the Leafs—much to the disgust of their coach, Hap Day—lost 4–2 and trailed two games to none heading to Detroit. Toronto's bad situation only got worse when the Red Wings banged five goals past Turk Broda, usually known as a top-drawer "money" goalie, and edged ever closer to a Stanley Cup triumph.

Some might say it was time for Toronto to panic; others would suggest the Leafs' difficult circumstances simply required extreme measures. In any event, coach Day yanked two of his stars—Drillon and Bucko McDonald—from the lineup in Game 4 and prayed the shakeup would work. It did. Trailing 2–0 in the second period, the Leafs scored twice in each of the next two periods to stave off elimination with a 4–3 win. Meanwhile, Detroit coach Adams became embroiled with referee Mel Harwood over perceived noncalls and—after attempting to

*Detroit coach Jack Adams was suspended for attacking ref Mel Harwood.*

physically assault the official—was suspended by league President Clarence Campbell for the rest of the playoffs.

Back home for Game 5, the Leafs still faced a huge task. No team in the history of the NHL had ever trailed three games to none in a series and come back to win. Nevertheless, they mounted an assault that seemed to crush Detroit's spirit. Drillon's replacement, Don Metz, notched three goals and two assists, Apps had two goals and three assists, and Nick Metz and Wally Stanowski each had a goal and two assists. The Leafs were ahead 9–1 before the Wings netted a pair of late goals. In Toronto, hope was alive. In Detroit, where Game 6 was scheduled, blood ran cold.

Dazed from their reversal of fortune, the Red Wings suffered a total collapse on home ice. Despite a valiant assault in the first period, the Wings could not squeeze the puck past Broda, who had regained his form and was surrendering nothing. Failing to pierce the armor of Toronto's great goalie, the Wings faded. Don Metz scored midway through the second period, and Broda notched his fifth career playoff shutout, as the Leafs won 3–0 to tie the series—with the deciding game in Toronto.

Syd Howe gave the Red Wings a glimmer of hope in Game 7 when he scored early in the second period to break a scoreless tie. But the Leafs had destiny on their side. Before the biggest crowd ever to watch an NHL game, counted at 16,240, the Leafs tied the game on Sweeney Schriner's goal early in the third period, then took the lead when Pete Langelle jumped on a rebound and rammed the game-winner past Detroit goalie Johnny Mowers—the final goal of Langelle's short career. Schriner scored a late goal, and the greatest comeback—or worst collapse—was complete.

### 1942 STANLEY CUP FINALS

| Game 1 | April 4 | @Toronto | Detroit 3, Toronto 2 | GWG Grosso |
| Game 2 | April 7 | @Toronto | Detroit 4, Toronto 2 | GWG Grosso |
| Game 3 | April 9 | @Detroit | Detroit 5, Toronto 2 | GWG McCreavy |
| Game 4 | April 12 | @Detroit | Toronto 4, Detroit 3 | GWG N. Metz |
| Game 5 | April 14 | @Toronto | Toronto 9, Detroit 3 | GWG Schriner |
| Game 6 | April 16 | @Detroit | Toronto 3, Detroit 0 | GWG D. Metz |
| Game 7 | April 18 | @Toronto | Toronto 3, Detroit 1 | GWG Langelle |

# MAPLE LEAFS 4, CANADIENS 1

## 1951 STANLEY CUP FINALS

When is a five-game series romp *not* a five-game series romp? When all five games are decided in sudden-death overtime. When every match hurls you back and forth on that one-of-a-kind emotional roller-coaster ride where one mistake, one momentary lapse, can mean everything. In 1951, Montreal and Toronto clashed in the Stanley Cup Finals and engaged in one of the most intense playoff series in history.

The Leafs were a better team than Montreal, having recently completed a far superior regular season, with 41 wins compared to the Canadiens' 25. Toronto had Vezina Trophy goalie Al Rollins ably succeeding Turk Broda, who was near his retirement, and Max Bentley leading the attack. The Habs, meanwhile, had the game's second-best goal-scorer, Maurice Richard, whose 42 tallies trailed only Gordie Howe's 43. The Maple Leafs had a comparatively easy road to the Finals, dispatching Boston four games to one in the semifinals. Meanwhile, the Canadiens shocked the first-place Red Wings in the semis, winning three of six games in Detroit.

In the championship series, it was immediately and abundantly clear that goals would be rare and valuable. A seesaw battle through two periods of Game 1 resulted in a 2–2 tie that held through regulation. Sid Smith and Tod Sloan scored for the Leafs, while Richard and tiny Paul Masnick tallied for Montreal.

*Leafs captain Ted Kennedy won Game 3 of the 1951 Finals when he beat Gerry McNeil in the fifth minute of overtime.*

Broda, who had taken Toronto past Boston, started in goal and was brilliant. His opposite number, rookie Gerry McNeil, played valiantly while Canadiens fans quietly lamented the early retirement of Bill Durnan, who had taken them to Cups in 1944 and 1946. In sudden-death, Sloan fed Smith for the game-winner at 5:51, giving Toronto the early advantage.

Game 2 did not lack for thrills. A pitched battle saw Masnick score in the first period and his diminutive mate, Billy Reay, extend the Habs to 2–0. Smith halved the lead late in the second period. Teeder Kennedy knotted the score at 2–2 in the third period, forcing another overtime. On this night, Rocket Richard, whose six playoff OT winners are the most ever, delivered. Richard, who had scored two OT goals in the 1951 semifinals against Detroit, ended it quickly, beating Broda just 2:55 into the extra session. This sent the series home even-up and gave Montreal home-ice advantage.

The usual suspects were on hand for the drama in Game 3, although Toronto coach Joe Primeau swapped Rollins for Broda in goal. Richard continued his torrid scoring when he put the Canadiens ahead just 2:18 into the game. But Toronto answered when Smith scored in the middle session. The game remained deadlocked for the rest of regulation. Kennedy collected the only sudden-death goal of his career, 4:47 into the extra frame, as the Leafs regained control of the series, if tenuously.

Game 4 saw the series' goal-scoring aces, Smith and Richard, trade first-period goals. Smith scored 38 seconds into the game, but the Canadiens found their balance and scratched back, tying it late in the session. Howie Meeker, a former rookie of the year whose dismal, injury-plagued season resulted in only six goals, converted Harry Watson's set-up in the second period, giving Toronto the lead. Rollins was a brick wall as he denied Montreal shot after shot. But the Canadiens refused to quit. And at 13:49 of the third period, Richard set up his old Punch Line center, Elmer Lach, who scored to tie the game. In the fourth straight sudden-death game, Watson scored to give the Leafs a three-games-to-one advantage, with Game 5 back in Toronto.

In the fifth matchup, the indomitable Richard skated around Leafs defenseman Jim Thompson and scored midway through the second period following a tense, scoreless first stanza. Just over three minutes later, however, Toronto's Sloan answered. In the third period, Paul Meger knocked home the rebound of a Doug Harvey point shot to give Montreal another lead.

Less than a minute remained on the clock when Kennedy, the best faceoff man in the game, won a draw and relayed the puck to Bentley, who found Smith for a shot on goal. Parked alone beside Montreal's goal, Sloan captured the rebound and scored the tying goal with just 32 seconds left. Amazingly, there would be a fifth overtime.

Revived, the Leafs attacked in the extra period, knowing they had to keep the puck from Richard. Then, after a goalmouth scramble at McNeil's feet, the puck skittered out toward the point, where defenseman Bill Barilko was stationed. He chanced diving for the loose puck and managed to launch a hard, accurate shot past McNeil's outstretched glove hand, into the net, ending the thrilling series.

Wild jubilation filled the arena as Toronto celebrated its eighth Stanley Cup. However, sadness would soon follow when Barilko, just 24, was killed later that summer in a plane crash.

*Toronto defenseman Bill Barilko (No. 5) abandoned his left point to charge in for a rebound, resulting in the Game 5 overtime goal that won the 1951 Stanley Cup.*

### 1951 STANLEY CUP FINALS

| Game | Date | Location | Result | GWG |
|---|---|---|---|---|
| Game 1 | April 11 | @Toronto | Toronto 3, Montreal 2 (OT) | GWG Smith |
| Game 2 | April 14 | @Toronto | Montreal 3, Toronto 2 (OT) | GWG M. Richard |
| Game 3 | April 17 | @Montreal | Toronto 2, Montreal 1 (OT) | GWG Kennedy |
| Game 4 | April 19 | @Montreal | Toronto 3, Montreal 2 (OT) | GWG Watson |
| Game 5 | April 21 | @Toronto | Toronto 3, Montreal 2 (OT) | GWG Barilko |

## ISLANDERS 4, PENGUINS 3

### 1975 STANLEY CUP QUARTERFINALS

The 1975 playoffs were only three games old before the first major upset occurred. In New York, the Rangers and Islanders clashed in the opening round, with the Rangers owning home-ice advantage in the best-of-three series. But after losing Game 1 at the Garden and winning Game 2 on Long Island, the Rangers became victims of one of the biggest shocks in New York sports history when J. P. Parise scored 11 seconds into sudden-death of Game 3 to propel the Islanders to the Cup quarterfinals.

The 4–3 OT win over the Rangers wasn't just a humiliating defeat for the favored Blueshirts, it was the dawn of a new era of play-off contention for the Islanders. In the fortnight that followed, this Islanders squad established itself as a team of historic proportions, one to be reckoned with for a long time.

The Isles' next foe was the Pittsburgh Penguins, stocked with snipers. Jean Pronovost led with 43 goals, followed by Rick Kehoe (32), former Ranger Vic Hadfield (31), and Pierre Larouche (31). The Penguins were at their best when they scored early, then played "Katy Bar the Door" the rest of the way. This was the very tactic they attempted against the Isles.

Bolstered by their Davidian victory over the Goliaths from Broadway, the Islanders skated into Pittsburgh on April 13, 1975, as a closely knit group

playing well together, rarely getting flustered. But then the Penguins scored just two minutes into Game 1—and led 3–1 by the end of the first period. The Isles closed to 3–2, but Pittsburgh scored

*Rookie Glenn "Chico" Resch, who didn't get to start until Game 4, won the last four games while yielding just four goals.*

twice more and won 5–4, negating a two-goal show by Parise in the final 20 minutes of play.

Denis Potvin, the Islanders' hard-hitting, high-scoring leader, turned up lame in Game 2 with a painful groin injury. He played, but without his usual presence, and after a scoreless first period Pronovost put Pittsburgh up just 24 seconds into the second period. Lowell MacDonald, one of Pittsburgh's nine 20-goal scorers, added two goals. New York's Clark Gillies spoiled Gary Inness's shutout bid with a late goal, but it was small consolation in a 3–1 loss.

In Game 3, for the third time in the series, the Islanders fell behind 3–0 before getting on track. The result was a 6–4 loss and imminent ruin. When the Rangers had been eliminated, Derek Sanderson bitterly predicted that the Islanders wouldn't win another playoff game. After dropping Game 3 to Pittsburgh, the Isles were in deep trouble indeed.

Isles coach Al Arbour swallowed hard and yanked goalie Billy Smith in favor of rookie netminder Glenn "Chico" Resch. It was a move that eventually turned the series around. In Game 4, the Isles' defense held Pittsburgh to 28 shots, and Andy St. Laurent ended Pittsburgh's first-goal reign by scoring just 3:18 into play. Gillies and Parise scored 39 seconds apart in the third period, and New York won 3–1 to avoid the sweep.

On April 22, the teams returned to Pittsburgh, where the Pens had lost only one of their previous 33 home games. The Isles had their backs against the proverbial wall, but they responded with a pair of goals in the first 5:24 of play, from Billy Harris and Ralph Stewart. The Penguins went for the jugular and outshot the Isles 38–19, but Resch was magnificent in goal, carrying his team to a 4–2 nail-biting win. For the first time, there were whispers about the 1942 Toronto Maple Leafs, who had won four consecutive games over Detroit after trailing three games to none in the Finals.

For Game 6 in New York, Arbour made another major shift, putting Stewart on the Gillies-Harris line in Bob Bourne's spot. After a scoreless first period, Stewart scored. Larouche answered back 49 seconds later, but the Isles moved ahead once more when super-pest Garry Howatt scored a rare goal. Ed Westfall and Jude Drouin scored empty-net goals as New York cruised 4–1 and sent the series back to Pittsburgh.

The most intense contest of the series, Game 7 remained scoreless through two periods. Twice on one shift, Resch used

his facemask to stop certain goals from Pronovost and Syl Apps Jr. (Ironically, Apps's father was a member of the

*Known more for fighting than scoring, New York's Garry Howatt notched a pivotal goal against Gary Inness in Game 6.*

1942 Leafs who had stunned the Red Wings.) Late in the third period, veteran Islander defenseman Bert Marshall pinched in at the point and trapped the puck before it skittered out of the zone. After advancing it along the boards, he dished a neat cross-ice pass to captain Westfall, who was cruising in the high slot. A wily soldier in his own right, Westfall corralled the puck, calmly put a deke on goalie Inness, and lifted a backhander into the open net. It was the only goal of the game and it came with just 5:18 left to play. Resch completed the shutout and the ultimate comeback, and the Cinderella Islanders advanced to the Stanley Cup semifinals—in only their first year of playoff competition.

| 1975 STANLEY CUP QUARTERFINALS | | | | | |
|---|---|---|---|---|---|
| Game 1 | April 13 | @Pittsburgh | Penguins 5 Islanders 4 | GWG | Burrows |
| Game 2 | April 15 | @Pittsburgh | Penguins 3 Islanders 1 | GWG | MacDonald |
| Game 3 | April 17 | @New York | Penguins 6 Islanders 4 | GWG | Apps |
| Game 4 | April 20 | @New York | Islanders 3 Penguins 1 | GWG | Gillies |
| Game 5 | April 22 | @Pittsburgh | Islanders 4 Penguins 2 | GWG | Westfall |
| Game 6 | April 24 | @New York | Islanders 4 Penguins 1 | GWG | Howatt |
| Game 7 | April 26 | @Pittsburgh | Islanders 1 Penguins 0 | GWG | Westfall |

# CANADIENS 4, BRUINS 3

## 1979 STANLEY CUP SEMIFINALS

Prior to 1979, Montreal and Boston had met in the Stanley Cup playoffs a total of 17 times, with the Habs holding a resounding 15–2 edge. In 84 playoff games, Montreal had won 58 times. In 1977 and 1978, Montreal had beaten Boston in the Stanley Cup Finals, sweeping the Bruins in 1977 and erasing the Bruins in six games in 1978. In 1979, the Habs were three-time reigning Stanley Cup champs, playing the high-octane hockey that had earned their Flying Frenchmen reputation. But these Bruins were a hard-hitting group, with eight players scoring 20 or more goals.

*Coach Don Cherry's blunder in Game 7 (too many men on the ice) cost Boston the series.*

Montreal hosted the first two games of the series. The Canadiens opened Game 1 by spotting Boston a 2–1 lead before taking command in the final 20 minutes. "Lucky" Pierre Larouche, a seldom-used one-time 50-goal scorer, combined with hard-nosed Doug Risebrough on the game-winner at 12:17. Boston's speedy Rick Middleton had a goal disallowed in the third period, and the Habs held on for a 4–2 win.

In Game 2, Boston built a 2–0 lead in the second period before Stan Jonathan tangled with Risebrough and both players were penalized four minutes. Skating four-on-four, Boston's Bobby Schmautz was whistled for tripping. Jacques Lemaire scored on the power play to cut Boston's lead, and just 30 seconds later Montreal's Bob Gainey beat Gerry Cheevers to tie the game. Mario Tremblay, a grinder, scored less than a minute after Gainey's goal, giving Montreal a three-goal outburst in 1:24. En route to a 5–2 win, the Habs beat Cheevers five times on 20 shots.

Licking their wounds and wondering if they'd ever beat Montreal again, the Bruins returned to Boston for Games 3 and 4. Coach Don Cherry replaced Cheevers with Gilles Gilbert, and in the opening minutes of play Gilbert stoned Lemaire and Serge Savard on "sure" goals, then kicked aside a breakaway attempt from Risebrough. Meanwhile, the Bruins intensified their forechecking and held Montreal to just 18 shots. Boston's first-period lead held up until Larry Robinson solved Gilbert with 6:37 left in the game.

As the clock wound down, Boston's Brad Park and Jean Ratelle attacked. Park carried in, looking for Ratelle on the give-and-go, but Ratelle was covered. Park's defense partner, Mike Milbury, had joined the play but was also covered. So Park cut to the middle and ripped a low shot to Ken Dryden's stick side.

Dryden waved but missed, and the Bruins had their margin of victory.

At 38 years of age, Ratelle showed his skill and elegance in Game 4 when he put the Bruins ahead in the first period and added a second-period marker to tie the match. The Bruins led 3–2 with 2:06 to play when Guy Lapointe scored to force overtime. Knowing Montreal had the advantage of youth and speed, Boston struggled to end the game quickly. Middleton and Ratelle attacked in the fourth minute of sudden-death, and the crafty winger lifted a perfect pass to

*Jean Ratelle was spectacular in Game 4, scoring in the first, second, and fourth periods to defeat Montreal 4–3.*

Ratelle in the slot. Dryden backed in rather than coming out to challenge, and Ratelle sneaked a backhander past the goalie to complete the hat trick and draw the series even at two games apiece.

Undaunted, Montreal's superb firepower dominated Game 5 at home, as the Habs outshot Boston 40–22. Bolstered by the return of sniper Steve Shutt, out for two weeks with a bad knee, the Canadiens built a 5–0 lead before Boston's pain-ridden captain, Wayne Cashman, scored in the final moments. Meanwhile, hostilities were renewed between Terry O'Reilly and Risebrough, who fought twice with Risebrough suffering a broken nose.

Facing elimination in Game 6, the Bruins took advantage of the small ice surface at Boston Garden and smothered Montreal's high-speed attack. A busy first period ended 2–2, with Jonathan and Don Marcotte negating goals by Pierre Mondou and Robinson. Gilbert continued to shine, stopping Guy Lafleur and Mark Napier point-blank. Despite a shoulder harness, Jonathan emerged as a hero with his first-ever playoff hat trick, losing two teeth while crashing the net to score in the third period. Outshot 27–23, the Bruins nevertheless romped 5–2 to stay alive.

Game 7 was a nail-biter from the opening draw. Boston built a 3–1 lead on

*Gilles Gilbert's courageous performance gave the Bruins a fighting chance.*

a goal from Middleton and two from Cashman, but Montreal scored twice to even it at 3–3. Middleton's second goal put the Bruins up with 3:59 to play, but a crucial bench minor for too many men on the ice—for which Cherry appropriately accepted blame—gave Montreal a power play. With only 1:14 to play, Lafleur, who had set up the two earlier goals, fired a rocket from the right-wing boards, beating Gilbert and sending the game to OT. Ultimately, the beleaguered Bruins could not keep pace with Montreal's quicker skaters in the sudden-death session. The end came at 9:33, when Tremblay fed Yvon Lambert, alone at the side of Boston's net, for the game-winner, sending the Canadiens to the Stanley Cup Finals (where they would beat the Rangers in five) and once

again breaking the hearts of the ill-fated Bruins.

*Guy Lafleur scored 10 goals in the 1979 playoffs, none bigger than the one that tied Game 7 with a mere 1:14 to play.*

## 1979 STANLEY CUP SEMIFINALS

| | | | | |
|---|---|---|---|---|
| Game 1 | April 26 | @Montreal | Montreal 4, Boston 2 | GWG Larouche |
| Game 2 | Apirl 28 | @Montreal | Montreal 5, Boston 2 | GWG Tremblay |
| Game 3 | May 1 | @Boston | Boston 2, Montreal 1 | GWG Park |
| Game 4 | May 3 | @Boston | Boston 4, Montreal 3 (OT) | GWG Ratelle |
| Game 5 | May 5 | @Montreal | Montreal 5, Boston 1 | GWG Lafleur |
| Game 6 | May 8 | @Boston | Boston 5, Montreal 2 | GWG Cashman |
| Game 7 | May 10 | @Montreal | Montreal 5, Boston 4 (OT) | GWG Lambert |

# KINGS 4, OILERS 3

## 1989 SMYTHE DIVISION SEMIFINALS

Glen Sather, GM of the Edmonton Oilers, has never been anyone's fool. But he watched a giant sports no-no go down on August 9, 1988, when Oiler legend Wayne Gretzky was traded to the Los Angeles Kings. You never trade a star to a division rival; it always backfires. In 1988–89, Gretzky carried the Kings from 18th place (where they finished in 1987–88) to fourth overall. Moreover, as the 1989 playoffs commenced, Gretzky and the Kings, second in the Smythe Division, were poised to challenge the defending NHL champion Oilers, third in the division, in the opening round.

Gretzky had given the Kings the NHL's top-rated offense—an average of 4.70 goals a game. But without patience, discipline, and goaltending, their chances against Edmonton were slim. Conversely, the Gretzky-less Oilers had their poorest record since 1980–81, and Jimmy Carson, acquired in the Gretzky deal, was a disappointment.

The Kings hosted the first two games in Hollywood, and they jumped out to a quick lead when journeyman Chris Kontos scored just 1:01 into play. But even after taking a 3–2 lead in the third period, the nervous, inexperienced Kings could not hold off their wily foes. In the final four minutes, Edmonton's Esa Tikkanen and Craig Simpson beat Kelly

Hrudey, forging a 4–3 comeback win to draw first blood.

Kontos gave L.A. another first-period lead in Game 2, and the Kings poured three goals past Grant Fuhr in the middle period en route to a 5–2 series-tying win. Gretzky and his old buddy, Mark Messier, canceled each other with a goal and an assist each.

*Weak with the flu in Game 3, L.A. goalie Kelly Hrudey was sensational in a 4–1 Game 6 win.*

The final chapter in Gretzky's emotional severance from Alberta was completed in Game 3, played in Edmonton, when he was booed by the crowd at Northlands Coliseum. Flustered and back on their heels, the Kings managed only 26 shots, none finding the mark. The Oilers chased the flu-ridden Hrudey with two first-period goals 16 seconds apart, and two more in the second peri-

od just 1:11 apart, for a 4–0 victory. Midway through the opening period, Messier did what most NHLers couldn't or wouldn't do—he nailed Gretzky with a nasty open-ice bodycheck, sending the message: This is war; our friendship is on indefinite hold.

If Gretzky was intimidated, he didn't show it in Game 4. With the Oilers ahead 2–1 after the first period, No. 99 set up Kontos and Tom Laidlaw in the middle frame, putting the Kings back on top. But the feisty Oilers drew even in the final period and won it on Steve Smith's goal with just 26 seconds left in regulation, taking a commanding 3–1 series lead.

Had the Kings bowed out of the playoffs in Game 5, they likely would not have been too harshly criticized; after all, these were the defending champions they were facing. With Gretzky at the helm, however, the black-and-silver Kings showed new courage. Kontos, who had spent the year in Europe before returning for the playoffs, continued his red-hot scoring with another game-opening goal. Gretzky then assisted Bernie Nicholls for a 2–0 lead in the second period. Although the Oilers closed to 3–2 late in the third period, Gretzky personally put the game out of reach at 18:43, enabling the Kings to delay their exit from the playoffs—at least for one more game.

Back in Edmonton for Game 6, the Kings faced their biggest challenge: a hostile crowd, a savvy opponent, and huge stakes. After veteran Randy Gregg gave the Oilers a first-period lead, a parade of unlikely heroes stepped forward for the Kings. Defensive ace Mike Allison tied the score in the second period, and defenseman Jim Wiemer potted one of his five career playoff goals to put the Kings up 2–1 early in the third. Gretzky set up Kontos's seventh playoff goal for insurance, and Luc Robitaille added the final marker, as the Kings shocked the Oilers in their own building and forced a decisive seventh game.

A crowd of more than 16,000 rocked the Great Western Forum as Gretzky, in customary fashion, took command of Game 7. Just 52 seconds after the opening draw, No. 99 launched a shot that beat Grant Fuhr for a 1–0 lead. After Edmonton's Jari Kurri scored his 82nd career playoff goal, tying Rocket Richard for third all-time, the Kings retook the lead on another Kontos tally. Nicholls scored twice in the second session, and the Kings took a precarious 4–3 lead into the third period.

In a difficult season of transition that saw him single-handedly reinvent hockey enthusiasm in California, Gretzky enjoyed the crowning moment of this emotional series when he extended the Kings' 5–3 lead to 6–3 with a shorthanded goal with 1:35 to play. His goal—the final nail—thwarted any last-gasp hopes the Oilers might have entertained and knocked them painfully from their Stanley Cup throne. Just the sixth team in history to overcome a 3–1 series deficit, the Kings—led by their new monarch— had scaled new heights. Gretzky's greatness had rarely been more evident than in this dramatic comeback victory.

*With his typical dramatic flair, Wayne Gretzky scored the first and last goals of Game 7.*

## 1989 SMYTHE DIVISION SEMIFINALS

| | | | | |
|---|---|---|---|---|
| Game 1 | April 5 | @LA | Edmonton 4, Los Angeles 3 | GWG Simpson |
| Game 2 | April 6 | @LA | Los Angeles 5, Edmonton 2 | GWG Kontos |
| Game 3 | April 8 | @Edmonton | Edmonton 4, Los Angeles 0 | GWG Carson |
| Game 4 | April 9 | @Edmonton | Edmonton 4, Los Angeles 3 | GWG Smith |
| Game 5 | April 11 | @LA | Los Angeles 4, Edmonton 2 | GWG Robitaille |
| Game 6 | April 13 | @Edmonton | Los Angeles 4, Edmonton 1 | GWG Wiemer |
| Game 7 | April 15 | @LA | Los Angeles 6, Edmonton 3 | GWG Nicholls |

# RANGERS 4, DEVILS 3

### 1994 EASTERN CONFERENCE FINALS

**G**reat players don't just perform; they perform at top level under the most difficult circumstances. And they do it with a relentless confidence that effectively diminishes the opponents' belief in its own ability to survive. Mark Messier has always been just that kind of player, and in the 1994 Stanley Cup semifinals, when he captained the Rangers against New Jersey, he proved it.

The league's top regular-season team, the Rangers crushed the Islanders and Capitals to reach the semifinals. New Jersey, the second-best team, needed seven games to erase Buffalo and six more to eliminate Boston, setting up what many viewed as the real "championship" series.

Led by their respective goaltenders—Mike Richter and rookie sensation Martin Brodeur—the Rangers and Devils traded momentum back and forth from game to game, period to period, even shift to shift. Game 1 at Madison Square Garden should have gone to New York. The Rangers led 3–2 when Devil Claude Lemieux, a brilliant playoff performer, scored with only 43 seconds to play. His goal sent the game to OT, and the teams skated through one complete session of sudden death and 15:23 of double overtime before New Jersey's Stephane Richer lifted the puck over Richter's shoulder to end the marathon.

Two nights later, the Rangers rebounded pointedly. With tenacious checking and perfect goaltending from Richter, the Blueshirts carried a 1–0 lead to the third period, then added three more goals before the 10-minute mark to cruise 4–0 and tie the series. Messier scored the game's first (and eventual winning) goal and notched an assist.

In New Jersey for Game 3, the Devils and Rangers continued their tight checking. Trading goals for two periods, the teams were scoreless in the third and ended regulation play tied 2–2. Richter made 31 saves on 33 shots while Brodeur faced 50 shots from the Rangers. At 6:13 of the second OT, Stephane Matteau knocked the puck past Brodeur to give the Rangers the win and a 2–1 series lead. But there was no time to rest, no chance to breathe, for either team.

In Game 4, the Devils scored twice in the first 16:54 and chased Richter from the Ranger net. Though Matteau scored again to narrow the gap to 2–1, the Devils held on for a 3–1 victory, with Game 5 set for the Garden.

On May 23, 1994, more than 18,000 Garden denizens—fans who last celebrated a Rangers Stanley Cup in 1940—watched the Devils use their neutral-zone trap to neutralize the Blueshirts. Brodeur stopped everything that did get through, and by game's end the Devils were up 4–1 on the scoreboard and within one victory of advancing to the Stanley Cup Finals. But captain Messier wasn't having any. In a bold

*The 1994 Cup semifinals started well for the Devils, as sniper Stephane Richer (No. 44) beat Rangers goalie Mike Richter deep into double OT for a 4–3 win.*

move, the Rangers captain guaranteed—to the New York press corps—that the Rangers would win Game 6 in New Jersey.

Then he went out and made sure. After seeing the Devils build a 2–0 lead in the first period on a goal from defenseman Scott Niedermayer (that went in off a Rangers forward) and another from Lemieux, Messier went to work. In the second period, he carried the puck into Devils territory and dropped a pass for Russian winger Alexei Kovalev, who blasted a shot past Brodeur to cut the lead in half. In the third period, Messier led the assault against the Devils and the cruel powers of fate. At 2:48, he took a neat crossing pass from Kovalev in the faceoff circle to Brodeur's left and fired a nasty backhander to tie the game. Ten minutes later, on another high-speed rush, Messier cruised the slot and rammed home the rebound of Kovalev's left-wing blast, giving New York its first lead of the game.

With less than two minutes remaining in the game, the Devils, on the power play, pulled Brodeur to create a six-on-four skating advantage. Messier won a faceoff deep in his own zone, then retrieved the puck 10 feet in front of his own crease and fired it the length of the

*Mark Messier promised a win in Game 6, and he delivered with a hat trick and a 4—2 Rangers victory.*

ice into the vacated Devils goal, completing his hat trick and forcing a seventh game, at Madison Square Garden.

In a classic cliff-hanger, the Rangers led 1–0 with 7.7 seconds left in Game 7 when Valeri Zelepukin scored to tie the game and stop hearts throughout New York City. For 20 minutes of sudden-death, the teams battled scorelessly. Then, in the fifth minute of double overtime, Matteau carried the puck behind the Devils' net, sneaked out to Brodeur's left, and slipped the rubber between the goalie's skates for the series-clinching goal.

Powered by Messier, Richter, and eventual Conn Smythe winner Brian Leetch, the Rangers won a seven-game series

against Vancouver in the Finals, ending 54 years of Stanley Cup futility. But without Messier in Game 6 against the Devils, it never would have happened.

*For the first time since 1979, the Rangers reached the Finals following a dramatic, double-OT victory in Game 7.*

| 1994 EASTERN CONFERENCE FINALS | | | | |
|---|---|---|---|---|
| Game 1 | May 15 | @New York | Devils 4 Rangers 3 (2OT) | GWG Richer |
| Game 2 | May 17 | @New York | Rangers 4 Devils 0 | GWG Messier |
| Game 3 | May 19 | @New Jersey | Rangers 3 Devils 2 (2OT) | GWG Matteau |
| Game 4 | May 21 | @New Jersey | Devils 3 Rangers 1 | GWG Guerin |
| Game 5 | May 23 | @New York | Devils 4 Rangers 1 | GWG Peluso |
| Game 6 | May 25 | @New Jersey | Rangers 4 Devils 2 | GWG Messier |
| Game 7 | May 27 | @New York | Rangers 2 Devils 1 (2OT) | GWG Matteau |

# Chapter 5

# 10 Best Games

While so many hockey games have kept fans on the edge of their seats, a select few have left viewers breathless, seemed endless, and entered a realm of surrealism. Listed here are the 10 most heart-pounding, gut-wrenching hockey games of all time.

Above: *With two late goals, Team Canada defeated the Soviet Union 6–5 in the decisive Game 8 of their historic 1972 series. Opposite page: Two weeks after losing to the Soviet Union 10–3, the U.S. defeated the Soviets when it mattered, 4–3 in the medal round of the 1980 Olympics.*

# MAPLE LEAFS 1, BRUINS 0 (6 OT)

## 1933 STANLEY CUP SEMIFINALS, GAME 5

**D**edication, perseverance, and heartbreak: three vital ingredients for any recipe when heroics and history are to be made. In 1933, the Bruins won the American Division of the NHL after finishing last the previous season. Their star goalie, Tiny Thompson, was back in form, playing the kind of goal that earned him the Vezina Trophy in 1929–30 and would garner him another in 1932–33.

Thompson was just one of Boston's secret weapons as it faced Toronto, the defending Cup champ, in the 1933 semifinals. Eddie Shore anchored Boston's defense, and crafty veterans Nels "Old Poison" Stewart and Marty Barry led the attack. The Leafs countered with the potent Kid Line (Joe Primeau, Charlie Conacher, and Busher Jackson), King Clancy on defense, and Lorne Chabot in nets.

After the first three games of the best-of-five series went to sudden-death overtime, with Boston winning twice, Game 4 was decided in regulation when the Leafs won 5–3. The decisive fifth game, played in Toronto on April 3, 1933, came the night after New York had eliminated Detroit in their total-goals series. The Rangers, who had been swept by Toronto in the 1932 Finals, were resting up for their return to the title round, awaiting the survivor of the Boston-Toronto slugfest.

Game 5 was full of thrills, though short on goals. Chabot and Thompson were peppered with shots, but no player on either side could find the range, and

*Three shutouts in one night? Lorne Chabot practically turned the trick, holding Boston scoreless into the ninth period.*

after 60 minutes the teams headed for a sudden-death overtime yet again, tied 0–0. Did either team have an edge? In their history, the Bruins had won four of nine overtime games (with two ending in ties during the 1927 playoffs), while Toronto had taken three of five, with no ties. Boston held a slim psychological edge, having won Game 1 and Game 3 of this series in sudden-death, but the Leafs were disciplined and poised.

So while it was both frustrating and nerve-racking for the teams and their fans, it was no big surprise when the first

period of sudden-death yielded no winner. However, the second, third, and fourth periods were scoreless, too. The tough Bruin defense contained the Leafs, while the hard-hitting Toronto backline had a riposte for every Boston thrust.

As the night grew long, Thompson seemed destined to play the hero for the Bruins, a veteran who was recapturing his status as the game's premier puck-stopper. But early in the sixth overtime, Thompson suffered a crushing blow when the Leafs' diminutive Ken Doraty, author of just 15 goals in 103 NHL games, found the back of the net behind Thompson after nearly three games' worth of grueling play. Time of the goal: 4:46 of period No. 9.

As an interesting footnote, Barry was traded to Detroit in 1935 and skated in the playoff game on March 24, 1936, that eclipsed this one as the longest game in NHL history (won by Mud Bruneteau). Further, it was Chabot, finishing his career with the Maroons in 1936, who gave up Bruneteau's historic goal. Thompson, winner of a Stanley Cup as a rookie in 1929, never won another.

| TORONTO 1, BOSTON 0 (6OT) | | | | | | | | | | |
|---|---|---|---|---|---|---|---|---|---|---|
| Toronto | 0 | 0 | 0 | 0 | 0 | 0 | 0 | 0 | 1 | 1 |
| Boston | 0 | 0 | 0 | 0 | 0 | 0 | 0 | 0 | 0 | 0 |

# RED WINGS 1, MAROONS 0 (6 OT)

### 1936 STANLEY CUP SEMIFINALS, GAME 1

The 1936 Stanley Cup semifinals began with the Detroit Red Wings and Montreal Maroons, respective division champs, facing each other while quarterfinal matches pitting Toronto against Boston and the New York Americans against Chicago went on simultaneously. The Red Wings, who had led the league with 24 wins, were led by Marty Barry, Herbie Lewis, and Larry Aurie. Their goalie, Normie Smith, playing in his first-ever Stanley Cup playoff series, had led the league in wins and was one year away from winning his first Vezina Trophy. Montreal was paced by high-scoring Hooley Smith.

As Toronto and the Americans worked over their opponents in the quarterfinals, the Wings and Maroons settled in for the "main event." Game 1 of the series turned out to be a classic for the ages, one that shattered a record most believed would never even be approached.

Playing in Montreal, the teams went at each other hammer and tong from the opening faceoff. The goalies, Smith and Montreal's Lorne Chabot, were perfect for 60 minutes, turning aside each and every shot that came their way. When the final buzzer sounded, the teams were deadlocked at 0–0. Through one overtime period, nothing changed. The Wings attacked Chabot, and the Maroons countered with a vigorous assault on Smith, but neither team's snipers could pierce the armor of the opposition.

Through double overtime and triple overtime, the teams persevered, and despite the high-energy level of the game, the pace slowed only marginally as the players wore down and the night wore on. In the minds of some onlookers, the entire concept of "sudden-death" was replaced with a new idea, one more along the lines of "slow death." Still knotted 0–0, the teams skated through a fourth and then a fifth overtime period, creating good scoring chances but failing at both ends.

Then, with less than four minutes to play in the sixth period of overtime, the Red Wings mounted another attack. Hec Kilrea, a scrappy left winger who had won a Stanley Cup with the 1927 Ottawa Senators, lugged the puck into Montreal's end of the ice. On his flank was a rookie right winger named Modere Bruneteau, known as "Mud." Kilrea carried deep, cleverly drawing Chabot out of his crease. Then he flipped a neat little pass to Bruneteau. Without stopping, Bruneteau fired the puck into the empty net and brought a finish to the longest game in NHL history. Three years earlier, Toronto and Boston had played to the 4:46 mark of a sixth overtime period. Now the Wings and Maroons had eclipsed the record by nearly 12 minutes.

Bruneteau's goal was only his third as an NHLer, after a modest two-goal rookie display. He would score once more in the 1936 playoffs as Detroit ultimately would sweep the Maroons in three games and then win the Stanley Cup with a three-games-to-one series triumph over Toronto. Still, it was an auspicious playoff debut for Bruneteau and Smith, the latter setting the NHL playoff record for longest shutout sequence: 248:32.

*A hard-hitting but clean player, Detroit's Modere "Mud" Bruneteau scored the only goal in the longest game ever.*

| DETROIT 1, MONT. 0 (6OT) | | | | | | | | | | |
|---|---|---|---|---|---|---|---|---|---|---|
| Detroit | 0 | 0 | 0 | 0 | 0 | 0 | 0 | 0 | 1 | —1 |
| Montreal | 0 | 0 | 0 | 0 | 0 | 0 | 0 | 0 | 0 | —0 |

# RED WINGS 4, RANGERS 3 (2 OT)

## 1950 STANLEY CUP FINALS, GAME 7

The Detroit Red Wings were the class of the NHL in 1949–50, taking the season title by 11 points over second-place Montreal. Toronto finished third, with New York sneaking into the playoffs 21 points behind Detroit.

After knocking off Montreal in the semifinals, the Rangers faced Detroit, which needed seven games to shake the pesky Maple Leafs, in the Finals. Because the circus was in town, the Rangers had to play their Finals home games in Toronto. Still, in the face of extremely tough competition and difficult circumstances, the Blueshirts rode a Don Raleigh overtime goal in Game 5 to take a surprising lead in the best-of-seven series. Detroit knotted the series in Game 6 to force a showdown at Olympia Stadium, setting the stage for one of the greatest games of all time.

The upstart Rangers took a 2–0 lead with goals from Allan Stanley and tiny Tony Leswick 1:04 apart midway through the first period. But the Red Wings boasted the Production Line of Ted Lindsay, Sid Abel, and Gordie Howe, who had finished 1–2–3 respectively in league scoring during the season. This team wasn't going to roll over and play dead. Pete Babando, a former 23-goal scorer in his rookie season with Boston (1947–48) and who played only one season with the Red Wings, scored early in the second period. Just 21 seconds after Babando's goal, Abel banged one past Rangers goalie Charlie Rayner to tie the game and stir Detroiters into a frenzy.

The underdog Rangers remained cool, waiting for another chance to exploit Detroit's jitters. Their chance came in the 12th minute of the middle period when

*Rangers goalie Chuck Rayner looks back helplessly as Pete Babando's shot ends the 1950 Finals in double OT of Game 7.*

Buddy O'Connor, a two-time Stanley Cup winner during six seasons with the Montreal Canadiens, scored to give New York its second lead. But the Wings kept coming, this time when Belfast-born Jim McFadden, the 1948 Calder Trophy winner, scored his second playoff goal late in the period to tie the game at 3–3. After a back-and-forth scoreless third period, the teams entered sudden-death overtime.

In previous Stanley Cup history dating back to 1918, only four championships had ever been decided in overtime, and twice (1933 and 1940) it was the Rangers who had emerged victorious. Meanwhile, Detroit had lost to Chicago in double overtime in the 1934 Finals. Now, after one scoreless OT period in which the closest chance came when Ranger Nick Mickoski hit the post, Detroit took the edge in play in double overtime.

In the 29th minute of sudden-death, George Gee beat O'Connor on a faceoff deep in the Rangers' zone and dropped a perfect pass to Babando. Without pausing, the winger unleashed a shot through a maelstrom of sticks, legs, and bodies. Shockingly, the puck found its way past Rayner, who never saw it coming, and into the Rangers' goal. It was just one goal in one game, but it earned the Red Wings a must-win Stanley Cup title over a courageous Rangers team that played over its head and nearly stole a championship from a superior adversary. As for the game's hero, he would forever be known as Pete "Sudden Death" Babando.

| DETROIT 4, NEW YORK 3 (2OT) | | | | | | |
|---|---|---|---|---|---|---|
| New York | 2 | 1 | 0 | 0 | 0 | —3 |
| Detroit | 0 | 3 | 0 | 0 | 1 | —4 |

# MAPLE LEAFS 3, CANADIENS 2 (OT)

### 1951 STANLEY CUP FINALS, GAME 5

Bill Barilko's NHL career lasted only five years but included four Stanley Cup championships. He played 252 regular-season games and notched just 26 goals and 62 points. Known less for his grace than for his physical style, he earned 456 career penalty minutes.

Yet Barilko, even by modern standards, never would have been considered a goon, for the enthusiasm he brought to the rink overshadowed all transgressions. He was feared for his devastating hip checks and admired for the bravery he showed in dropping to the ice to block shots. Barilko was a consummate team player, and his last act in the NHL made him an enduring hero.

The 1951 Stanley Cup Finals featured Montreal and Toronto. By virtue of finishing 30 points ahead of the Habs, the Leafs enjoyed home-ice advantage. However, the Canadiens were no pushovers, having dethroned the defending-champion Red Wings in the first round. After the teams split the first two games in Toronto, with both games going into overtime, the tight-checking series went to Montreal. There, the Leafs pushed Montreal to the edge of elimination as Teeder Kennedy scored 4:47 into OT in Game 3 and Harry Watson scored 5:15 into Game 4.

Game 5 in Toronto was a classic goaltenders' duel, with Gerry McNeil protecting Montreal's net and Al Rollins rebuffing every Canadien assault. After a scoreless first period, Rocket Richard,

*The conquering hero is raised on high: Toronto's Bill Barilko celebrates the goal that ended the all-overtime Finals.*

whose overtime goal in Game 2 tied the series, broke through with his playoff-leading ninth goal midway through the second period to give Montreal a 1–0 lead. The seesaw battle raged on. Toronto's Tod Sloan sandwiched a pair of goals around Paul Meger's tally and, with the score deadlocked at 2–2, the teams completed regulation tied for the fifth straight game.

In the dressing room, Toronto coach Joe Primeau cautioned his troops—particularly young Barilko—to play smart, positional hockey. Barilko had earlier been guilty of chasing the puck and leaving his post unguarded. Primeau warned Barilko that he would be fined for any further roving.

In the sudden-death period, the Leafs dictated play, controlling the puck deep in Montreal's end, determined to keep it away from the ever-dangerous Richard. Battling for every inch of ice, Toronto's Howie Meeker corralled the puck behind Montreal's net and tried a wrap-around shot, but McNeil was quicker and covered the post. Watson jumped on the rebound but couldn't fire it home. This time, the puck skittered loose. Forgetting his instructions, Barilko charged in from his point position, snared the puck, and pulled the trigger on a hard, accurate wrist shot that flashed past McNeil's glove hand and into the net, ending the game and giving Toronto the Cup.

At 24, Barilko was a national hero (and he wasn't fined by Primeau after all). However, he enjoyed only a brief turn in the spotlight, as a plane crash took his life in the summer of 1951. His final NHL game was one of the most exciting ever played, one on which he left his indelible mark.

| TORONTO 3, MONT. 2 (OT) | | | |
|---|---|---|---|
| Montreal | 0 1 1 0 | — | 2 |
| Toronto | 0 1 1 1 | — | 3 |

# CANADIENS 3, BRUINS 1

### 1952 STANLEY CUP SEMIFINALS, GAME 7

For a player who never won a scoring title, Maurice "Rocket" Richard was hockey's most dangerous goal-scorer throughout most of his 18 years in the NHL. The reason: He could beat you so many different ways. In the 1952 Stanley Cup semifinals, Richard was rendered nearly unconscious from a stunning blow to the head suffered early in the seventh game of his team's series with Boston, yet he summoned powers from an unknown source and delivered his Canadiens to victory. It was a performance that helped cement the legend of the Rocket.

Montreal and Boston finished the 1951–52 season second and fourth, respectively, and faced each other in the first round of the Stanley Cup playoffs, with Montreal enjoying home-ice advantage. But after winning twice in Montreal, the Habs dropped the next three games—two in Boston and Game 5 at home. Only a double-overtime goal by Paul Masnick in Game 6 saved them from elimination and forced a decisive Game 7.

In the second period of a 1–1 battle that saw both teams attack and counter-attack, Richard was victimized by a savage hit from Leo Labine, a nasty winger who recorded 688 penalty minutes and 128 goals in 11 NHL seasons. Using his stick to open a gash on Richard's skull, Labine also used his knee to knock the air from the Rocket's lungs. Eventually, Richard regained con-

*Boston goalie Jim Henry shakes the hand of Rocket Richard, who has just beaten him with the greatest goal ever scored.*

sciousness and staggered from the rink to receive medical aid. Remarkably, he soon returned to the Habs' bench—his forehead stitched together, complaining of dizziness and a ringing in his ears, and

asking for the license plate of the truck that ran him down.

In the third period, Richard was back on the ice, still suffering the effects of his injuries but locked into a typical "zone,"

sniffing out the puck with every turn. Then it happened. After stealing the puck in his own end from Woody Dumart, Richard put on a one-man display that sent even his own teammates into mild delirium. Racing along the right-wing boards, he zeroed in on defenseman Bill Quackenbush. A left-handed shooter, the Rocket cradled the puck to the outside to avoid a diving poke-check from Quackenbush. Not only did he elude the check, but Richard maintained control of the puck and dug his skates into the ice to cut sharply toward the middle of the rink, toward the Boston goal.

Bruins goalie Sugar Jim Henry, his eyes blackened from a recently broken nose, hugged the left post, anticipating Richard's sharp-angle shot on goal. But the Rocket didn't release. Instead, he closed on Henry and fired the puck to the long side, beating the surprised goalie and giving Montreal a 2–1 lead. According to some accounts, Richard's former linemate, Elmer Lach, watching from the bench, fainted. It wouldn't be surprising since he witnessed what is generally considered the most incredible goal ever scored. As for the Canadiens, they won 3–1 and advanced to the Finals, where they lost to Detroit.

| MONTREAL 3, BOSTON 1 | | |
|---|---|---|
| Montreal | 1 0 2 | —3 |
| Boston | 1 0 0 | —1 |

# CANADIENS 3, BLACK HAWKS 2

## 1971 STANLEY CUP FINALS, GAME 7

In 1969, Montreal trounced St. Louis to win its fourth Stanley Cup in five years. The next year, the Canadiens failed even to qualify for the playoffs. By the spring of 1971, the Habs were determined to reclaim their status. However, the Chicago Black Hawks, with Stanley Cup dreams of their own, stood firmly in the way.

Scanning the rosters, it was difficult to judge which team had the greater weaponry. The Hawks were led by Bobby Hull while Montreal boasted three of the top four playoff scorers: Frank Mahovlich, Yvan Cournoyer, and Jean Beliveau. In goal, the showdown between Hawks ace Tony Esposito and Habs rookie Ken Dryden took on classic proportions as the teams battled through six games, with each team winning three times—all in its own building. With Game 7 at the noisy Chicago Stadium, the advantage went to the Black Hawks, who had gone 30–6–3 at home in the regular season and lost only one of nine home playoff games (in overtime) during this Stanley Cup year.

As Game 7 began, the Hawks attacked relentlessly. Only a brilliant first period by Dryden kept Montreal from being swamped. As it was, Chicago took a late lead when Dennis Hull banked a rebound off Dryden's shoulder, convert-ing a power-play advantage. In the eighth minute of the second period, the Hawks increased the lead. This time it was the crafty Pit Martin who orchestrated the goal. He sped past Montreal's defenders to retrieve the puck behind Dryden's cage before centering to Danny O'Shea, who blasted the puck past Dryden. With

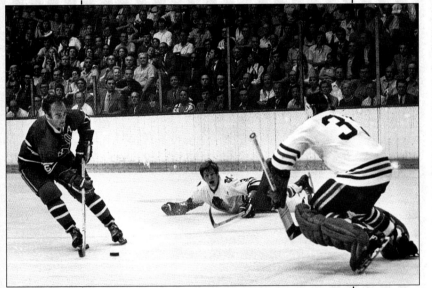

*Montreal's Henri Richard scores the Cup-clinching goal against Chicago's Tony Esposito in Game 7 of the 1971 Finals.*

Esposito appearing unbeatable, the Hawks seemed poised to win their first Stanley Cup in a decade.

With just over five minutes to play in the second period, however, Jacques Lemaire, the Habs' hard-shooting center, uncorked a rocket and appeared to catch Esposito napping. The goalie later insisted he saw it all the way but missed it. Thus inspired, the Habs reverted to the style that had earned them their nickname, the "Flying Frenchmen," and stormed the Hawks, firing shot after shot at Tony O.

With under two minutes to play in the second period, Lemaire and Henri Richard (whose feud with coach Al McNeil made headlines and caused many to question the team's unity) exploited a broken play deep in Chicago's zone when Eric Nesterenko and defenseman Bill White bobbled the puck. When it bounced to Lemaire, the quick-witted center found Richard alone in front, fed him the puck, and Henri buried it for a 2–2 tie.

In practical terms, the third period was sudden-death overtime. With the scarcity of scoring, the consensus was that the next goal would win the Cup. At 2:34 of the period, Richard capped a masterful rush with a deke around the defense and a clever wrist shot past Tony O. Meanwhile, Dryden proved to be a fortress the Hawks could not penetrate. Despite a brave effort, the Hawks fell short, and the underdog Canadiens survived to raise their 16th playoff trophy.

| MONTREAL 3, CHICAGO 2 | | | |
|---|---|---|---|
| Montreal | 0 | 2 | 1—3 |
| Chicago | 1 | 1 | 0—2 |

# TEAM CANADA 6, SOVIET NATIONAL TEAM 5

## 1972 EXHIBITION SERIES, GAME 8

Perhaps arrogant, perhaps just overconfident, an entire nation could be heard chuckling to itself when Alan Eagleson, former boss of the NHL players' union, announced that a team of NHL All-Stars would play an eight-game series against the Soviet national team in the autumn of 1972. With four games in Canada and four in Moscow, this first-of-its-kind series would actually be a stunning eye-opener for hockey enthusiasts across North America.

For the impossible happened not once but twice within a week. The Soviets actually beat the NHLers at their own game, and in their own rinks. Appearing out of shape and only marginally inspired, the NHL squad lost 7–3 in Montreal and 5–3 in Vancouver before mustering a 4–4 tie in Winnipeg. It managed only one win, by 4–1 in Toronto, before heading to Moscow down 1–2–1.

In Game 5, the disciplined Soviets overcame a 4–1 deficit in the third period to win 5–4 and take what seemed an insurmountable edge. After playing so poorly for so many games, how could the All-Stars hope to rebound, particularly against such a well-oiled machine that seemed impervious to the Canadians' physical abuse? But then a star emerged for Canada. A crafty winger named Paul Henderson scored the winning goal in Game 6, then broke a 3–3 tie late in

Game 7 to bring the series dead even at 3–3–1 and set the stage for the final confrontation.

More than 14,000 fans (among them 3,000 Canadians) filled Luzhnicki Sports Palace in Moscow for the historic showdown, and they were not bored. The first

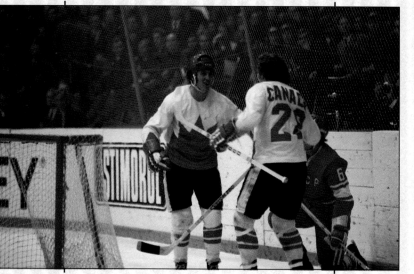

*Paul Henderson (left) emerged as a hero when he scored game-winners in Games 6, 7, and 8 against the Soviets.*

period was a tense melee with four goals (two apiece) and plenty of controversy. Minnesota North Star J. P. Parise was ejected for threatening West German referee Joseph Kompalla with his stick after a disputed penalty call. (Published reports claimed he told the official, "You're going to die.") Later, Eagleson became embroiled with a Moscow policeman, and even mild-mannered Rangers winger Rod Gilbert engaged in fisticuffs, taking on Yevgeny Mishakov.

The Soviets pulled ahead 5–3 in the second period and maintained a 5–4 lead with less than 10 minutes to play. With 7:04 to play, Montreal Canadien Yvan Cournoyer launched a rocket past Vladislav Tretiak, but the red light did not initially go on, triggering another maelstrom of hostility. Eventually the goal was credited. But the NHLers needed another goal to break the deadlock. A tie in the series would be considered a loss— no two ways about it.

As action swept back and forth, Canada pressed the Soviets while the technically superior USSR squad countered, using the same game plan it had employed throughout the series. The Soviets' ability to maintain focus regardless of the scoreboard earned them admiration from the Canadians, if grudgingly. With the clock ticking off the final excruciating minute of play, the NHLers finally broke through when Henderson, perched beside the net, slammed the rebound of Phil Esposito's shot past Tretiak for his third straight game-winner, lifting his team—and his country—to a difficult, elusive, and highly educational victory.

| CANADA 6, USSR 5 | | |
| --- | --- | --- |
| Canada | 2 1 3 | 6 |
| USSR | 2 3 0 | 5 |

# SOVIET RED ARMY 3, CANADIENS 3

### 1975 SUPER SERIES, GAME 3

With two summit series under their belts, the NHL and Soviets were well acquainted with each other when the "Super Series" between two Soviet teams (Wings and Red Army) and eight NHL clubs commenced on December 28, 1975. On that day, the Red Army humiliated the New York Rangers 7–3 at Madison Square Garden. The featured match of the series took place on New Year's Eve in Montreal, as the great Canadiens hosted the most dangerous team in the world not playing in the NHL.

A highly anticipated showdown between two of the world's greatest goalies, Ken Dryden and Vladislav Tretiak, the match also pitted Montreal's creative and at times highly improvisational offense against the flashy skating and immutable teamwork of the Soviets. If the pressure on the Habs wasn't great enough already, particularly after the Rangers debacle, Alan Eagleson, chief organizer of the event, told the Habs they carried the pride of Canada on their shoulders.

Surprisingly, the Canadiens were considered underdogs entering the match—such was the respect being paid the balletic yet tough-minded Soviets. Nearly 19,000 fans packed the Montreal Forum for the game, and all were delighted by the dominance of the Habs and virtuoso goaltending at both ends of the rink.

Montreal clearly controlled play, unleashing three shots on goal for the Soviets' one. The Habs got the first break of the game in the first period when Viktor Kuzkin coughed up the puck in his own zone and Pete Mahovlich found sniper Steve Shutt alone in front. Shutt

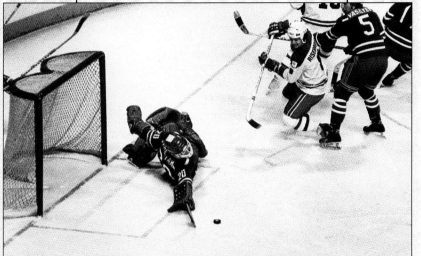

*Vladislav Tretiak befuddled Montreal with numerous sensational saves, including this one in the first period.*

made no mistake, firing the puck past Tretiak for a 1–0 lead. Yvon Lambert combined with Doug Risebrough and Serge Savard in the eighth minute of play to build a 2–0 lead. But everyone on the ice and in the stands and watching at home on TV knew no such lead was safe against this foe.

In the second period, Boris Mikhailov and Valeri Kharlamov bookended goals around Yvan Cournoyer's mid-frame tally, as the Soviets scored twice on just

three shots. Though the Habs held a 22–7 advantage in shots after two periods, Tretiak rejected them at virtually every turn. Cournoyer's goal came while one Soviet player sat in the penalty box and another had just been released following an abbreviated two-man advantage.

Early in the third period, the Canadiens were caught deep in the offensive zone and the Soviets counterattacked, three on one, with only Savard back to defend. Boris Aleksandrov played give-and-go with his linemates and finally buried the puck behind Dryden, who was left virtually helpless in the face of such elegant passing. Aleksandrov's shot was only the ninth of the game for the Red Army team, but it knotted the score 3–3.

In the closing minutes of play, Montreal pressed for the victory, pouring shot after shot on Tretiak, but to no avail. With less than a minute to play, Shutt once more found himself open with a chance to net the winner, but he fanned and the contest ended 3–3. Many historians still refer to this game as the greatest in hockey history.

| USSR 3, MONTREAL 3 | | | |
| --- | --- | --- | --- |
| USSR | 0 | 2 1 | —3 |
| Montreal | 2 | 1 0 | —3 |

# USA 4, USSR 3

## 1980 OLYMPICS, MEDAL ROUND

As the 1980 Winter Games began in Lake Placid, New York, two decades separated the U.S. Olympic hockey program from its last gold medal. But Herb Brooks, hockey coach at the University of Minnesota, brought his underdog squad to upstate New York prepared to compete, prepared to win. Though seeded seventh in the 12-nation pool, the Americans showed they were no patsies, eking out a surprise tie with Sweden in their first game.

In their next four games, the Americans stunned Czechoslovakia 7–3, then beat Norway, Romania, and West Germany. Finishing the round at 4–0–1, they earned a berth in the medal round along with Finland, Sweden, and the defending gold-medal champion Soviet Union. The Soviets were winners of the previous four gold medals and five of the last six. The only team to beat them since 1956 was the American squad in 1960.

The Americans' first medal-round game promised to be the toughest, as they faced the Soviets. But if the Americans were intimidated, they didn't show it. In fact, early in the game, Valeri Kharlamov attempted to split the USA defense. The defenders closed on the Russian star and hammered him rudely to the ice. The crowd of 10,000 cheered deafeningly.

Undaunted as always, the stoic Soviets went about their business in the methodical, fast-paced manner that had become customary in recent years. Working the puck with magical control, they peppered USA goalie Jim Craig, formerly of Boston University, with 39 shots. Throughout the game, they did their best to swarm the young and untested Americans, who had only one player

*Defenseman Mike Ramsey was one of several Americans who parlayed a stunning gold-medal win into an NHL career.*

(Buzz Schneider) with previous Olympic experience.

In the first period, Valery Krutov, standing in the slot, redirected a slap shot from Alexei Kasatonov past Craig to open the scoring. But Schneider answered with a laser-beam shot over the shoulder of Vladislav Tretiak minutes later. Sergei Makarov scored to give the Soviets another lead, but Mark Johnson pounced on a rebound of Ken Morrow's shot and tied the game with just one second left in the first period.

Showing signs of panic, the Soviets yanked Tretiak, one of the greatest goalies in the world, and installed Vladimir Myshkin. In the second period, the Americans managed only two shots while Alexander Maltsev scored to put his Soviet squad on top.

Still, the Americans battled relentlessly, matching the Soviets hit for hit. Early in the third period, Johnson scored again to tie the game. And with 10 minutes to play, captain Mike Eruzione, who'd been playing in the IHL before joining the Olympic team, made history. Taking a pass from John Harwrington inside the Soviets' blue line, the stocky winger cruised to the middle of the ice and unleashed a 30-foot slap shot that sneaked through a screen and beat Myshkin to give USA its margin of victory.

The final 10 minutes were the longest in U.S. hockey history, but the Americans held on, amazingly, and two days later won a shocking gold medal with a 4–2 win over Finland. But their 4–3 win over the Soviets was the real miracle.

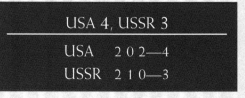

| USA 4, USSR 3 | | | |
| --- | --- | --- | --- |
| USA | 2 0 2 | — | 4 |
| USSR | 2 1 0 | — | 3 |

# ISLANDERS 3, CAPITALS 2 (4 OT)

### 1987 PATRICK DIVISION SEMIFINALS, GAME 7

The 1986–87 season was filled with special moments, including a midseason break during which the NHL hosted a two-game series against the Soviet national team, called "Rendez-Vous 1987." But for sheer thrills, the Stanley Cup play-offs, with 12 overtime games, were the capper, and no series provided more drama than the Patrick Division semifinals between the Islanders and Capitals.

In 1975, the Islanders had shocked the Pittsburgh Penguins by winning their second-round series in seven games after trailing three games to none. Down three games to one 14 years later, they staged yet another of their classic comebacks, winning Game 5 in Washington and then knotting the series with another must-win Game 6 victory on home ice. This set up the all-or-nothing finale. Although the game was scheduled for April 18, 1987, it would not end on that date.

In Game 7, the Islanders trailed 2–1 with less than six minutes to play when their leader, Bryan Trottier, a former Hart Trophy winner, fired the puck past Caps goalie Bob Mason to tie the game and force overtime. With Mike Bossy, Denis Potvin, and Brent Sutter—three of their top players—out of the lineup nursing injuries, the Islanders were severely depleted. The Caps had outshot New York 36–21 in regulation.

The Capitals, who had owned the series in the early stages, did not fold

their tents, either. As sudden-death play began, the teams played evenly, firing 11 shots on goal apiece. When no winner was determined after 20 minutes, the ice

*As the bizarre story on the scoreboard signals, it took seven periods for the Isles and Caps to decide this "Easter Epic."*

was resurfaced and the teams returned for double overtime. The Caps took the edge in shots, but Isles goalie Kelly Hrudey—who finished the night with 73 saves—was in a rhythm that could not be disrupted even by Washington's relentless riflemen. At the far end,

Mason allowed nothing, so the teams went to a third session of OT after receiving oxygen and potassium tablets from their training staffs. Still tied after 120 minutes of play, the teams retired once more to prepare for quadruple overtime. By the time they returned to the ice, the arena clock read 1:30 A.M.—and it showed in the slowness of the skaters and the brevity of their shifts.

In the ninth minute of quadruple overtime, the Islanders swarmed Washington's zone. Low-scoring defenseman Gord Dineen carried the puck behind the Caps' net, then sneaked out to the right faceoff circle and unleashed a shot. Washington's Kevin Hatcher read the play and went down to block the shot, sending the puck skittering toward the blue line. Retreating to cover for Dineen, Pat LaFontaine captured the puck and whirled, firing a 45-foot slap shot that struck the post and ricocheted into the net behind Mason, leaving the goalie, his teammates, and more than 18,000 die-hard fans in stunned silence.

To date, this contest stands as the fifth-longest game in NHL history. It ended at 1:56 A.M. on Easter Sunday, and it was soon dubbed the "Easter Epic."

| NEW YORK 3, WASH. 2 (4OT) | | | | | | | | |
|---|---|---|---|---|---|---|---|---|
| New York | 0 | 1 | 1 | 0 | 0 | 0 | 1 | —3 |
| Washington | 1 | 1 | 0 | 0 | 0 | 0 | 0 | —2 |

# Chapter 6

# BEST OF THE REST

Who had the scariest slap shots? Who were the toughest goons? Which goalies had the coolest facemasks? This section answers these and 23 other intriguing hockey questions. Here are the fastest skaters, biggest blowouts, best arenas, etc. in hockey history.

Above: *The Bread Line of Bill Cook, Frank Boucher, and Bun Cook (left to right) was among the 10 Best Forward Lines in NHL history. Opposite page: Only the foolish messed with Bob Probert, one of hockey's 10 Best Goons.*

# 10 BEST FORWARD LINES

## BIG, BAD BRUINS

**K**en Hodge, Phil Esposito, Wayne Cashman. Like a locomotive with a bad attitude, the Bruins terrorized the NHL during the early 1970s thanks to Esposito and wingmen Cashman and Hodge, two strong-arm guardians who fed Espo from the corners. A five-time scoring champ, Esposito set new standards when he ripped 76 goals in 1970–71. The Bruins smashed the NHL team scoring record by 96 goals (399 vs. 303) in 1970–71.

## BREAD LINE

**B**un Cook, Frank Boucher, Bill Cook. There was no meaner or more hard-nosed player than 1927 NHL scoring champion Bill Cook. Nor was there a more gentlemanly or elegant skater than Cook's center, Boucher, winner of seven Lady Byng Trophies. The Bread Line, filled out by Bill's kid brother Bun, gelled instantly when the Rangers debuted in the NHL in 1927–28. They won Stanley Cups that year and in 1933, with Bill and Frank each scoring a Cup-clinching goal.

## FRENCH CONNECTION LINE

**R**ick Martin, Gilbert Perreault, Rene Robert. Grace and speed— and no shortage of shooting power— propelled the French Connection Line and enabled the Buffalo Sabres to rise from expansion doormats in 1970–71 to Stanley Cup finalists just four years later.

*Rene Robert (No. 14), Rick Martin (No. 7), Gil Perreault (No. 11)*

In 1974–75, Perreault (Buffalo's all-time leading scorer), Martin (whose 52 goals and 95 points set a team mark for left wingers), and Robert (with 100 points) all made it to the NHL's list of top 10 scorers.

## GAG LINE

**V**ic Hadfield, Jean Ratelle, Rod Gilbert. Ratelle's elegant playmaking at center, Gilbert's explosive skating and shooting from the right wing, and Hadfield's battering ram, nononsense approach on the port side gave the New York Rangers potent weapons in the early 1970s. They earned the nickname "Goal-A-Game Line" during the 1971–72 season when they combined for 139 tallies (including 50 from Hadfield) and went all the way to the Stanley Cup Finals.

## KID LINE

**B**usher Jackson, Joe Primeau, Charlie Conacher. From 1929–35, Primeau, Conacher, and Jackson were among the NHL's most productive units and the Leafs one of hockey's premier teams. In 1931–32, the Kid Line shone brightest when Primeau (the playmaker) led the league in assists, Conacher (the finisher) paced the league in goals, and Jackson (the all-around threat) won the scoring championship. On the strength of this trio, Toronto annexed the Stanley Cup in 1932.

## KRAUT LINE

Woody Dumart, Milt Schmidt, Bobby Bauer. Rarely in the history of the NHL have synergy and chemistry been more apparent as in Boston in the late 1930s and early 1940s. Childhood buddies Schmidt, Bauer, and Dumart combined to give the Bruins an attack potent enough to win two Stanley Cups. Despite missing three seasons while serving in World War II, Schmidt, Bauer, and Dumart combined for 365 goals and 781 points in 350 games before Bauer retired in 1947.

## PONY LINE

Doug Bentley, Max Bentley, Bill Mosienko. What they lacked in size, Chicago's Pony Line made up for with speed, playmaking, and vitality. Doug and Max Bentley notched 543 and 544 career points, respectively, and won three scoring titles between them despite playing on weak Black Hawks teams. Mosienko added scoring and a touch of class. The Pony Line was Chicago's only hope for five seasons before Max was dealt to Toronto in 1947–48.

## PRODUCTION LINE

Ted Lindsay, Sid Abel, Gordie Howe. In 1947–48, Detroit coach Tommy Ivan assigned Howe to the team's top line with Abel and Lindsay. Two years later, Lindsay led the league in scoring with Abel second and Howe third. In 1950–51, Howe took the triple crown, leading in goals, assists, and points. Led by the Production Line,

*Reg, Max, and Doug Bentley*

Detroit won two Stanley Cups (1950 and 1952). After Alex Delvecchio replaced Abel, the line produced two more Cups (1954 and 1955).

## PUNCH LINE

Toe Blake, Elmer Lach, Maurice Richard. Few offensive units in NHL history enjoyed more compatibility than Montreal's truculent but gifted Punch Line. A crafty playmaker, Lach won two scoring titles while Blake (once a scoring champ) rode shotgun and Richard simply rewrote the record books. Lach, Richard, and Blake finished 1–2–3, respectively, in NHL scoring in 1944–45 and carried Montreal to two Stanley Cups (1944 and 1946).

## TRIPLE CROWN LINE

Charlie Simmer, Marcel Dionne, Dave Taylor. Years of struggle and minimal fan support were briefly forgotten in 1979–80 when the Los Angeles Kings rode the scoring of their high-octane Triple Crown Line. Simmer tied for the league lead in goals (56), Dionne won his only Art Ross Trophy with 137 points, and Taylor added 90 points, enabling the line to outscore Edmonton's top line (with Wayne Gretzky) and Montreal's first unit.

# 10 HARDEST SHOOTERS

*Bathgate*

## ANDY BATHGATE

Although others, like Bobby Hull and Boom Boom Geoffrion, were more celebrated for the flash and drama of their fearsome shots, Bathgate was among the first NHLers to perfect the art of the slap shot. On November 1, 1959, Bathgate blasted the puck into the face of Montreal goalie Jacques Plante, who left bleeding. Plante later returned to the game wearing a protective mask, and he never played without it again.

## MIKE BOSSY

Sleek and fast, Bossy was one of hockey's premier right wingers from his debut season (1977–78), when he set an NHL mark with 53 rookie goals, until his premature retirement in 1987 due to back trouble. Bossy's wrist shot was as deadly accurate as his slap shot was powerful, enabling him to put together nine consecutive 50-goal seasons. He also reached the 60-goal mark five times.

## RAYMOND BOURQUE

Nobody told Bourque it would be easy to follow in the footsteps of Bobby Orr. But since he arrived in Boston in 1979–80 and won the Calder Trophy, he's been making it look easy. One of the greatest power-play quarterbacks ever, Bourque's tremendous shot from the point and his willingness to unleash it (he's always among the league leaders in shots on goal) earned him more than 300 goals in his first 16 seasons.

## CHARLIE CONACHER

The finisher on Toronto's Kid Line, The Bomber had one of hockey's most feared cannons, which he used to lead the league in goals five times. Against the New York Americans on January 19, 1932, Conacher ripped five goals past Shrimp Worters during an 11–3 win. It was the greatest individual effort of his career. Later that same year, he assisted Ace Bailey's Cup-clinching goal.

## BERNIE GEOFFRION

His nickname, "Boom Boom," derived from the noise of his stick hitting the puck and the puck rico-

*Geoffrion*

cheting off the boards. On March 16, 1961, Geoffrion blasted the puck past Toronto goalie Cesare Maniago, doing what only Rocket Richard had managed before him: Score 50 goals in a season. While Richard did it with fire and relentless puck-handling prowess, Geoffrion used a different weapon—his awesome slap shot.

*Bobby Hull*

## GUY LAFLEUR

In the tradition of the Flying Frenchmen, Lafleur followed in the footsteps of Rocket Richard and Boom Boom Geoffrion when he made his debut in 1971. He immediately wowed NHL fans with his rifle shot off the right wing. From 1974–80, he enjoyed six successive 50-goal seasons and led the NHL with 60 tallies in 1977–78, winning one of his three scoring titles.

## AL MacINNIS

For most of the 1980s and early 1990s, MacInnis was recognized as the hardest-shooting defenseman—perhaps the hardest shooter, period—in the NHL. In the 1989 Stanley Cup playoffs, he demonstrated his terrific offensive skills when he carried the Calgary Flames to a championship and led all scorers with 31 points, earning the Conn Smythe Trophy as playoff MVP. He reached the 28-goal mark three times and, in 1990–91, notched 103 points.

## BOBBY HULL

Known respectfully around the NHL as the "Golden Jet," Hull combined foot speed with powerful shooting to become the game's first player to score 50 goals twice. Starting in 1961–62, he put together five 50-goal seasons. On February 21, 1970, Hull, inventor of the curved stick blade, used his frightening slap shot to beat Rangers goalie Ed Giacomin and became the NHL's third-ever 500-goal scorer, joining Rocket Richard and Gordie Howe.

## BRETT HULL

Heredity? Environment? Hard work and desire? Some or all of these factors are clearly at work in the mastery shown by Hull, whose goal-scoring ability has given him Hall of Fame qualification years before his career is approaching its conclusion. During a three-year span (1989–92), the Golden Brett, son of Bobby Hull, blasted 228 goals. Brett relies on a nasty slap shot and a quick-release, one-time wrist shot that few goalies can handle.

## FRANK MAHOVLICH

In 1960–61, Mahovlich, a 23-year-old left winger skating for the Toronto Maple Leafs, scored 38 goals in his first 35 games. Everyone watching felt that the Big M, with his graceful skating stride and powerful shot, was going to break Rocket Richard's 50-goal record. But Mahovlich buckled under the awesome pressure and fell just short, with 48 goals. In 1968–69, he scored 49 goals for Detroit. A six-time Stanley Cup champ, he scored 533 career goals.

# 10 FASTEST SKATERS

## PAUL COFFEY

Coffey's combination of instant acceleration, incomparable agility side-to-side, and the knack for shifting into reverse with seamless ease has gone a long way toward making him the NHL's all-time leading scorer among defensemen. Credited with possessing the "extra gear" common to all classic speed merchants, he also navigates in tight quarters without showing the least discomfort. He is a one-man skating clinic.

Cournoyer

## YVAN COURNOYER

A Flying Frenchman in all senses of the term, Cournoyer was famous for his blinding speed. A winner of 10 Stanley Cups during his 16-year NHL career, The Roadrunner stood just 5'7". He had to be fast to elude the thundering hits of defensemen who typically outweighed him by 40 or 50 pounds. He notched 428 career goals, plus the Stanley Cup-winning goal against Chicago in 1973, when he led all playoff scorers.

Fedorov

## SERGEI FEDOROV

North American hockey fans got a preview of the "new breed" of players from the Soviet Union during recent Olympic and World Championship tournaments, but little could prepare them for the speed and mobility of Fedorov, who carries the banner for all Russian skating masters. Fedorov's ability to skate and handle the puck at top speed often leaves defenders sprawling in his wake. Sergei earned a Hart Trophy in 1993–94.

Gartner

## MIKE GARTNER

Gartner has won several "Fastest Man in Hockey" competitions held at All-Star Games. A key to his quickness is his off-season training, during which he spends countless hours patrolling backcountry roads on in-line roller skates, keeping his legs—his money-makers—in top condition. In 1996–97, Gartner staged a major assault on his 700th career goal.

## BOBBY HULL

Goaltenders feared him for his terrifying slap shot, but defensemen also shared many moments of high anxiety when Bobby Hull came barreling down the wing. Hull, whose blond hair and quick feet earned him the nickname "Golden Jet," was powerfully built and low to the ice. He created countless scoring chances simply by outskating the opposition to open ice. And if he could not go around you, he was strong enough to go straight through you.

*Lafleur*

## GUY LAFLEUR

At the height of his career, Lafleur won three straight scoring titles (1976–78), leading the NHL once in goals and once in assists. It was his speed and grace as a playmaker and as a finisher that enabled The Flower to dominate. His ability to do everything at high speed—whether streaking down the ice and blasting the puck on net or creating a goal-scoring chance for a teammate—was his greatest gift.

## RICK MIDDLETON

Rangers fans still lament the day budding superstar Middleton was traded to Boston for an aging Ken Hodge. Middleton, called "Nifty" for his dazzling footwork, was a monument to finesse. His ability to race the puck through traffic and turn defensemen inside out was the key to his goal-scoring success. Middleton netted 448 goals and the 1982 Lady Byng Trophy, when he scored 51 goals and tallied only 12 penalty minutes.

## HOWIE MORENZ

In an era when it was common for NHL shooters to fire the puck from long range, then storm the net for rebounds, Morenz was a rarity. He would carry the puck deep and use his gifts of speed and agility to rebuff defenders. Tragically, a broken leg ended the career of this mythic superstar, and a fatal heart attack during his subsequent hospitalization ended his life at just 35.

## DENIS SAVARD

When Montreal drafted Doug Wickenheiser first overall in 1980, it bypassed Savard, who spent that year tearing up the Quebec juniors. Savard went to Chicago and dazzled fans for a decade. Savard created the "spin-o-rama"—a 360-degree turn, with the puck—which he used to elude defenders and discourage goalies. The fleet-footed center returned to Chicago in 1995 after winning a Stanley Cup in 1993—with Montreal!

## CYCLONE TAYLOR

Despite the claim of modern historians that "the game was different then," meaning slower, there is no diminishing the agility and savvy of Taylor. Cyclone once vowed to skate through an entire enemy lineup backwards and score a goal, and then went out and did it. Taylor, who used a stick with a bent shaft, played in the pre-NHL era with Ottawa, Renfrew, and Vancouver and once scored six goals in a game.

*Morenz*

# 10 BEST DEFENSIVE FORWARDS

*Carbonneau*

## GUY CARBONNEAU

The adage "offense wins games, but defense wins championships" is at the heart of most NHL teams' strategies. Carbonneau, one of the NHL's finest defensive forwards, won a pair of Stanley Cup titles with Montreal (in 1986 and 1993) and balanced that team's great offense. Small but fast, tenacious and tough, Carbonneau's ability to neutralize the opposition's best scoring threat earned him three Frank Selke Trophies (1988, 1989, 1992) as well as runner-up status twice more.

## SERGEI FEDOROV

Some critics suggest that the Frank Selke Trophy is a nonglamour award. Fedorov disproved the notion when, in 1994, he was voted the MVP of the NHL by the press and the players, taking the Hart Trophy and Lester B. Pearson Award thanks in part to his 120 points. That he was also selected as hockey's preeminent defensive forward, taking the Selke in a three-trophy sweep, was a clear celebration of his brilliance as a legitimate two-way threat.

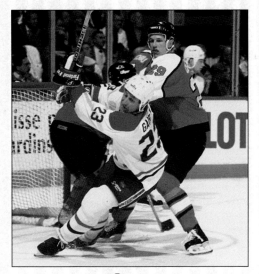

*Gainey*

## BOB GAINEY

Some historians insist that the Frank Selke Trophy was invented as homage to Gainey. In the late 1970s and 1980s, Gainey was hockey's best defensive forward, combining offensive skill—four 20-goal seasons—with a blanket of forechecking that stifled the opposition's offense. In the 1979 playoffs, Gainey earned the Conn Smythe Trophy by shutting down Phil Esposito and the Rangers in the Finals. He won the first four Selke Trophies (1978–81) as well.

*Kasper*

## STEVE KASPER

Ironically, Kasper came to the NHL from the Quebec juniors, a league notorious for its lack of defensive play. Yet during his 13-year career with Boston, Los Angeles, Philadelphia, and Tampa Bay, Kasper was one of the game's most skilled defensive centers, a superb faceoff man, and a low-to-the-ice skater with speed and quick wits. He was the second NHLer to win the Frank Selke Trophy, in 1982.

*Kelly (right)*

### RED KELLY

When Toronto acquired Kelly from Detroit in 1960, it converted the former Norris Trophy defenseman into a center and put him on a line with Frank Mahovlich. And while Kelly was a brilliant playmaker with the puck—helping the Leafs win four Stanley Cups—he was equally skilled away from the puck, using his speed and intelligence to read the opponents' developing attack and successfully interrupt its flow.

### DAVE KEON

Had he spent less of his 18-year career shadowing the opposition's top lines, Keon's own numbers might have been even more impressive.

As it was, the multifaceted center was no slouch, with 396 NHL goals on his way to a Calder Trophy, two Lady Byng Trophies, and a Conn Smythe Trophy as MVP of the 1967 playoffs. Keon won four Stanley Cups with Toronto and was celebrated for his terrific skating and tireless checking.

### DOUG MOHNS

Mohns, who earned the nickname "Diesel" because of his quick feet, was a talented skater who could play defense or left wing. In 1959–60 with Boston, he became only the second defenseman ever to score 20 goals. After 11 seasons in Boston, he was traded to Chicago, where he skated with Stan Mikita and Kenny Wharram. Thanks to his defensive experience, he was a skillful, reliable forechecker.

### CLAUDE PROVOST

A pit bull on skates, Montreal's Provost was small at 5'9" but had a tenacious spirit. In an era when Gordie Howe and Bobby Hull patrolled the NHL, Provost's assignment was to negate the superstars, which he did while scoring himself. In 1961–62, he clicked for 33 of his 254 career goals. In 15 NHL seasons, he helped Montreal win nine Stanley Cups.

### CRAIG RAMSAY

In the mid–1970s, when Buffalo was building its team into a Stanley Cup contender, the Sabres boasted a defensive Butch Cassidy-and-Sundance Kid duo up

front in Ramsay and Don Luce, who were considered by many to be the NHL's best penalty-killers and checkers. A gentlemanly forward, Ramsay put together eight straight 20-goal seasons (1973–81) and won the Frank Selke Trophy in 1985, in the finale of his 14-year career in Buffalo.

*Ramsay (left)*

### ED WESTFALL

When the Islanders came into existence in 1972–73, veteran winger Westfall was immediately snatched off the Bruins' roster in the expansion draft. It was around Westfall, a crafty defensive ace who had given balance to two Stanley Cup winners in Boston, that the Isles built their future. A modest scorer whose 25 goals in 1970–71 and 1975–76 were career highs, Westfall provided confidence to a young Islanders team on the Stanley Cup charge.

# 10 CLASSIEST PLAYERS

## SYL APPS

Putting aside his legendary accomplishments—one Calder Trophy, three Stanley Cups, and the self-sacrifice of leaving the NHL at the height of his career to serve in World War II—what made Apps a hero to a nation was his skill and unparalleled sportsmanship. In 423 NHL games, he scored 201 goals, sat out just 56 penalty minutes, and won the 1942 Lady Byng Trophy. He was renowned for his refusal to play dirty— or even to swear on the bench!

## JEAN BELIVEAU

It wasn't just his talent that captured the imagination of Montreal fans— for they had seen Aurel Joliat, Howie Morenz, and Rocket Richard before. The quality Beliveau emanated was one of intense sportsmanship and grace. He was big, but he moved with elegance. He was strong but never clumsy. His hands were as soft with the puck as they had once been punishing in a fight.

## FRANK BOUCHER

Arguably the most gentlemanly player ever to perform in the NHL, Rangers center Boucher enjoyed such a firm grip on the Lady Byng Trophy that the NHL ultimately decided to give him the trophy permanently while a new piece of hardware was commissioned for subsequent annual winners. Boucher, who took part in three Stanley Cups in New York, won seven Lady Byng Trophies from 1928–35, interrupted by Joe Primeau in 1932.

*Bucyk*

## JOHNNY BUCYK

Often lost in the tumult of Phil Esposito, Bobby Orr, and the high-powered Stanley Cup champion Bruins of 1970 and 1972 was the quiet presence of Bucyk, a one-time member of the Uke Line with Bronco Horvath and Vic Stasiuk. Bucyk scored 556 career goals in 23 seasons, won a pair of Lady Byng Trophies, and was a 51-goal scorer in 1970–71, sitting out just eight penalty minutes while his Big, Bad Bruins were terrorizing the NHL.

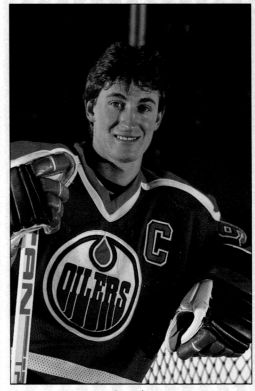

*Gretzky*

## WAYNE GRETZKY

When he wasn't demoralizing the competition with his one-of-a-kind scoring talent, Gretzky served as the game's clean-cut ambassador. Comporting himself in majestic fashion, slip-sliding through the NHL's mine field of would-be assassins, and demonstrating an advanced level of sportsmanship, the Great One captured four Lady Byng Trophies and finished second in voting five other times.

## RED KELLY

Despite spending most of his career as a defenseman, Kelly won four Lady Byng Trophies and took an average of one minor penalty (two minutes' worth) every eight games! An outstanding offensive defenseman, Kelly relied on his grace and intelligence to win the nightly David-and-Goliath wars he fought against bigger, stronger NHLers. He finished his career with 823 points and just 327 penalty minutes in 1,316 games. He also won eight Stanley Cups.

*LaFontaine*

## PAT LaFONTAINE

Playing clean and playing tough are not mutually exclusive. Consider LaFontaine, a small, fleet-footed play-making genius who regularly stands up to the toughest players in the NHL without backing down. He has never been a finalist for the Lady Byng Trophy, and has earned his share of penalty time, but he's also nearing his 500th goal. He's a courageous symbol of hockey's grace and elegance.

## FRANK NIGHBOR

Ottawa Senators pivot Nighbor, who played 13 years in the NHL, took home the inaugural Hart Memorial Trophy in 1924. A hard-working two-way player who never coasted and never threw a cheap shot, Nighbor was also the first player to win the Lady Byng Trophy, which was presented initially in 1925. Nighbor also won four Stanley Cups with Ottawa.

## BILL QUACKENBUSH

In 1948–49, Quackenbush tallied 23 points while playing defense for Detroit. Only Boston's Pat "Boxcar" Egan (24) had more points among NHL defensemen. Quackenbush, long recognized as one of the game's cleanest and best backliners, won the 1949 Lady Byng Trophy. Perhaps the Red Wings thought him too clean, for they abruptly traded him to Boston prior to the 1949–50 season. Quackenbush played 774 NHL games and sat out 95 penalty minutes.

## JEAN RATELLE

Precious few players ever enjoy an unofficial "free pass" from abuse by the opposition. But Ratelle, who starred on Broadway before completing his 21-year career in Boston, was so widely respected for his finesse and clean play that he rarely was targeted for cheap shots or excess punishment. Finishing his NHL run just nine goals shy of 500, Ratelle won two Lady Byng Trophies for sportsmanship (he was also runner-up twice) and a Masterton Trophy for dedication. Over his career he sat out just 276 penalty minutes.

*Ratelle*

# 10 GRITTIEST PLAYERS

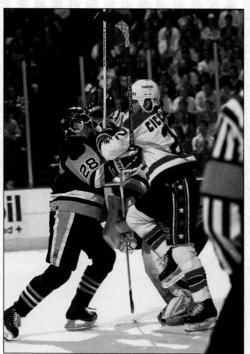

*Ciccarelli*

## DINO CICCARELLI

After a badly broken leg sidelined him during his second year of junior hockey, Ciccarelli was abandoned as an NHL prospect. No team would draft him. When his OHL career ended, he signed a free-agent deal in Minnesota. As a second-year man, he scored 55 goals, then reached 52 goals five years later. On January 8, 1994, he scored his 500th career goal. Small but tough, Ciccarelli has proven his courage on a nightly basis.

## BOBBY CLARKE

As a teenager, Clarke was viewed skeptically by NHL experts— even those who admired his talent and enthusiasm—for Clarke suffered from diabetes and required daily insulin injections. With his toothless grimace and curly hair, he had a boyish veneer, but that was quickly peeled away to reveal a fervent competitor. Clarke played 1,144 games and won three Hart Trophies, a Frank Selke Trophy, a Masterton Trophy, a Lester B. Pearson Award, and two Stanley Cups.

*Ezinicki*

## BILL EZINICKI

Wild Bill Ezinicki once had four teeth knocked out in a game, then returned later in the contest to score the game-winning goal. His insurance policy paid him $5 for every stitch he took—which he considered a boon to his finances, such was his style. Long before the concept of being "hard to play against" became vogue, Ezinicki was the ultimate warrior. He was loved in Toronto and hated (though respected) everywhere else.

## GORDIE HOWE

As the NHL's leading goal-scorer and predominant power forward for many years, Howe enjoyed public accolades and no shortage of "industry respect." However, he also suffered the nuisance of defensive shadows as well as a parade of young gunfighters anxious to prove their mettle against the master. Thus, Howe ran a perpetual gauntlet of physical abuse, suffered many concussions, and absorbed hundreds of stitches. Nevertheless, the great winger rarely missed a game.

## STEVE LARMER

Larmer was the Frank Sinatra of his own NHL destiny, doing it "his way." He made a decision to leave the Blackhawks in 1993 (for the Rangers), which cost him a consecutive-games streak that had reached 884—third best in NHL history. Larmer won the Calder Trophy in 1983 and had five 40-goal seasons. He quit with 441 goals, 1,012 points, and a Stanley Cup ring. The Rangers tried to talk him out of retirement, but Larmer, as always, marched to his own drum.

### TED LINDSAY

A scrapper who stood only 5'8", Terrible Ted Lindsay once referred to his hockey stick as "the great equalizer." Not only could he score goals (he won the scoring title in 1949–50), but he was also a fearsome pugilist who in 1958–59 led the league in penalty minutes (with 184, the second-highest total ever to that point). A classic "disturber," Lindsay played more than 1,000 NHL games and scored 379 goals. Away from the rink, he tried to organize the first players' union.

*Messier (bottom)*

### MARK MESSIER

The law-enforcement branch of the NHL has had an eye on Messier for many years, and he has paid several fines and sat out several suspensions for ramming players viciously into the boards or cutting them with his stick. More than any modern-era player, Messier is a throwback to a bygone style of NHL combat. He combines speed, enormous talent, and a lethal mean streak. Next to Gordie Howe, Messier is the most dangerous superstar ever.

*O'Reilly*

### TERRY O'REILLY

When the Bruins ascended to Stanley Cup contention in the late 1970s with a squad of muckers and diggers known as the "Lunch Pail Gang," the leader was O'Reilly, a hot-tempered Irish kid who cruised the right wing looking for, finding, and ending any trouble the opposition might start. A willing and able fighter, O'Reilly ultimately developed into an offensive threat as well, leading the Bruins in scoring (90 points) in 1977–78.

### MARCEL PRONOVOST

Among his claims to fame, Pronovost was long considered to be the most injured man in hockey, suffering countless fractures, sprains, cuts, and bruises. And yet he never changed one iota the reckless, self-sacrificial style of his play. One of the best defensemen of his time (1950–70), Pronovost won four Stanley Cups with Detroit and one with Toronto in his long career. His puck-rushing skills and toughness got him to the Hall of Fame.

### MAURICE RICHARD

It wasn't only brilliant skating and puck-handling that led to Rocket Richard's fame. Just as important were his qualities of irascibility and physical courage. He would drop the gloves and fight just about any time, anywhere. His legendary goal against Boston in the 1952 playoffs, when he was dazed from a serious head wound, exemplified his grit. Rival goalie Glenn Hall said Richard would come at him with "his eyes all lit up, flashing and gleaming like a pinball machine. It was terrifying."

# 10 BEST PERSONALITIES

## TURK BRODA

Long after he had served in World War II, Broda fought the real battle of the bulge—his own. Toronto boss Conn Smythe decided prior to the 1949–50 season that Broda was too fat, and he gave his goalie less than a week to trim down from 197 to 190 pounds. Always a happy-go-lucky performer, Broda fasted and sweated and, come the weigh-in, barely made it, grinning all the way. In his next game, he shut out the Rangers.

*Cherry*

## DON CHERRY

Loud and at times obnoxious, Cherry is one of hockey's most vocal and opinionated observers. His

*Joliat*

ostentatious clothing (loud, checkered jackets; wide, colorful ties; tie pins; and flashy cufflinks) and "old-time hockey" rhetoric combine to give Canadian hockey broadcasts an almost burlesque aspect. Once a respected coach who took the Bruins to the brink of the Stanley Cup, "Grapes" is equally famous for his bull terrier, Blue.

## AUREL JOLIAT

Not only was he a brilliant little player for Montreal in the early days of the NHL, but Joliat was also a quirky gent. One of his trademark oddities was his insistence on wearing a black baseball cap on the ice at all times. If someone knocked it off, he'd chase the hat before chasing the puck. The "Little Giant" pleased crowds everywhere.

## LANNY McDONALD

On March 21, 1989, with a trademark blast that eluded Islanders goalie Mark Fitzpatrick, McDonald ensured that his tremendous mustache—a big, red Yosemite Sam number that obliterated the bottom half of his face—would be but a footnote to his brilliant career, not the main story. The hard-shooting winger scored 500 goals (Fitzpatrick surrendering the last one) and, on his final night in uniform, raised the Stanley Cup with Calgary.

## JACQUES PLANTE

The record book is full of reasons Plante went to the Hall of Fame, but it doesn't mention his inventiveness

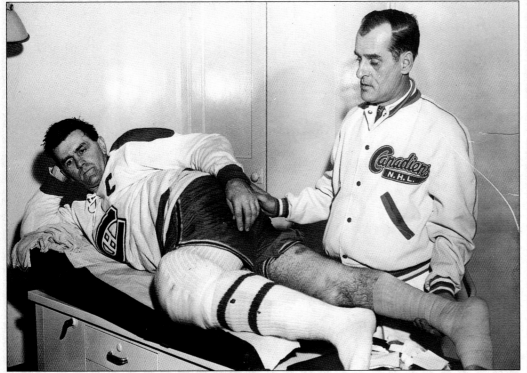

*Richard (left)*

or his reputation as a brainy, analytical man whose understanding of hockey was at the heart of his greatness. When he wasn't spending his free time knitting wool caps, Jake the Snake was concocting ways to improve his game; e.g., leaving the crease to handle the puck, a previously unheard-of practice.

## MAURICE RICHARD

Never a shrinking violet, Richard was a scene-stealer throughout his NHL career, as on the night Elmer Lach, his center on the Punch Line, notched his 200th career goal. Less than a minute later, while the crowd at the Montreal Forum cheered Lach, Richard skated alone on Chicago goalie Al Rollins and fired in his 325th goal to become the NHL's all-time leading goal-scorer. As with everything he did, Richard stole the show.

## DEREK SANDERSON

Flamboyant but tough, Sanderson was the chip on the collective shoulder of the Big, Bad Bruins of the 1970s, taunting the enemy and smirking at his victims as he beat them with a goal or with a flurry of punches. A brilliant penalty-killer and checker, Sanderson also had a touch with the puck and a hunger for the fast lane. Long-haired and mustachioed, the Turk was Boston's answer to New York's Joe Namath, pro sports' original high-profile ladies' man.

## EDDIE SHORE

The encyclopedia of adventures that shaped the legend of Shore includes an all-night drive through a blizzard to play a game in Montreal, a frenzied attack that nearly killed Ace Bailey, four MVP awards, a pair of Stanley Cups, and a reputation as hockey's most colorful character ever. Driven and inflexible, Shore did everything his way.

## TIGER WILLIAMS

As a student in high school, Dave "Tiger" Williams was asked to complete a vocational aptitude form. In the space regarding his choice of profession, he wrote "NHL." There was never any doubt. Rambunctious and ferocious, Williams set the NHL record for career penalty minutes. An unrepentant hooligan at times, he was known to ignore the handshake line at the end of playoff series.

## GUMP WORSLEY

About his profession, Lorne "Gump" Worsley once said, "If you want to be a good goaltender, it helps to be a little crazy. Not all goaltenders are nuts . . . only about 90 percent of them." A fun-loving goalie who admitted his favorite postgame meal was a beer and a cigarette, Worsley won four Cups in Montreal.

# 10 BEST EUROPEAN PLAYERS

*Bure*

## PAVEL BURE

Vancouver GM Pat Quinn took the NHL all the way to the Canadian courts of law to secure Bure, the 1989 Soviet Rookie of the Year, for his Canucks. In 1991–92, Bure scored 34 NHL goals and won the Calder Trophy. In each of the next two years, he ripped 60 goals—leading the league in 1993–94. Injuries have hampered him but not diminished his skills. A high-speed center, Bure is nicknamed the "Russian Rocket."

## SLAVA FETISOV

Called "the Bobby Orr of Soviet hockey," Fetisov was the anchor of the Soviet national and Central Red Army teams, winning three Soviet Player of the Year Awards (1982, 1986, and 1988). Teamed with Alexei Kasatonov, Fetisov was for more than a decade considered the best offensive defenseman in the world not playing in the NHL. He signed with the New Jersey Devils in 1989 and enjoyed modest success in the NHL.

## DOMINIK HASEK

Before he came to the NHL with Chicago in 1990, Hasek had established himself as the top goalie in eastern Europe, winning five Czechoslovakian Goalie of the Year Awards (1986–90) and three Czech Player of the Year Awards (1987, 1989, and 1990). After a slow start in the NHL, he was swapped to Buffalo for Daniel Berthiaume. In Buffalo, he won two Vezina Trophies (1994 and 1995).

*Hasek*

*Jagr*

## JAROMIR JAGR

Wayne Gretzky and Mario Lemieux notwithstanding, Jagr, winner of the 1995 Art Ross Trophy, is considered the most dangerous one-on-one player in the NHL. At 6'2" and 216 pounds, Jagr is big, strong, and exceedingly creative with the puck. After debuting in the NHL in 1990 at just 18, he steadily grew into a superstar. In 1995–96, he scored a career-high 62 goals, was second overall in points to Lemieux, and became an idol with his long, flowing hair.

## VALERI KHARLAMOV

Sadly for North American fans, Kharlamov played during the Cold

War. They rarely witnessed this creative genius, who led the Soviet national and Central Red Army teams to their greatest victories in Olympic and international play—especially against NHL All-Star teams in the 1970s. Tragically killed in a car accident, Kharlamov was the Soviet Union's best player ever.

## JARI KURRI

Not only is Kurri one of the greatest European players, but the Finnish sniper who enjoyed his greatest years on Wayne Gretzky's right flank in Edmonton is one of the greatest players ever to skate in the NHL. As the 1996–97 season (his 16th) began, he was 13th all-time in points (1,341). In 1985–86, he led the NHL in goals (68), setting a record for right wingers.

## KENT NILSSON

Nilsson was a tall, smooth-skating center who played with the finesse that typified the Swedish style of play. Nilsson made his NHL debut in 1979–80, after two seasons in the WHA. As a 23-year-old rookie, he scored 40 goals, then flirted with 50 the next year (falling just one short) while finishing third overall in points (131). He ended his NHL tenure with the Stanley Cup champion Oilers in 1987, then resumed his career in Europe.

## BORJE SALMING

When Salming arrived in Toronto from Sweden in 1973, his coun-

*Salming*

trymen had a reputation for shrinking away from the NHL's physical play—not being able to "take it." Over the next 17 years, the smooth-skating offensive defenseman shattered the stereotype, proving he was tough enough to survive and skilled enough to thrive. In 1,099 games in Toronto, he notched 768 points, third all-time behind Darryl Sittler and Dave Keon. He finished his career in Detroit in 1989–90.

## PETER STASTNY

Stastny was a 24-year-old defector from Czechoslovakia when he took the NHL by storm in 1980–81, setting NHL rookie records with 70 assists and 109 points. Stastny went on to a brilliant career that included five 40-goal seasons. He retired in 1995 with 450 goals and 1,239 points. Hall of Famer Stan Mikita is the only Czech-born player ever to amass more NHL points (1,467) than Stastny.

## VLADISLAV TRETIAK

Had it not been for the acrobatic goaltending of Tretiak, who was the first Soviet player inducted into the Hall of Fame, games between the Soviet Union and the NHL might never have become the tooth-and-nail battles that thrilled international hockey fans throughout the 1970s. Tretiak's showdown against Montreal's Ken Dryden on New Year's Eve, 1975, is considered one of the greatest games ever played.

# 10 BEST AMERICAN PLAYERS

## HOBEY BAKER

Baker, for whom the annual award for the best U.S. college player is named, never skated in the NHL. However, during his Ivy League tenure at Princeton University (1910–14), he led the Tigers to a pair of collegiate titles. He once took a team of U.S. amateurs to play in Quebec, where they beat the Montreal Stars. Observers on hand were sure Baker had to be Canadian, so high was the level of his play (and their arrogance).

## TOM BARRASSO

When the Buffalo Sabres called his name with the fifth pick at the 1983 draft, Barrasso, a native of Massachusetts, joined two others as the highest-drafted goalies in NHL history. Just 18 when he made his NHL debut in 1983–84, Barrasso quickly proved himself, winning both the Vezina and Calder Trophies. Later traded to Pittsburgh, the tall butterfly goalie helped the Pens win two Stanley Cups (1991 and 1992), setting a record with 11 straight wins in 1992.

## FRANK BRIMSEK

Boston fans were not happy when Tiny Thompson was banished to Detroit five games into the 1938–39 season to make way for 23-year-old rookie Brimsek, from Eveleth, Minnesota. But in his first month as a regular, Brimsek tossed three straight shutouts. En route to Calder and Vezina honors, Brimsek posted 10 of his 40 career shutouts, which earned him the nickname "Mr. Zero."

*Broten*

## NEAL BROTEN

One of three brothers to play in the NHL, Broten turned pro following his Hobey Baker Award-winning season at the University of Minnesota—just a year after helping the U.S. win a gold medal at the 1980 Olympics. As an NHL rookie in 1981–82, he notched 98 points. Four years later, the speedy center topped the century mark with 105 points. In 1995, Broten put his name on the Stanley Cup with New Jersey.

*Chelios*

## CHRIS CHELIOS

Many insist Chelios, a three-time Norris Trophy-winning defenseman, is the most talented American ever to skate in the NHL. Widely respected for his ability to play every facet of the game with courage, strength, and consistency, Chelios was a star at the University of Wisconsin and a member of the 1984 U.S. Olympic team before turning professional. Before his trade to the Blackhawks in 1990, the Chicago native won a Stanley Cup with the 1985–86 Canadiens. Chelios earned his Norris hardware in 1989, '93, and '96.

## PHIL HOUSLEY

When he came out of South St. Paul (Minnesota) High School as the sixth player chosen in the NHL's 1982 draft, Housley was favorably compared to Bobby Orr. In 1982–83, Housley jumped to the NHL at 18 without so much as a sniff of the minor leagues. After 14 years in Buffalo, Winnipeg, St. Louis, Calgary, and New Jersey, he spent the 1996–97 campaign with the Washington Capitals, chasing his 300th goal and 1,000th point.

## PAT LaFONTAINE

Unlike many U.S.-born players who apprentice at the college level, St. Louis native LaFontaine went to the Quebec juniors, where in 1982–83 he outplayed Mario Lemieux and led the QMJHL in scoring (104–130–234 in 70 games). After a year with the U.S. Olympic program, he played seven years with the Islanders. Traded to Buffalo in 1991, he became team captain and reached the 53-goal mark in 1992–93.

*Mariucci*

## BRIAN LEETCH

When the Rangers won the Stanley Cup in 1994, Leetch became the first American ever named playoff MVP. Born in Texas and raised in Massachusetts, Leetch came to New York from Boston College, where he was the top player in his conference as a freshman in 1986–87. After setting an NHL record for goals by a rookie defenseman (23), he won the 1989 Calder Trophy, then added the Norris in 1991–92.

## JOHN MARIUCCI

The godfather of Minnesota amateur hockey, Mariucci, who grew up with future Hall of Famer Frankie Brimsek, made his legend at the University of Minnesota in the 1930s. A tough-as-nails defenseman, he played five seasons with the Black Hawks from 1940–48, his career interrupted by a stint in World War II. A promising NFL prospect, "Maroosh" stuck to hockey because it was "more fun."

## JOE MULLEN

An NHL star from the mean streets of New York City? That's Joe Mullen. After four years at Boston College, Mullen signed with St. Louis and made a meteoric rise from farmhand to eventual 50-goal scorer (1988–89). A Stanley Cup winner in Calgary (1989) and Pittsburgh (1991 and 1992), he was the first American with 1,000 NHL points. In 1996–97, he became the first U.S. product to score 500 goals.

# 10 BEST GOONS

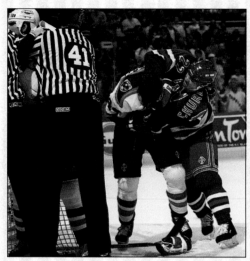

*Churla (right)*

## SHANE CHURLA

The single-season NHL record for penalty minutes is 472. In 1990–91, Churla played in just 40 games for the Minnesota North Stars and brawled his way to 286 PIM. Over an 80-game schedule, Churla's rate of misconduct would have earned him 572 PIM. In his first 10 years of NHL hockey, the cranky winger scored 26 goals while sitting out 2,195 minutes in penalties. Ironically, he has never led the league in penalty minutes.

## STEVE DURBANO

A journeyman defenseman who bounced around the NHL for six years, Durbano was notorious throughout major and minor pro hockey for his miscreant deeds both on and off the ice. Arrested on several occasions, "Demolition Durby" also touched off some of hockey's worst brawls, including a bench-clearing melee in 1972–73 when he ran over Atlanta goalie Phil Myre. Durbano sat out 1,127 PIM in his 220 NHL games, averaging more than five minutes per game.

## LOU FONTINATO

A muscular defenseman dubbed "Leaping Louie" for his energetic style, Fontinato lived by the sword and died by the sword. In 1955–56, he set an NHL record when he eclipsed the 200 mark in penalty minutes. He led the NHL in PIM three times during nine seasons with New York and Montreal. In 1959, he lost the most lopsided bout of his career, to Gordie Howe, and was never the same after.

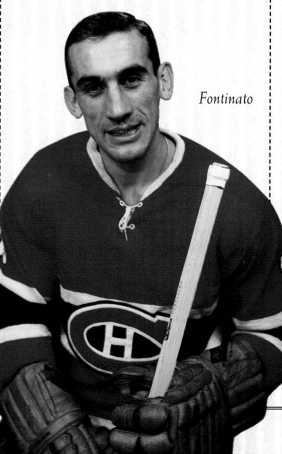

*Fontinato*

## JOEY KOCUR

Known for two things—his destructive punch and his staunch refusal to fight cousin Wendel Clark—Kocur is one of the most feared fighters in hockey. Kocur started fast, leading the NHL in penalty minutes during his rookie year (377). On February 21, 1989, he punched Islanders winger Brad Dalgarno and caved in Dalgarno's eye socket, sending the fallen winger into a one-year retirement. Kocur's career penalty minutes have outpaced his goal-scoring by a ratio of 32–1.

## JOHN KORDIC

A troubled young man who battled drug dependency and died at 26 as a result of an overdose, Kordic was a torpedo on skates during an eventful seven-year NHL career. After showing some promise in Montreal, he was traded several times and always was plagued by instability on the ice—where he would fight anyone, any time—and off. He scored just 17 goals in 244 NHL games while sitting out 997 penalty minutes (4.1 minutes per game).

## CHRIS NILAN

Earning the nickname "Knuckles" for his prodigious punching ability, American-born Nilan patrolled the wing in Montreal, New York, and Boston during a 13-year career. Hot-tempered and quick to fight, Nilan twice led the league in penalty minutes. Once, after a fight with Paul Baxter, he hurled a puck at his adversary and nailed the unsuspecting enemy for 10 stitches in the head. Nilan finished his career with 3,043 penalty minutes, among the top five all-time.

*Probert*

## BOB PROBERT

Though he has neither the hardest punch nor the meanest temperament in the game, Probert is widely recognized as hockey's best fighter, principally for his ability to endure long battles. He will wait for his chance, then demolish his adversary with a flurry. In 1987–88, he led the NHL in penalty minutes (398) but also scored 29 goals,

putting him in a higher class of "enforcer." In his first 552 NHL games, he sat out 2,327 minutes—the equivalent of nearly 39 games.

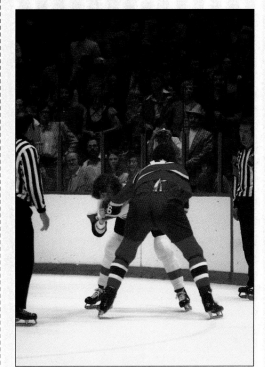

*Schultz (left)*

## DAVE SCHULTZ

Typically soft-spoken off the ice, Dave "The Hammer" Schultz began fighting late in his junior career when he realized he was good at it. Later, as the main act in the Philadelphia Flyers' traveling goon review, he rewrote the record books with 472 penalty minutes in one season (1974–75), marking the third straight year in which he led the league. He averaged 4.4 penalty minutes per game during his career.

*Williams*

## TIGER WILLIAMS

Unlike some pugilists who turn pussycat away from the rink, Dave "Tiger" Williams was as ornery in civvies as he was in full pads. An outspoken antagonist whose "do anything to win" attitude bred contempt in his foes, Williams retired as the NHL's all-time penalty leader with 3,966 minutes in 962 games. In addition to taking on the NHL's heavyweights, he often launched attacks against players recognized for their noncombative style of play.

## HOWIE YOUNG

Unpredictable. A loose cannon. A head case. These are just some of the descriptions used to paint the colorful picture of Young, a talented skater with a huge shot who terrorized the NHL in the 1960s. As a third-year NHLer in 1962–63, he broke Lou Fontinato's penalty record with 273 minutes. Struggles with alcohol resulted in Young's career fizzling out prematurely. Though he would eventually reform, he wasted his best years in the minors.

# 10 BEST HOT STREAKS—SKATERS

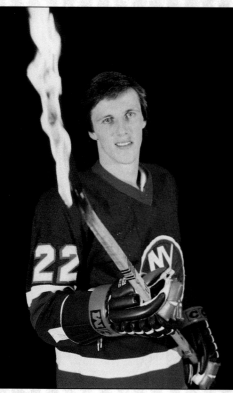

*Bossy*

## MIKE BOSSY

In the 1983 Stanley Cup semifinals, the Islanders rode Bossy's brilliant scoring to a six-game victory over the Bruins, propelling them into the Finals for the fourth straight year. Bossy, who finished the playoff season with a league-high 17 goals, scored the game-winning goals in Games 1, 3, 4, and 6, giving him an NHL-record four game-winners in a single series.

## PUNCH BROADBENT

The 1921–22 Ottawa Senators won 14 of 24 games thanks to the explosive skill of Harry "Punch" Broadbent, a rugged right winger whose league-high 32 goals and 46 points earned him the scoring championship. During one stretch, Broadbent scored at least once in 16 straight games, setting an NHL record that has lasted 75 years. During the streak, Broadbent bent the twine 25 times.

*Broadbent*

## WAYNE GRETZKY

On December 30, 1981, in just his third season, Gretzky became the fastest 50-goal scorer in history after ripping five goals against the Philadelphia Flyers. It took the Great One just 39 games to reach 50, smashing the record of 50 games shared by Maurice Richard and Mike Bossy. While Gretzky admitted his NHL was less defense-oriented than Richard's, he went on to finish the 1981–82 season with 92 goals!

## WAYNE GRETZKY

When the Oilers finally dethroned the Islanders and won their first Stanley Cup in 1983–84, Gretzky racked up points in a stunning 51 consecutive games, shattering his own previous record of 30 games, which he had set in 1982–83. Beginning on opening night, Gretzky's lengthy barrage included 61 goals and 153 points. He didn't take his first doughnut until the Kings stopped him on January 28, 1984.

## MEL HILL

In the 1939 Stanley Cup semifinals between Boston and the Rangers, a new hero emerged, rookie Mel Hill. In Game 1, he broke a 1–1 tie with just 35 seconds left in triple overtime. Two nights later, he scored to end Game 2, again in overtime. Though the Rangers battled from a three-game deficit to force Game 7 in Boston, Hill once again proved a hero. His series winner came at 8:00 of OT and earned him the nickname "Sudden Death."

*Kurri*

## JARI KURRI

Playing with Wayne Gretzky, right winger Kurri blasted his way into the record books during the 1985 play-offs when he scored 12 goals against the Black Hawks in the conference finals (during which Edmonton outscored Chicago 44–25). He finished the playoff season with a record four hat tricks, including one four-goal outburst. In the postseason, Kurri tallied 19 goals, tying the league record.

## REGGIE LEACH

Rarely does a player win the Conn Smythe Trophy in a year when his team fails to win the Stanley Cup. In 1976, when the defending-champion Flyers were swept by Montreal in the Finals, Leach led all scorers with a record 19 goals. Nine of his goals came against Boston in the semifinals—five in the series-clinching sixth game. Though the Flyers were ultimately shot down, Leach, with a nine-game goal-scoring streak, won playoff MVP honors.

## RICK MIDDLETON

Boston barely sneaked past Buffalo in the 1983 Adams Division finals, needing an OT goal from Brad Park in Game 7 to advance. Without Middleton, their top-scoring center, it's doubtful they'd have gone that far. Against the Sabres, "Nifty" set an NHL single-series record with 19 points (five goals, 14 assists). Though Boston was eliminated by the Islanders in the Cup semifinals, Middleton was the second-leading play-off scorer with 33 points.

## MAURICE RICHARD

In a six-team league where defense was emphasized and the goalies were the best in the world, Richard's goal-scoring prowess was nothing short of sensational. On March 18, 1945, on the final night of the 1944–45 schedule, Richard capped a brilliant season when he scored on Boston's Harvey Bennett in a 4–2 win and became the first NHLer ever to score 50 goals in 50 games. Richard's hot streak, which included a five-goal game against Detroit, lasted all season.

## BRYAN TROTTIER

Trottier is living proof that Wayne Gretzky doesn't hold every playoff scoring record. In 1981, when he led his Islanders to their second of four straight Cups, Trotts had a record 18-game points streak, with 11 goals and 29 points. Those 18 games were just part of a 27-game points streak that had begun with the last seven games of the 1980 playoffs and would extend through Trottier's first two playoff games in 1982.

*Richard*

# 10 BEST GAMES—SKATERS

## BOBBY BAUN

With his team facing elimination in the 1964 Cup Finals against Detroit, Toronto's Baun was crumpled by a shot to his right leg above the ankle with Game 6 tied and time running out. Unable to stand, he was carried from the ice. Refusing X-rays, he ordered doctors to freeze the leg, then went back into action. In overtime, Baun scored the winning goal. Toronto went on to win Game 7 and the Cup. Baun, with a fractured fibula, spent the next six weeks in a cast.

*Berenson (No. 7)*

## RED BERENSON

Gordon "Red" Berenson was a bench jockey in Montreal and New York before the expansion St. Louis Blues acquired him early in 1967–68. Emerging as a major scoring threat the following year, he exploded at Philadelphia on November 7, 1968, scoring six goals. He tied Busher Jackson's and Max Bentley's joint record of four goals in a period. Berenson remains the only NHLer ever to score six goals in a road game.

## WAYNE GRETZKY

As the 1989–90 season began, the Kings' Gretzky needed just 14 points to eclipse Gordie Howe as the NHL's all-time leading scorer. On October 15, 1989, in Edmonton no less, he matched Howe's 1,850 points with an early assist, then led his Kings in a late-game rally, tying the game at 4–4 with less than a minute to play for his 1,851st point. After ceremonies halted play, the game went into overtime. At 3:24 of sudden-death, Gretzky himself scored the dramatic winning goal.

## MARIO LEMIEUX

With Lemieux leading the charge, Pittsburgh seemed poised to knock off the Flyers in the 1989 playoffs. On April 25, 1989, with the series tied 2–2, Lemieux went on a rampage, scoring three times in the first seven minutes and adding a fourth goal before the first period ended. Before the night was over, he assisted three more goals and scored into an empty net for a record five-goal, eight-point night. Pittsburgh won the game 10–7 but lost the series 4–3.

## JOE MALONE

On the last day of January 1920, with temperatures dipping to -25 Fahrenheit, the Quebec Bulldogs iced the Toronto St. Pats 10–6. The Bulldogs got the bulk of their offense from the spry, speedy "Phantom" Malone, who scored seven goals—an NHL record that has endured for more than 75 years. Malone scored three of his seven goals in a two-minute span, thrashing the highly respected Jake Forbes, in goal for Toronto.

## BILL MOSIENKO

Chicago's Mosienko didn't just break the record for fastest hat trick in NHL history; he shattered it. On March 23, 1952, in the final game of the season, Mosienko slipped three goals past rookie goalie Lorne Anderson in just 21 seconds, destroying the record of three goals in 1:52, set by Detroit's Carl Liscombe in 1938.

*Mosienko*

## MAURICE RICHARD

After being shut down by Toronto in the first game of the 1944 playoffs, Richard warned Leafs goalie Paul Bibeault that things would soon change. The ever-dramatic Richard then went on a tear. In the second period of Game 2, he scored twice in 17 seconds and completed the hat trick before the period ended. Richard added two more goals in the third stanza. The final score was Rocket 5, Toronto 1.

## DARRYL SITTLER

It's unlikely anyone will ever surpass Sittler's NHL record of 10 points in a single game. On February 7, 1976, the Toronto center was a one-man wrecking crew, scoring six times against Boston and adding four assists in an 11–4 home-ice triumph. By his own admission, it was "one of those nights," when everything he touched turned to gold. En route to immortality, Sittler eclipsed Rocket Richard and Bert Olmstead, who had eight-point games.

## PATRIK SUNDSTROM

On April 22, 1988, the Cinderella New Jersey Devils were locked in second-round playoff combat with the Washington Capitals when their leading scorer, Sundstrom, caught lightning in a jar. In Game 3, the Swedish sensation notched a hat trick and set up five other goals, becoming the first man in league history to score eight points in a postseason match. The Devils won 10–4.

## IAN TURNBULL

Nearly 60 years after Toronto's Harry Cameron became the first NHL defenseman ever to score four goals in a game, another Leafs backliner came along and wrote a new chapter in the history books. On February 2, 1977, Turnbull, a gifted offensive defenseman who had gone 30 games without a goal, took his frustrations out on the visiting Red Wings, blasting five goals—the most ever by a defender.

*Sundstrom (right)*

# 5 BEST HOT STREAKS—GOALIES

### GERRY CHEEVERS

Besides wearing a stylish facemask, with all the potential stitches he might have suffered drawn in with indelible ink, Hall of Fame goalie Cheevers took the Bruins to a pair of Stanley Cups (1970 and 1972). In 1971–72, he appeared in 41 games and put together a league-record 32-game undefeated streak, winning 24 and tying eight. This broke the previous NHL mark of 23 games set by former Bruins goalie Frank Brimsek in 1940–41.

### ALEX CONNELL

Twice in his 12-year career, Connell led the NHL with 15 shutouts, setting a record that only George Hainsworth (with 22 in 1928–29) would ever beat. In 1927–28, while tending goal for the defending-champion Ottawa Senators, Connell registered six straight shutouts and kept the puck out of his goal for a record 461 minutes and 29 seconds. Connell won 20 games that year, and 15 of them were white-washes.

### KEN DRYDEN

After playing only six regular-season games in 1970–71, rookie Dryden went between the pipes for Montreal in the 1971 playoffs, while Phil Myre and Rogie Vachon sat and watched. In one of the greatest debut performances ever, Dryden carried the Habs past the defending-champion Bruins

in seven games and the North Stars in six. He then outdueled Chicago's splendid Tony Esposito in a nail-biting seven-game Finals series, earning the Conn Smythe Trophy as playoff MVP.

### PATRICK ROY

Going into the 1993 playoffs, the Canadiens' best weapon was clearly their incomparable "money" goalie, Roy. After losing Game 1 of their opening-round series to Quebec in overtime, the low-scoring Habs found themselves in 10 additional sudden-death games (two against Quebec, three against Buffalo, two against the Islanders, and three against L.A. in the Finals). En route to a "surprise" Stanley Cup, Roy set an NHL record by winning 10 straight sudden-death games.

### TERRY SAWCHUK

The tradition of throwing an octopus on the ice in Detroit goes back to the 1952 playoffs, when the powerful Red Wings were backstopped by the unbeatable Sawchuk. In Detroit's eight straight playoff wins—the first-ever such postseason sweep—Sawchuk tossed four blanks (two each against Toronto and Montreal) and posted an 0.62 goals-against average, the lowest since Lorne Chabot's 0.50 in 1935. The eight-armed octopus was homage to Sawchuk's eight-game excellence.

*Connell*

# 5 BEST GAMES—GOALIES

## CHARLIE GARDINER

Sadly, the most courageous game of Gardiner's life, Game 4 of the 1934 Stanley Cup Finals between his Black Hawks and the Red Wings, was also his last. A two-time Vezina honoree, Gardiner held Detroit scoreless through four-and-a-half periods despite suffering from a painful infection that had spread through his body and would soon claim his life. When Mush March scored at 10:05 of double OT, Gardiner was a champion. Two months later, he was dead.

## SAM LoPRESTI

Hailing from the same Minnesota town that sent Frank Brimsek to the NHL, LoPresti had a much shorter NHL career than Mr. Zero—just two seasons with Chicago. But on the night of March 4, 1941, the Eveleth goalie gave a heroic performance in Boston—against Brimsek's Bruins. Powered by Bill Cowley, Dit Clapper, and the Kraut Line (Schmidt-Bauer-Dumart), the Bruins launched an NHL-record 83 shots at LoPresti. Sam set his own record with 80 saves, though he lost 3–2.

## ALFIE MOORE

Prior to April 1938, Moore's NHL résumé listed all of 18 games with the lowly Americans. When Chicago goalie Alex Karakas turned up lame on the eve of the Stanley Cup Finals between the Hawks and Toronto, Moore was summoned. Allowing just one goal, he miraculously beat the Leafs 3–1. A protest from Toronto GM Conn Smythe kept Moore out of Game 2. Eventually, the Hawks won the Cup. Moore, whose "15 minutes" had expired, retreated into obscurity.

*Turk Broda, Smith*

## NORM SMITH

After taking the Red Wings to a league title in 1935–36, Smith entered the playoffs hotter than Ted Lindsay's temper. In Game 1, he notched a shutout against the Montreal Maroons as the teams battled to six overtimes before Modere "Mud" Bruneteau finally ended the longest game in NHL history. Two nights later, he blanked Montreal again. He didn't give up a goal until 12:02 of Game 3, ending a span of 248:32 of shutout hockey.

*Pierre Larouche, Tretiak, Dan Grant*

## VLADISLAV TRETIAK

On December 31, 1975, hockey fans everywhere were treated to an exhibition of sheer acrobatic brilliance when Central Red Army goalie Tretiak, the best goalie in the world who never played in the NHL, stood the Montreal Canadiens on their ears. Tretiak earned his team a 3–3 tie in what has been called the greatest game ever played. Tretiak, lithe and technically masterful, stopped 35 shots and inspired Montreal defender Serge Savard to quip, "Tonight, God was Russian."

# 10 BIGGEST DRAFT BUSTS

## NEIL BRADY

No. 3, 1986. A big, physical center, Brady was a member of two Memorial Cup championship teams at Medicine Hat (WHL) after New Jersey picked him third overall in the 1986 draft. However, Brady's scoring never developed. He scored 33 AHL goals in 1990–91 but was traded to Ottawa and later signed as a free agent with Dallas. He spent the bulk of his time in the minors, with just nine goals in his first 90 NHL games.

*Chapman*

## BLAIR CHAPMAN

No. 2, 1976. Pittsburgh had high hopes for right winger Chapman when it used the second pick in the 1976 draft to acquire him from Saskatoon of the WHL. He fired 14 goals as an NHL rookie in 1976–77, then added 24 as a sophomore. Traded to St. Louis in 1979–80, he recorded a pair of 25-goal seasons with the Blues. However, his scoring soon began to tail off and his NHL career ended in 1983, after just seven mediocre seasons.

*Chyzowski*

## DAVE CHYZOWSKI

No. 2, 1989. The Islanders used the second pick of the 1989 draft to grab 56-goal scorer Chyzowski from Kamloops (WHL). Rugged and willing, Chyzowski was, however, a terrible skater—a problem the Isles thought they could fix. After five unsuccessful attempts to earn a permanent NHL job, Chyzowski signed with Detroit in 1995, with whom his minor-league career continued.

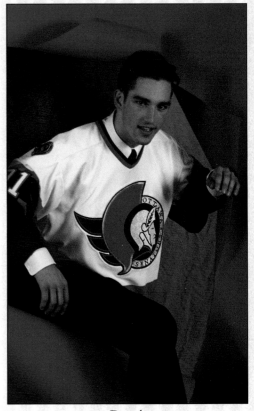

*Daigle*

## ALEXANDRE DAIGLE

No. 1, 1993. After collecting 247 points in 119 games at Victoriaville (QMJHL), Daigle was picked first overall by Ottawa in 1993 and signed to a $12-million deal that was the catalyst for an eventual rookie salary cap. Daigle struggled badly in the years after a 20-goal rookie season. He appeared on the verge of a breakthrough before 1995–96, but a broken arm ended his season with just five goals in 50 games. In 1996–97, he began to score with some regularity.

*Joly*

### BARRY DEAN

No. 2, 1975. When Kansas City spent the second pick in the 1975 draft on Medicine Hat scoring ace Dean, they thought they were getting an offensive sparkplug. Instead, Dean rejected them for Phoenix of the WHA and didn't play in the NHL until 1976–77, when he found the net just 14 times in 79 games. Traded to Philadelphia, Dean managed only 11 goals over his remaining two seasons.

### GREG JOLY

No. 1, 1974. When defenseman Joly led Regina to the Memorial Cup in 1973–74, there was every reason to think he'd be an impact player in the NHL, and expansion Washington drafted him first overall in 1974. Over the next nine seasons, he played 365 NHL games—only nine with the Caps, who traded him to Detroit in 1976—but scored just 21 career goals, as he was unable to translate his junior success to the pros.

*Lawton*

### BRIAN LAWTON

No. 1, 1983. When North Stars GM Lou Nanne drafted Lawton first overall in 1983, he gave the Rhode Island high school star a jersey with No. 98 on it, insisting Lawton was that close to another Wayne Gretzky. Lawton played nine NHL seasons with six teams and scored 112 goals in 483 games. The 21 goals he collected in 1986–87 were a career best. Following his retirement in 1993, he became a sports agent.

### WAYNE McBEAN

No. 4 1987. Drafted fourth overall by Los Angeles in 1987, McBean was a high-speed, offensively skilled defenseman. In his 211 NHL games over seven years, it became clear that McBean wasn't physically suited for the big leagues. Tall but lanky, he couldn't establish himself and spent most of his disappointing career shuttling between the NHL and the farm, notching just 10 NHL goals.

### JACQUES RICHARD

No. 2, 1972. When they used their first-ever draft pick on QMJHL scoring champion Richard, the expansion Atlanta Flames hoped they were getting a franchise star who'd lead them to prominence. Instead, the Flames picked a vastly gifted winger who was just as likely to score 10 goals (Buffalo, 1978–79) as he was to score 52 (Quebec, 1980–81). In 556 NHL games, Richard scored 160 goals, about half of what had been projected.

### DOUG WICKENHEISER

No. 1, 1980. It was hard to argue with Montreal when it selected Wickenheiser—the WHL's top scorer and MVP—with the first pick in the 1980 draft, passing up Denis Savard, Larry Murphy, Paul Coffey, and Brent Sutter to get him. Wickenheiser had scored 89 goals at Regina in 1979–80. Little could they have known that he would net just 111 goals in 556 NHL games over the next decade.

# 10 BEST GENERAL MANAGERS

## PUNCH IMLACH

You didn't have to like the irascible Imlach—many of his players didn't—to appreciate his savvy as a bench boss and personnel manager. Imlach took over the struggling Maple Leafs in 1958 and, over the next decade, fashioned hockey's first "dynasty," as his Leafs won three straight Stanley Cups (1962–64). Short-tempered and cocky, Imlach's "my way or the highway" approach didn't win him many friends, but it helped Toronto to four Stanley Cups.

*Imlach*

*Adams*

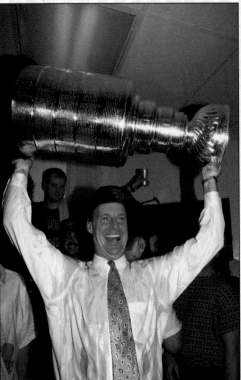

*Craig Patrick*

## JACK ADAMS

Brash and confident, Adams turned a successful playing career into an even more impressive tenure as an executive for the Red Wings. Taking over as GM-coach in 1927–28, he spent the next 34 years building championship teams, bringing home seven Stanley Cups. With the financial backing of James Norris, who bought the team in 1933, Adams shaped 12 first-place teams, including seven straight from 1948–55.

## CRAIG PATRICK

Patrick, grandson of Lester Patrick, wasn't around when the Penguins chose Mario Lemieux in 1984. Instead, his defining moment as Pittsburgh's GM came when he acquired Ron Francis from Hartford and gave the team a 1–2 punch at center that took them to consecutive Stanley Cups (1991 and 1992). A player of modest skill, Patrick proved his aptitude as a talent judge when he served successfully as the Rangers' GM (1981–86) before going to Pittsburgh in 1990.

## LESTER PATRICK

Thanks to the "difficult" nature of Conn Smythe, its original GM, the Rangers franchise was in some disarray even before its first season, 1926–27. Patrick was called in from the PCHL, and he not only calmed the Rangers' seas but he built the team into a Stanley Cup winner in just its second year. As GM, he served for 18 years, won three playoff titles, and developed some of the greatest players ever, including Frank Boucher and Bill Cook.

## SAM POLLOCK

Pollock had the unenviable task of following Frank Selke as GM of the Canadiens in 1964–65. Under Selke, the team had won six Stanley Cups. Pollock was expected to deliver, and did he ever! From 1964–77, his hand-built Habs won eight silver mugs. Pollock made his reputation in the expansion era by fleecing his NHL colleagues—trading declining veterans for high draft picks.

## ART ROSS

Among the most creative minds ever to bless hockey, Ross was responsible for designing the modern-day hockey puck and goal net. And he was the chief architect of the powerful Bruins teams that dominated the NHL in the 1920s. As Boston GM for three decades (1924–54), Ross built three Cup champions (1929, 1939, and 1941). He was immortalized in 1947, when the NHL's annual scoring champion was first presented with the Art Ross Trophy.

## GLEN SATHER

Glen "Slats" Sather may only have been an average player, but he survived 10 years on crafty intelligence and wit. As GM of the Edmonton Oilers, he showed masterful skill with draft picks, selecting Kevin Lowe, Mark Messier, Glenn Anderson, Paul Coffey, Jari Kurri, Andy Moog, Grant Fuhr, Steve Smith, Jeff Beukeboom, and Esa Tikkanen. He won five Stanley Cups from 1984–90.

## FRANK SELKE

Unlike his more garish colleagues, Selke was dignified as well as crafty. In his first NHL job, as Conn Smythe's right-hand man in Toronto, he swapped Frank Eddolls to Montreal for Ted Kennedy. Smythe was serving in World War II at the time and later forced Selke's resignation for insubordination. Selke had the last laugh when Kennedy went to the Hall of Fame. Meanwhile, Selke became GM of Montreal and won five Cups from 1946–64. He also built the great Canadiens farm system, which cranked out the NHL's best talent for three decades.

## CONN SMYTHE

A colorful, dauntless advocate of hockey, Smythe starred at the University of Toronto and was a World War I hero long before he came to the NHL. In 1927, a year after his falling out with the owner of the expansion Rangers franchise (for whom he had signed a batch of talented players), Smythe took over as GM of Toronto. In the next three decades, Smythe's Leafs won seven Stanley Cups, including three straight (1947–49) and six of 10 from 1942–51.

*Smythe*

## BILL TORREY

After apprenticing in minor pro hockey, Torrey took the reins as GM of the first-year New York Islanders in 1972. A graduate of St. Lawrence University, Torrey used his business and psychology training to craft a well-balanced team made up of future Hall of Famers Denis Potvin, Mike Bossy, Bryan Trottier, Billy Smith, and others. Torrey built the Isles into a four-time Stanley Cup champion (1980–83), and he later worked his magic on the Florida Panthers in the 1990s.

# 10 BEST ARENAS

## BOSTON GARDEN

Dirty, rat-infested, and lacking such modern conveniences as air-conditioning, Boston Garden was nonetheless an almost holy site for hockey. With its fading banners honoring Shore, Hitchman, Orr, Clapper, Esposito, Bucyk, and Schmidt—as well as five Stanley Cups—the "Gah-den" was a relic but also a museum as venerable as its many treasures.

*Boston Garden*

## CHICAGO STADIUM

One of the loudest buildings in North America, the now-demolished Chicago Stadium was replaced in 1994 by the United Center as the home of the Blackhawks. The Stadium was a gigantic indoor bowl with an overhanging press box (that caused many nosebleeds), indoor brick walls, and a massive pipe organ, which added to the acoustic bedlam. Called the "Madhouse on Madison Street," the building stood for 65 years and was home to three Stanley Cup champs (1934, '38, and '61).

*Chicago Stadium*

## JOE LOUIS ARENA

Despite enduring two generations without a Stanley Cup, the Detroit Red Wings are one of the hottest tickets and boast one of the best hockey-watching arenas in the NHL. Joe Louis Arena, which opened in 1979, seats more than 18,000 and offers SRO options to allow for nearly 20,000. Without a bad seat in the house, the building is replete with banners honoring seven Stanley Cup teams and the retired numbers of five Hall of Fame Red Wings.

## MADISON SQUARE GARDEN

Smoke-filled and loud, the original Madison Square Garden, on 49th Street and Eighth Avenue in New York, was a building whose atmosphere yelled out, "Anything goes!" With chicken wire instead of Plexiglas as well as shared penalty boxes (in the early days), the Garden was home to both the Rangers and, for a couple of years, the rival Americans. Lester Patrick's Rangers won three Stanley Cups (1928, '33, and '40) but never clinched the Cup on home ice.

## MAPLE LEAF GARDENS

The last of the "Original Six" arenas still in operation, Toronto's Maple Leaf Gardens lacks all of the splash and pizzazz of 1990s sports architecture, but it nevertheless qualifies as hallowed ground in the NHL. Built in 1931, it is both an active arena and a museum, with exhibits recalling past teams and celebrating the Leafs' long, storied history as champions, with 11 Stanley Cup titles.

*Maple Leaf Gardens*

## OLYMPIA STADIUM

They were still called the Cougars when Detroit's Johnny Sheppard scored the first home goal at Olympia Stadium on November 22, 1927. Renamed the Red Wings, the team spent the next 52 years on Grand River Avenue, winning six Stanley Cups and clinching at home in 1937, '50, '52, '54, and '55. The Olympia was a loud but intimate building with lots of atmosphere.

## THE POND OF ANHEIM

Called the "Taj Mahal of NHL arenas," The Pond of Anaheim, home of the Mighty Ducks, boasts an extravagance of elegance, with great marble concourses, polished granite exteriors, huge glass archways, and gleaming brass fittings. This distinctly Disneyesque operation features "Wild Wing," the Mighty Ducks' mascot, sailing down from the rafters during the pregame show.

## MET CENTER

Famed for its multicolored seats arranged with party-mix randomness, the Met Center in Bloomington, Minnesota, was situated to best accommodate fans from Minneapolis and St. Paul. Clean and viewer-friendly, the Met Center had excellent sight lines from every seat. The stadium's sole melancholy feature was the No. 19 banner to honor Bill Masterton, fatally injured during a game in 1968.

## MONTREAL FORUM

Before the official opening of Le Centre Molson, the Montreal Forum was the NHL's most revered temple. The Habs' dressing room was famed

*Montreal Forum*

for its portraits of past heroes, high above the players' lockers, looking down on the current Canadiens and reminding them of their duty. Home of 23 Stanley Cup winners in 70 years, the Forum was also known for serving the best grilled hot dogs in the NHL.

## THE SPECTRUM

Its interior detailed in blood red, the Philadelphia Spectrum—currently home of the Flyers' AHL affiliate—is a tall, loud building with lobby exhibits commemorating its past champions. There is also a statue of Rocky Balboa, another of fabled good-luck charm Kate Smith, and several others that reenact key goals in Flyers history. The only NHL arena with genuine cheese steaks and hoagies, the Spectrum is all about "atmosphere."

# 10 BEST TRADITIONS

## CHICAGO STADIUM'S PIPE ORGAN

Built in the 1920s, Chicago Stadium was one of the loudest and most majestic NHL arenas for nearly seven decades. Part of its majesty came from the massive Barton pipe organ built into one end of the building. When the Blackhawks moved to the United Center in 1994, great pains were taken to recreate the organ's sounds, which were recorded and then programmed into the new Allen organ.

*Hats on ice*

## HATS ON THE ICE FOR HAT TRICKS

In 1943, Toronto boss Conn Smythe told his photographers (the Turofsky brothers) that if they took any pictures showing empty seats, they'd have to buy Smythe a new hat. Local Stetson dealer Sammy Taft took it one step further, offering a new chapeau to any NHLer who scored three goals in a game—a hat trick. Soon, fans became aware of the promotion and began throwing their own hats on the ice when a player hit the trifecta.

## HOCKEY NIGHT IN CANADA

Ask most modern players where they got their first inkling of a dream to play in the NHL and they'll tell you it was while sitting in front of the family television on Saturday night, watching *Hockey Night in Canada*. Hosted by Dave Price, the nationwide broadcast was first aired on November 15, 1952, by the Canadian Broadcasting Company, sponsored solely by Imperial Oil. Broadcasting legend Foster Hewitt did the play-by-play.

*Kate Smith*

## KATE SMITH SINGS "GOD BLESS AMERICA"

Among the more eccentric features of the Flyers of the mid–1970s was "good luck charm" Kate Smith, the veteran radio and TV singer. Smith first sang "God Bless America" before Philly's home opener in 1973–74 (a 2–0 win over Toronto) and was there to sing before the Flyers' Cup-clinching win against Boston on May 19, 1974. Philly was hard to beat when Smith sang.

*Octopuses in Detroit*

## OCTOPUSES IN DETROIT

From 1942–68, the NHL playoffs lasted two rounds; eight wins were needed to hoist the Stanley Cup. In the 1950s, the Red Wings were frequent entrants in the Finals, and in 1952 Terry Sawchuk won eight straight games to win the Cup. On April 15, 1952, Jerry Cusimano, whose father was in the fish business, tossed an octopus on the ice at Olympia Stadium, its eight tentacles representing the eight wins. The practice has endured in Detroit for five decades.

## THE PENALTY SHOT

From 1934–35 (when the penalty shot was introduced) through 1995–96, the NHL staged 4,300 games, during which only 567 penalty shots were awarded. Habs winger Armand Mondou missed on the first try ever, against Toronto's George Hainsworth, on November 10, 1934. Three days later, St. Louis defenseman Ralph Bowman beat Maroons goalie Alex Connell.

*Bill Durnan, Turk Broda*

## PLAYOFF HANDSHAKE LINE

One thing that sets the NHL apart from other major sports is the traditional handshake line at the conclusion of playoff series. As far back as can be recalled, teams have put aside their differences and shared genuine congratulations at series end. But once in 1954, when Montreal and Detroit battled in the Finals, the Habs refused to shake

hands after Tony Leswick's OT goal beat them in Game 7 of their bitterly fought series.

*Rats on ice*

## RATS AT MIAMI ARENA

Early in the 1995–96 season, the Florida Panthers were preparing for a practice when a rat scurried through their locker room. Scott Mellanby, a hard-shooting winger, intercepted the rodent and fired it into a cement wall, killing it. Mellanby instantly became known as "Ratman." Fans at Miami Arena soon began celebrating goals by throwing plastic rats on the ice—hundreds of them—which ultimately forced the NHL to install delay-of-game rules to discourage further littering.

## ROGER DOUCET'S "O, CANADA"

Though small in stature, Roger Doucet, with his shock of white hair, was huge in the resonance and drama of his singing voice. When he stepped onto the ice at the Montreal

Forum to deliver "O, Canada"—typically in French—it was as though he was heralding the arrival of yet another triumph for the Flying Frenchmen. Doucet was a fixture at the Forum for years.

*Roger Doucet*

## THREE STARS OF THE GAME

In 1936, *The Hot Stove League*, a radio show aired across North America and sponsored by Imperial Oil, began the practice of naming three stars for each hockey game it broadcast as a way of helping the sponsor advertise its Imperial Three-Star gasoline. In its early years, the three selections were often made by former NHL stars. According to legend, Joe Primeau and Syl Apps were two of the original three-star judges.

# 10 BIGGEST BLOWOUTS

*Bruins 10, Maple Leafs 0*

## BRUINS 10, MAPLE LEAFS 0

In Game 1 of Boston's 1969 Stanley Cup quarterfinal series against Toronto, Phil Esposito scored four goals and John Bucyk and Derek Sanderson each had a pair as the Bruins humiliated the Maple Leafs 10–0. The game was marred by fights after Leafs defender Pat Quinn knocked Bobby Orr unconscious with an elbow late in the second period. Boston swept the series.

## CANADIENS 16, BULLDOGS 3

On March 3, 1920, the Canadiens set an NHL record when they scored 16 goals against Quebec while surrendering just three. The game featured a showdown between the league's top two goal-scorers—the Canadiens' Newsy Lalonde and Quebec's Joe Malone. On this night, Lalonde enjoyed a small moral victory, although it was Malone who eventually won the goal-scoring championship, 39–36.

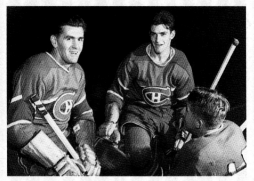

*Rocket Richard (left)*

## CANADIENS 11, MAPLE LEAFS 0

On March 30, 1944, Montreal crushed the Maple Leafs 11–0 and knocked them out of the Stanley Cup semifinals. Led by Rocket Richard and Ray Getliffe (two goals and five points each), the Habs erupted before a record Forum crowd of 13,215. Leading 5–0, Montreal netted five goals in less than four minutes in the third period. Meanwhile, goalie Bill Durnan stymied Toronto for his first career playoff shutout.

## MAPLE LEAFS 14, RANGERS 1

The Rangers had fourth place (and the final playoff berth) locked up when they visited Toronto on March 16, 1957. Their effort that night against the fifth-place Leafs was, at best, half-hearted as they lost 14–1. Brian Cullen and Syd Smith had hat tricks, while Teeder Kennedy—on the eve of retirement—notched four assists. Eight different Leafs scored against Gump Worsley while only Ron Murphy could solve Toronto goalie Ed Chadwick.

## NORTH STARS 15, JETS 2

On November 11, 1981, the Minnesota North Stars grounded the Winnipeg Jets with an eight-goal outburst in the second period and cruised to a 15–2 win. Bobby Smith had four goals and seven points, while 11 different North Stars beat Jets goalie Doug Soetaert—who faced 51 shots, 27 of them in the second period alone.

## OILERS 10, FLAMES 2

Not surprisingly, Wayne Gretzky was at the heart of Edmonton's lopsided 10–2 triumph over Calgary in Game 3 of the 1983 Stanley Cup quarterfinals. After being held scoreless in the series' first two games, Gretzky notched four goals and three assists. Lost in the glow of Gretzky's one-man show was a three-goal performance by Mark Messier.

## OILERS 13, KINGS 3

En route to their third Stanley Cup in four years, Edmonton faced Los Angeles in the opening round of the 1987 playoffs. In Game 2, Edmonton handed the Kings their crowns in a humiliating 13–3 rout. Jari Kurri scored four goals and Wayne Gretzky added a goal and six assists (one of his three career seven-point playoff games), while Mark Messier and Kent Nilsson each scored twice. Edmonton scored its 13 goals on just 45 shots.

Sabres 14, Capitals 2 (Don Luce, No. 20; Bill Clement, No. 10)

*Jari Kurri*

## RED WINGS 15, RANGERS 0

The most decisive victory in NHL history saw Detroit skate into Madison Square Garden on January 23, 1944, and blast 15 goals past rookie Rangers netminder Ken McAuley. Three Red Wings—Murray Armstrong, Don Grosso, and Syd Howe—had five points (Howe notched a hat trick), and Joe Carveth had four assists. The only Red Wings not to figure in the scoring were defenseman Cully Simon and goalie Connie Dion, who notched his only career shutout.

## SABRES 14, CAPITALS 2

Talk about breaking out of a slump! The Buffalo Sabres went through a difficult stretch in December 1975, losing three of four games as their fearsome French Connection Line was temporarily disconnected. On December 21, however, they fired 50 shots at Washington goalies Ron Low and Bernie Wolf. Rick Martin scored four goals, Fred Stanfield had three, and Gil Perreault and Don Luce each scored twice as Buffalo humbled the Caps 14–2. For Washington, the game was a microcosm of their season. The expansion club finished 8–67–5 while being outscored 446–181.

## SENATORS 23, DAWSON CITY 2

When Joe Boyle brought his Dawson City team from the Yukon to Ottawa to challenge the Silver Seven in 1905, little could he have known that the 4,000-mile journey would end in the worst beating any Stanley Cup "contender" has ever absorbed. In the second game of their two-game set, Ottawa's Frank McGee ripped 14 goals against goalie Dave Finney as Ottawa cruised 23–2. McGee's record has never been approached, much less matched.

*Note: Category includes NHL regular-season and Stanley Cup playoff games only.*

# 10 UGLIEST FIGHTS

*Boucha vs. Forbes*

## BOUCHA VS. FORBES

On January 4, 1975, Minnesota's Henry Boucha and Boston's Dave Forbes fought and were sent to the penalty box, with Forbes vowing revenge. When their penalties expired, Forbes attacked Boucha with the butt end of his stick, opening a 25-stitch gash over Boucha's eye, then hammered him with punches as he lay bleeding on the ice. Forbes was subsequently indicted for aggravated assault, while Boucha missed 19 games after surgery to repair his fractured eye socket.

## CANADIENS VS. RANGERS

For sheer bloodletting mayhem, few donnybrooks in NHL history have rivaled the brawl staged on March 16, 1947, between the Canadiens and Rangers at the Garden. Longtime enemies Ken Reardon and Cal Gardner were the catalysts, but the bloodiest of the simultaneous bouts featured Rocket Richard against Bill Juzda, Bill Durnan against Bill Moe, Leo Lamoureux against Hal Laycoe, and Butch Bouchard in a dizzying one-punch knockout of Bryan Hextall.

## GREEN VS. MAKI

Few men tougher than Ted Green ever played in the NHL, but on September 21, 1969, Green met his match. During an exhibition game between his Bruins and St. Louis, Green engaged in a stick fight with Wayne Maki. Maki speared Green in the abdomen, while Green whacked Maki below the shoulder. When Maki brought his stick down on Green's skull, the burly defenseman collapsed. Rushed to the hospital, his life was saved by emergency surgery. "there was a rumor that he died," said teammate Ed Westfall. Green didn't play again for a year.

*Maki (left) vs. Green*

## HOWE VS. FONTINATO

On February 1, 1959, Lou Fontinato stood up for a teammate by going to the aid of Eddie Shack, who was being mauled by Fontinato's hated rival, Gordie Howe. "Leapin' Louie" challenged Howe and connected with three huge punches before the Detroit legend countered. Then, in the most one-sided devastation ever witnessed on an NHL rink, Howe smashed Fontinato with a series of piston-driven punches, rerouting his nose and sending him to the hospital.

## KOCUR VS. DALGARNO

On February 21, 1989, Detroit's notorious brawler, Joey Kocur, dropped his gloves to fight rugged Islander winger Brad Dalgarno, who had earlier thrashed Red Wing forward Shawn Burr. Against Kocur, however, Dalgarno was badly overmatched. With one of his patented rock-hard punches, Kocur crushed the bone around Dalgarno's left eye and sent him to the hospital. Dalgarno didn't skate again for more than a year.

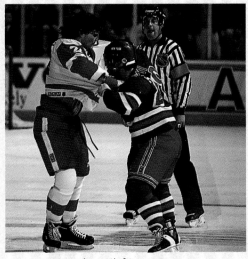

*Probert (left) vs. Domi*

## PROBERT VS. DOMI

On December 2, 1992, at Madison Square Garden, Rangers hitman Tie Domi and Detroit brawler Bob Probert engaged in a rematch of an earlier bout in which Domi had bloodied the Red Wing's nose. Thanks to Domi's brash pre-bout jaw-flapping, fans knew a marquee rematch was about to unfold. One witness counted 60 punches thrown, with Probert narrowly declared the winner—and still heavyweight champ.

## RICHARD VS. BRUINS

Though he stood only 5'7", Henri Richard was plenty tough and fearless. On January 1, 1958, against Boston, he fought three Bruins in succession. First, he dropped reputed hitman Leo Labine with a punch that cost Leo eight stitches in the eyebrow. When big Jack Bionda came to Labine's rescue, Richard delivered a punch that spread Bionda's nose across his face. Finally, Fern Flaman waded in but Richard more than held his own, earning new respect around the league.

## RICHARD VS. LAYCOE

On March 13, 1955, the ever-combustible Rocket Richard tangled with archenemy Hal Laycoe after the Bruin defenseman sliced opened Rocket's scalp with a high stick. Richard reacted by hacking viciously at Laycoe, then unleashing a flurry of punches at linesman Cliff Thompson. Richard was banned for the rest of the season and the playoffs, costing him his only scoring title and resulting in a riot at the Montreal Forum on March 17.

## SCHULTZ VS. ROLFE

The 1973–74 Rangers were high-salaried and talented, but many saw them as "fat cats." In the playoffs against the Flyers, Philly hitman Dave Schultz attacked Dale Rolfe early in Game 7 and mercilessly pummeled New York's tall-but-placid defenseman. None of the Rangers went to Rolfe's rescue, and the team exited the playoffs in resounding shame.

## SHACK VS. ZEIDEL

The blood feud that simmered hotly between Eddie Shack and Larry Zeidel for more than a decade exploded on March 7, 1968. The longtime enemies became embroiled after exchanging cheap shots and immediately resorted to swinging their sticks. When it was over, both were bleeding freely from head wounds. Zeidel accused Shack and the Bruins of inciting him with anti-Semitic taunts. The Bruins denied the charge, but Zeidel soon thereafter left the NHL.

*Richard Riot*

# 10 WORST INJURIES

### ACE BAILEY

A case of mistaken identity nearly cost Irvin "Ace" Bailey his life. On December 12, 1933, in Boston, Bailey's Maple Leafs were embroiled with the Bruins when King Clancy tripped Eddie Shore. Shore looked around and spotted Bailey, thinking he'd found the culprit. Shore charged Bailey, checking him viciously from behind and flipping him over backwards. Bailey crashed headfirst into the ice, suffering a fractured skull. Surgery saved his life, but he never played again.

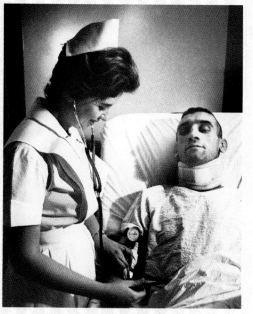

*Fontinato*

### LOU FONTINATO

Fontinato was rugged and fearless, always sacrificing for the team. On March 9, 1963, while skating for Montreal at the Forum, Lou's career came to a sudden end when he and the Rangers' Vic Hadfield crashed into the boards while chasing a loose puck. Though Fontinato smartly ducked to avoid Hadfield's inevitable elbow, he slammed headfirst into the wall and suffered a career-ending broken neck.

*Gordie Howe*

### GORDIE HOWE

On March 28, 1950, with the playoffs only just begun, Detroit's Howe took a run at Toronto center Ted Kennedy. But Gordie missed Kennedy, lost his footing, and slid into the boards, striking his head against the base of the wall. Carried from the ice on a stretcher, Howe was rushed into surgery with a life-threatening fractured skull. Incredibly, he made a full recovery and won the 1950–51 scoring title.

### MARK HOWE

An eventful 5–5 tie in Hartford between the Islanders and Whalers on December 27, 1980, took a scary turn late in the third period. Hartford defenseman Howe crashed heavily into the goal cage and impaled himself on the metal center post of the net. Taken away on a stretcher, he was treated at a hospital for a deep laceration of his upper left thigh and buttock—a serious puncture wound that only narrowly missed the base of his spine.

### PAT LaFONTAINE

Late in a November 16, 1991, game in Calgary, speedy Sabres center LaFontaine was skating in alone on goalie Mike Vernon when Jamie Macoun slashed him from behind. LaFontaine went down with a double fractured jaw and a severed facial artery. He underwent immediate surgery to stop the bleeding, and doctors inserted a metal plate to stabilize his jaw. Unrepentant, Macoun insisted LaFontaine, who missed 13 games, was hurt when he fell to the ice.

### CLINT MALARCHUK

One of the bloodiest, most frightening injuries in NHL history was suffered by Sabres goalie Clint Malarchuk on March 22, 1989. In the midst of a goalmouth scramble, the skate of St. Louis winger Steve Tuttle slashed across Malarchuk's throat, severing his external jugular vein. As a fountain of blood spurted from the wound, doctors raced to stop the flow and stabilize the wound. After repairs, Malarchuk was released from the hospital the following day.

## BILL MASTERTON

A well-liked journeyman player, Masterton was playing with the expansion North Stars in 1967–68. On January 13, 1968, in just his 38th NHL game, he was trying to split the Oakland Seals' defense when Larry Cahan and Ron Harris converged on him. Though Masterton prepared for the hit, he flipped backwards and crashed headfirst to the ice. Masterton, age 29, died after laying in a coma for two days. He became the first NHLer ever to lose his life in a league game.

## OWEN McCOURT

In 1907, organized hockey suffered its first game-related fatality when McCourt, a skilled scorer from Cornwall, was attacked by Montreal's Charles Masson, who allegedly used his stick to render McCourt bloody and unconscious. The following morning, McCourt died in a hospital. Masson later faced a murder charge, but he was acquitted when the judge could not determine that, in fact, it was Masson's stick that dealt the fatal blow.

## HOWIE MORENZ

The legendary Morenz was in his second tour of duty with the Canadiens when, on January 28, 1937, he crashed into the boards, broke his ankle, and shattered bones in his leg. Morenz,

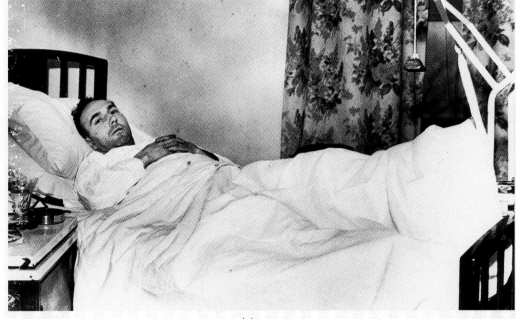

*Morenz*

age 34, was hospitalized for several weeks. As he watched his hockey days end, he lapsed into severe depression. On March 8, he died in his sleep from a coronary embolism. Those who knew him, however, said Morenz died of a broken heart.

## BORJE SALMING

Maple Leaf defenseman Salming experienced his worst nightmare on November 26, 1986, in a game in Detroit. In the middle of a pileup in front of his goal, Salming was flat on his back, protecting the puck, when his defense partner shoved Detroit's Gerard Gallant. Out of balance, Gallant stepped on Salming's face, opening a gash that started above Borje's right eye and continued down his face to his chin. It required

nearly 300 stitches and three hours of surgery to close.

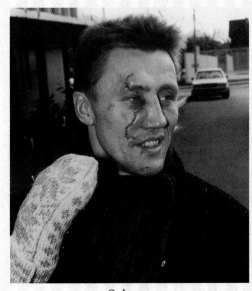

*Salming*

# 10 BEST GOALIE MASKS

*Belfour*

## ED BELFOUR'S "SCREAMING EAGLE"

The bright red paint that shines like so many coats of lacquer is just the beginning of Belfour's magnificent creation. On either side of his "helmet" portion, Eddie the Eagle sports a screaming eagle painted with striking precision. The aggression in the hunting bird is an apt analogy for the intensity of Belfour the goalie.

## CLINT BENEDICT'S "PHANTOM OF THE OPERA"

Thanks to a shot from Howie Morenz that mashed his nose and cheekbone, Benedict became the first NHL goalie to wear a mask, if only briefly, in the early 1930s. His leather protector was fashioned after models taken from football and boxing gear. However, it proved a terrible experiment, as his vision was impaired by the wide nose piece.

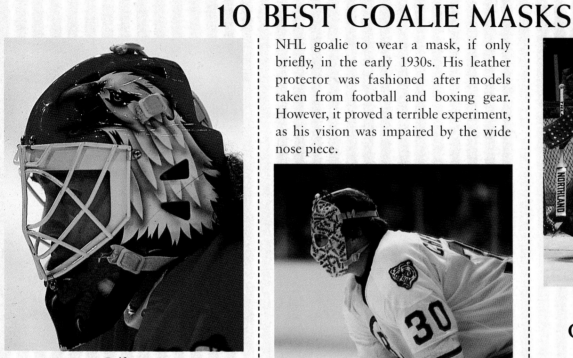

*Cheevers*

## GERRY CHEEVERS'S "STITCHES"

When Cheevers put the mask on in the early 1970s, he was the goalie for the Big, Bad Bruins. In keeping with the team's general attitude, Cheevers began to draw the actual stitches he would have received—had he not put on the mask—onto the plastic, creating a pseudo-Frankenstein persona that would have done well on any Halloween night.

*Gratton*

## GILLES GRATTON'S "LEO"

Playing just two NHL seasons, with St. Louis and the Rangers, Gratton was a free spirit who was known to streak at practices. He also had one of the NHL's first artistic masks, beautifully painted with the face of a wide-mouthed snarling lion—a tribute to his astrological sign, Leo.

## RON HEXTALL'S "PHILLY MONTAGE"

As technology improves, one area, goalie masks, continues to bear the mark of mankind's brilliant handiwork—and nowhere more so than on Philadelphia goalie Hextall's headgear. Though he's known as a dirty player, Hexy's mask—depicting the Philadelphia skyline and Liberty Bell done in black, gold, and red—is the epitome of class.

## GARY SIMMONS'S "COBRA"

A tall, beefy goalie who toiled with weak NHL teams, Simmons distinguished himself mostly with his ostentatious facemask. His fiberglass mask, painted basic black, featured a neon-green Cobra in striking position, with its jaws gaping and its tongue extended.

## JOHN VANBIESBROUCK'S "PANTHER"

V anbiesbrouck chose a red, white, and gold panther mask after joining the expansion Florida Panthers in 1993. The panther's mouth frames the Beezer's face, with shiny white teeth atop and below. Beady red eyes give the snarling cat a sinister visage.

*Plante ("Mummy")*

## JACQUES PLANTE'S "MUMMY"

T he Rangers' Andy Bathgate forever changed Plante's approach when he bounced a slap shot off the Montreal goalie's face on November 1, 1959. After repairs, Plante reemerged with a brown fiberglass mask that he'd worn in practice. Against his coach's wishes, he continued to wear the mask and continued to win games, and he never played barefaced again.

## JACQUES PLANTE'S "PRETZEL"

P lante, who was always on the cutting edge of innovation, continued to experiment with different kinds of face shields. In the early 1960s, Plante switched from his solid fiberglass mask to a "pretzel" style that resembled a more intricate football facemask, with horizontal and vertical bars. Ken Dryden would wear a similar mask.

## MIKE RICHTER'S "STATUE OF LIBERTY"

R angers goalie Richter chose New York's greatest symbol for his ornately detailed headgear. Front and center on Richter's red, white, and blue facemask is a kind of star burst of the head of the Statue of Liberty. Along the jaw lines of his mask are the words "New York" and "Rangers."

*Vanbiesbrouck*

# 5 BEST BROADCASTERS

*Cusick*

### FRED CUSICK

Calling hockey games for nearly 45 years, Cusick, voice of the Boston Bruins, is the current dean of hockey broadcasters. A former player at Northeastern University, Cusick has been a regular voice on TV and radio ever since. He called the first nationally televised Bruins game on CBS in 1957 and was elected to the Hall of Fame in 1984.

### JOHN DAVIDSON

A thinking man's goalie, Davidson played 10 seasons in the NHL with St. Louis and the Rangers. After hanging up his skates, J. D. moved to the broadcast booth as "color man" on Rangers telecasts. His insider's knowledge and candid assessments earned him immediate praise. In addition to Rangers games, he serves as a TV commentator for FOX.

*Gallivan*

### DANNY GALLIVAN

Longtime voice of the Canadiens, Gallivan brought such colorful phrases as "eeee-normous save" to his typical hockey call. After modest beginnings in Nova Scotia, he got his break in 1950 when Habs broadcaster Doug Smith fell ill. After two years as a "substitute" in the booth, Gallivan took over full-time in 1952, and he remained with the Habs until 1984.

### FOSTER HEWITT

Hewitt was only 20 years old when he turned a novice newspaper job at the *Toronto Star* into a trailblazing broadcasting career. On March 22, 1923, via telephone hookup in a glass booth, he recounted the events of a local game for CFCA radio. Later, from his perch in the famed gondola at Maple Leaf Gardens, he became the voice of hockey, calling games on TV and radio for 55 years. Hewitt is credited with coining the phrase, "He shoots . . . he scores!"

*Hewitt*

### DAN KELLY

A former host of *Hockey Night in Canada*, Kelly spent two decades as the play-by-play man for the St. Louis Blues. Many credit the vastly knowledgeable and affable Kelly with teaching U.S. hockey fans how to watch the game. Kelly was elected to the Hall of Fame in 1989.

# 5 BEST MOVIES

## THE BOYS ON THE BUS

In the late 1980s, the Edmonton Oilers were the subject of a documentary by Canadian movie and record producer Dave Mackenzie. The 85-minute, behind-the-scenes film followed the Oilers from their disastrous playoff loss to Calgary in 1986 through their Stanley Cup victory (their third) in 1987. It's a candid, intimate, and sometimes funny portrait of a championship team.

## THE DEADLIEST SEASON

Michael Moriarty is oddly cast as a marginal talent who resorts to violence to stay in the majors. Filmed in the 1970s, *The Deadliest Season* attempts to take a hard line on sports violence (specifically hockey violence), but at times it seems ill-informed. Moriarty's character becomes first a goon and then a killer. Far-fetched in its dramatic license, it is nevertheless a well-intentioned and thought-provoking effort.

## GROSS MISCONDUCT: THE BRIAN SPENCER STORY

Brian "Spinner" Spencer lived by the sword, playing a hard-hitting game of contained violence for 10 NHL seasons. He also died by the sword, surviving a murder charge in Florida before ultimately losing his life as a robbery-shooting victim. *Gross Misconduct* is the dramatic retelling of Spencer's tragic life,

based on a 1988 biography by Toronto journalist Martin O'Malley.

## MIRACLE ON ICE

With Karl Malden leading a cast of recognizable Hollywood stars, *Miracle on Ice* is a well-filmed if disappointingly written account of the U.S. Olympic hockey team's 1980 win over the Soviet Union. Malden steals the show as coach Herb Brooks, while the story itself is fairy-tale material. A notable bright spot is the realistic action sequences, which are often very poor in hockey movies.

## SLAP SHOT

Profane and hilarious in equal measures, *Slap Shot* isn't so much a portrait of minor pro hockey as it is a devastating depiction of human frailty—of the lengths to which desperate people will go to survive. Starring Paul Newman as aging player-coach Reg Dunlop, this alternately funny and heartbreaking romp follows the travails of the Charlestown Chiefs, whose players are fighting (literally) for their lives in a corporate-driven era when winning takes a back seat to finances. *Slap Shot* was directed by the acclaimed George Ray Hill.

Slap Shot *(Paul Newman)*

# 5 BEST BOOKS

### BEHIND THE CHEERING

**B**y **Frank Selke.** Published in 1962, *Behind the Cheering* is a warm and well-written insider's look at the NHL from its beginnings through more than five decades. Recognized as one of the greatest managers in the history of hockey, Selke saw it all. He became associated with Conn Smythe in 1918 and was running the great Canadiens into the 1960s.

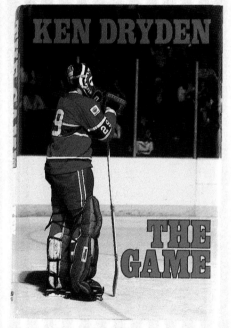

The Game

### THE GAME

**B**y **Ken Dryden.** Astonishingly honest and consistently insightful, *The Game* is the first book authored by Hall of Fame goalie Dryden. It's about his penultimate season with the Canadiens

(1978–79), when age, team complacency, and the onset of self-doubt began to make him contemplate not only what had been a marvelous career in hockey, but what the future might hold.

### REQUIEM FOR REGGIE

**B**y **Earl McRae.** McRae's 149-page *Requiem for Reggie* was published in 1977, and it instantly catapulted McRae to the status of most-admired (among colleagues) and most-hated (among his subjects) sports writer in North America. The title refers to a moving portrait of Reggie Fleming at the sad end of his violent career, but the book also contains biting features on Phil Esposito and goal judge Derek Sanderson—plus the story of goal judge Eddie Mepham.

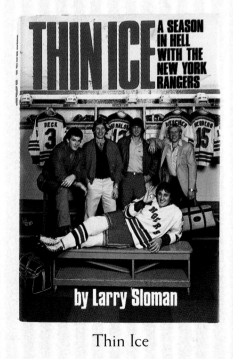

Thin Ice

### THIN ICE

**B**y **Larry Sloman.** Larry "Ratso" Sloman, author of *On the Road with Bob Dylan*, spent the 1979–80 season with the New York Rangers. The result was *Thin Ice: A Year in Hell with the New York Rangers*. Far from flattering, it is a forthright account of underachievement and disappointment in the most demanding of sports markets.

### TRAIL OF THE STANLEY CUP

**B**y **Charles L. Coleman.** *Trail of the Stanley Cup* is one of the very few remaining original source materials that recount the early years of professional hockey. It chronicles the game from the birth of the Stanley Cup in 1893 through 1967, when the league expanded from six teams to 12. In three volumes, this tome is highly regarded among historians both for its breadth of content as well as its attention to detail.

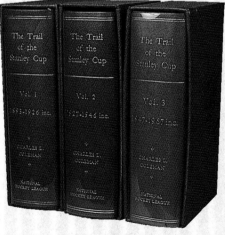

Trail of the Stanley Cup

# BEST NICKNAMES

Eddie "The Eagle" Belfour
Max "Dipsy Doodle Dandy" Bentley
Johnny "China Wall" Bower
Frank "Mr. Zero" Brimsek
Harry "Punch" Broadbent
Modere "Mud" Bruneteau
Steve "The Puck Goesinski" Buzinski
Bill "Big Whistle" Chadwick
Don "Grapes" Cherry
Charlie "The Big Bomber" Conacher
Fred "Bun" Cook
Harold "Baldy" Cotton
Yvan "The Roadrunner" Cournoyer
Alex "Fats" Delvecchio

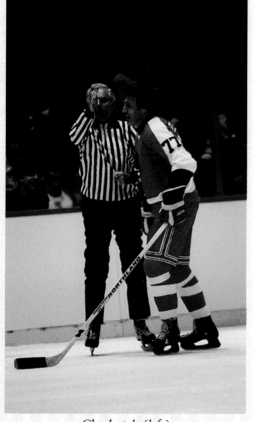

*Chadwick (left)*

"Leapin' Louie" Fontinato
Emile "The Cat" Francis
Johnny "Black Cat" Gagnon
Bernie "Boom Boom" Geoffrion
Wayne "The Great One" Gretzky
Glenn "Mr. Goalie" Hall
"Bad Joe" Hall
Camille "The Eel" Henry
"Sugar Jim" Henry
Mel "Sudden Death" Hill
Larry "Suitcase" Hillman
Bill "Flash" Hollett
Ed "Boxcar" Hospodar
Gordie "Mr. Hockey" Howe
Bobby "The Golden Jet" Hull
Ted "Stinky" Irvine
Alex "Killer" Kaleta
Bob "Battleship" Kelly
Bob "Hound Dog" Kelly
Jerry "King Kong" Korab
Edouard "Newsy" Lalonde
Pierre "Lucky" Larouche
"Terrible Ted" Lindsay
Ken "Rat" Linseman
Harry "Apple Cheeks" Lumley
Hubert "Pit" Martin
Ken "Tubby" McAuley
John "Pie" McKenzie
Rick "Nifty" Middleton
Howie "The Stratford Streak" Morenz
Bernie "Pumper" Nicholls
Frank "The Pembroke Peach" Nighbor
Chris "Knuckles" Nilan
Didier "Cannonball" Pitre
Jacques "Jake the Snake" Plante
Don "Bones" Raleigh
Chuck "Bonnie Prince Charlie" Rayner
Henri "Pocket Rocket" Richard
Maurice "Rocket" Richard
Don "Big Bird" Saleski

*Buzinski*

Dave "The Hammer" Schultz
Eddie "The Entertainer" Shack
Fred "The Fog" Shero
Brian "Totally" Skrudland
Brian "Spinner" Spencer
Nels "Old Poison" Stewart
Dave "Stitch" Taylor
Fred "Cyclone" Taylor
Georges "Chicoutimi Cucumber" Vezina
Mike "Shaky" Walton
Bryan "Bugsy" Watson
Dave "Tiger" Williams
Lorne "Gump" Worsley
Roy "Shrimp" Worters
Larry "The Rock" Zeidel